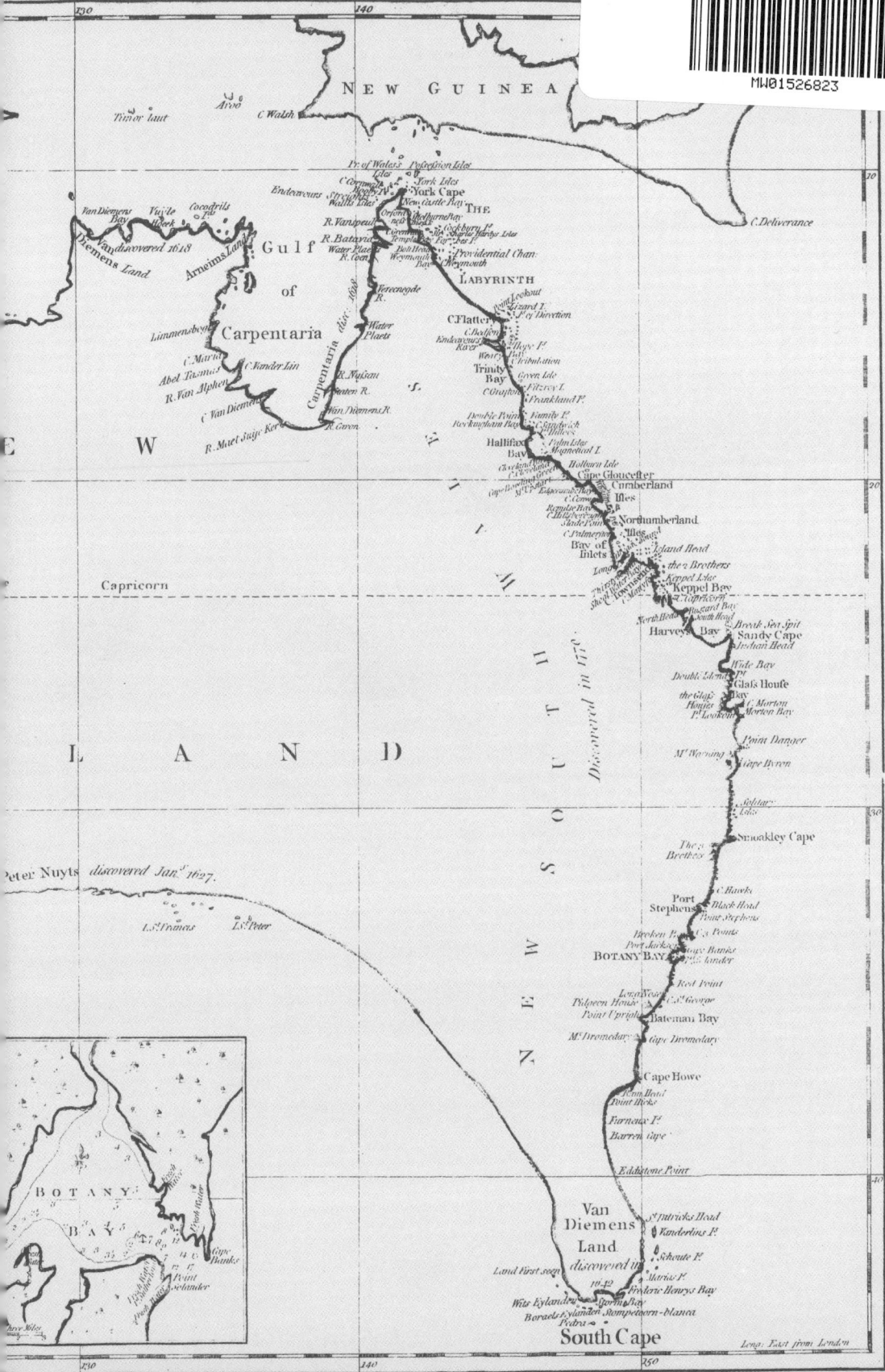

King Bungaree

Fig. 44.

BUNGAREE
C. Pye, c. 1834 (after Charles Rodius?).
Lithograph, 24.7 x 15.5 cm.
[Caption] *This singular countenance is an authentic Likeness from
an original Drawing of the Chief of the Broka Bay Tribe, New
South Wales, well known at Sidney .*

London, Published by J.B. Ashley, 23 Hanway Street, Oxford
Street, Printed by J.B. Ashley.
Mitchell Library, Sydney.

King Bungaree

*A Sydney Aborigine meets the great
South Pacific explorers, 1799–1830*

Keith Vincent Smith

Kangaroo Press

For Irene

Acknowledgments

King Bungaree could not have been written without the help of many people.

I am grateful to:

The staff of the Mitchell Library, State Library of New South Wales, Sydney, where I researched Bungaree's life for nearly four years.

Richard Neville, Curator, Pictures Research, Mitchell Library, Sydney, for his advice on the portraits of Bungaree and for permission to quote from his article 'The Many Faces of Bungaree' in *The Australian Antique Collector*, July-December 1991.

Dr Frederick McCarthy, for his friendly encouragement and the loan of his research notes.

Glynn Barratt, Professor of Russian at Carleton University, Ottawa, for his helpful comments about the sketches of Bungaree's family by Russian artist Pavel Mikhailov.

Tim McCormick, who generously allowed me to study colour transparencies of Mikhailov's original sketches of Aborigines in Sydney in 1820, now in the Russian State Museum, St Petersburg.

Leslie Lino, for her translations of the French texts.

My friend Leigh Mackay, who read the manuscript and made many helpful suggestions.

The Mitchell and Dixson Libraries, State Library of New South Wales, Sydney, are the major sources for the illustrations in this book. I thank the Library Council of New South Wales for permission to reproduce original and rare works from these collections. Many colour plates and black and white illustrations are reproduced by courtesy of the National Library of Australia, Canberra.

The cover portrait 'King Bungaree' by John Carmichael is reproduced by the kind permission of Denis Joachim of Melbourne.

Quotations from 'Two Voyages to the South Seas', by Jules Dumont d'Urville, published by Melbourne University Press in 1987, are reprinted by courtesy of Helen Rosenman.

Quotations from 'The Voyage of Captain Bellingshausen to the Antarctic Seas, 1819–1821', by Frank Debenham, are reprinted by courtesy of the Hakluyt Society, London.

Quotations from 'The Russians at Port Jackson, 1814–1822', Glynn Barratt, are reprinted by courtesy of the Australian Institute of Aboriginal and Torres Strait Islander Studies (AIATSIS), Canberra, ACT, who also helped me with biographical details.

© Keith Vincent Smith 1992

First published in 1992 by Kangaroo Press Pty Ltd
3 Whitehall Road (P.O. Box 75) Kenthurst NSW 2156
Typeset by Midland Typesetters Pty Ltd, Maryborough, Victoria
Printed in Singapore by Global Com Pte Ltd

ISBN 0 86417 470 5

Contents

Part 1: 1799–1819
The Go-Between

1	Images of Bungaree	8
2	A Boy at Broken Bay	15
3	Sailing with Matthew Flinders	26
4	Voyage of the Investigator	45
5	'The Most Intelligent of That Race'	65
6	Macquarie's Favourite	72
7	Voyage of the *Mermaid*	87

Part 2: 1820–30
His Sable Majesty

8	The Russians at Kirribilli	103
9	The Native Settlers	116
10	French Connections	124
11	'A King of Shreds and Patches'	133
12	An Actor in the Streets	149
13	Images of Bungaree (2)	159
14	Epilogue: Black Ulysses	166

Appendixes:

I The Name Bungaree	168
II Picturesque Voyage	170
III 'The Rum Cove'	174

Notes	177
Bibliography	183
Index	188

Fig. 33.

Buggery Roi dela tribu du Port Jackson—N^lle Hollande
(Buggery King of the Port Jackson Tribe—New Holland)
Jules Lejeune, 1824.
Pen and ink sketch, 19 x 24 cm.

[Caption] *C.P. almost black. some red on the forehead and on the cheeks.*
Service Central Hydrographique de la Marine, Paris.

Part 1: 1799–1819
The Go-Between

1 Images of Bungaree

The Panorama

Sketching one day on the summit of Calton Hill, overlooking Edinburgh, an Irish artist named Robert Barker (1739–1806) opened up an umbrella to shade himself from the sun. Looking around, his eye was struck by the effect of the circle framing the horizon and the town laid out below. He hit upon the idea of creating a kind of 'seamless' circular topographical painting with no beginning or end. By trial and error, he solved the problems of capturing 'nature at a glance' with apparently straight lines drawn or painted on paper pasted on linen over a curved surface.[1]

Barker showed his first huge watercolour view of Edinburgh at 28 Haymarket, London, on 14 March 1789. His invention evolved into the Panorama, which opened in Leicester Square in 1793.[2] Before photographs, or the moving pictures of the cinema, the Panorama was the best way to experience the illusion of actually being part of a particular place. It was a great novelty and soon became one of London's most popular attractions.

Londoners got their first glimpse of the colony of New South Wales in 1822 in the panorama of *The Town of Sydney* which incorporated three topographical drawings by Major James Taylor of the 48th Regiment. These were shown by Henry Barker, who managed the Panorama after his father's death.[3]

Landscape painter Robert Burford (1791–1861) acquired the Panorama in 1823 and was the proprietor until the 1850s. He painted topographic views in oils of such exotic places as Hong Kong, Macao and Canton from sketches made by travelling artists. These were presented to the public in two small displays and one huge circle 42 feet high and 90 feet in diameter which completely surrounded the viewers.[4]

In 1829 Burford's Panorama in Leicester Square was given over to a view of *The Town of Sydney, New South Wales; The harbour of Port Jackson, and surrounding country*.[5] Reared on tales of brutality at 'Botany Bay', the audience no doubt expected to see transported convicts in leg irons toiling under the lash in a half-wild land 16,000 miles away at the other side of the world. Instead, the tranquil scene revealed a provincial township whose 10,000 inhabitants lived in a jumble of houses and cottages around Port Jackson with its 'blue waters and green islands'. There were sturdy Regency-style buildings, including Fort Macquarie, St James's church, the Commissariat Store and separate barracks for soldiers and convicts. The view did not show the narrow, winding laneways and steps of the Rocks on the western side leading to the waterfront, where inns and sly grog shops with names like The Brown Bear or The Sheer Hulk were the haunt of sailors, pickpockets and prostitutes.

The panorama of Sydney was based on a series of eight overlapping watercolour views, painted in February 1827 by Augustus Earle (1793–1838), a young artist who wandered the world painting portraits and landscapes. To obtain a bird's-eye view, Earle climbed to the top of the Old Government Windmill on Palmer's Hill, the highest part of the Government Domain.[6] The Australian newspaper had heard that the artist would receive 100 guineas for his work.[7] The stone tower grain-grinding windmill was built in the Governor's Domain on land granted to Commissary John Palmer by Governor Philip Gidley King in 1802. It stood close to the bronze statue of Governor Arthur Phillip erected in 1897 near the Garden Palace Gates in Macquarie Street, Sydney.[8]

'No possible means could have been devised to render the colony of New South Wales more notorious to the people of Great Britain than a Panorama of Sydney,' commented Dr Roger Oldfield in the first number of The South-Asian Register in October 1827. 'No work that has been published can compare with it,' added Oldfield, after seeing Earle's sketches before they were shipped to London on the Mary Hope.[9]

'The Panoramic view of Sydney attracts a great many persons to it,' remarked John Richardson in a letter from London in April 1829 to the Rev. Samuel Marsden at Parramatta, New South Wales. 'It is very correct but taken from a bad spot (the old Government windmill)—Earle took it.'[10]

A group of naked Australian natives appear in the landscape, but only three persons were depicted and named. The first two were the governor of New South Wales Sir Ralph Darling and his brother-in-law and private secretary Lieutenant Colonel Henry Dumaresq (pronounced Dummerick), riding near the entrance to the Government Gardens. The third person, rigged out in a similar uniform to the horseback riders, was a black man, sketched in a characteristic pose, extending his hat to greet them.

This picturesque character was Bungaree, an Aborigine from Broken Bay, who was for many years one of the best known people of Georgian Sydney. As soon as any ship dropped anchor in Port Jackson, Bungaree arrived in his fishing boat rowed by two of his wives. Dressed like a Napoleon in rags in a cast-off military dress jacket with shiny brass buttons, tattered trousers and bare feet, he climbed on board to welcome the newcomers to 'his' country. His trademark was a stiff black cocked hat decorated with gold ribbons and a feather plume. Doffing his hat, bowing deeply and grinning widely to all, he would ask to drink the captain's health in rum or brandy. Afterwards, he inspected the ship's pantry and levied his 'tribute', which he received in the form of 'presents' or 'loans'.[11]

On his chest, hanging from a copper chain around his neck, shone his treasured badge of office, a brass gorget or breastplate shaped like a crescent which had been presented to him by Governor Lachlan Macquarie.[12] It was inscribed:

BOONGAREE
Chief of the
Broken Bay Tribe
1815

Bungaree's flamboyant costume, his good nature and elaborate manners set him apart from other Aborigines living on the fringes of the British convict settlement. He was witty, intelligent and diplomatic enough to keep one foot in each of the black and white camps. Like Shakespeare's clown in Twelfth Night, Bungaree was 'wise enough to play the fool' and used his natural talents to obtain most of his needs. A clever mimic, Bungaree could imitate the walk, gestures and expression of past governors of the colony of New South Wales.

Bartering fish and trading in Aboriginal weapons also helped Bungaree to support himself, his wives and his people. The coins he was 'loaned' were used to buy old clothes, bread, butter and sugar for his ragtag tribe and brandy (his favourite tipple), other spirits, Cooper's beer, tea and tobacco for himself. Over the years he had come to depend on these European stimulants.

Macquarie, his great patron, had twice built huts for Bungaree and his people at Georges Head, opposite the entrance to Port Jackson. In a vain attempt to persuade the 'friendly' Aborigines to settle down and become farmers, the governor gave them clothes, agricultural implements, seeds and a fishing boat. Bungaree preferred to use the boat to ambush ships entering the harbour.

Although he made himself useful to the European settlers, by tracking escaped convicts and guiding naval explorers, Bungaree also exerted considerable influence in Aboriginal tribal life. He often took part in corroborees and ritual battles which sometimes degenerated into drunken brawls. At such times he abandoned his European finery, armed himself with a shield and spears, and smeared his naked body with a dusting of red ochre. Bungaree also made it his business to meet Aborigines visiting Sydney from far-off places.

Nothing remains of the original great canvas of the panorama in which Earle and Burford captured Sydney Town, Port Jackson and the 'life size' figure of King Bungaree. The rather crude engraving, *PANORAMA OF SYDNEY N.S.W. in the Year 1829, as painted by Robert Burford, and Exhibited in Leicester-square, LONDON* (Plate 1), in which Bungaree is merely a 'stick' figure, conveys only a vague notion of the colour and spectacle of the original. This is a hand-coloured version of the engraved folding frontispiece of the sixpenny printed catalogue, *Description of a View of the Town of Sydney*, published in London in 1829. This is how Robert Burford described Bungaree:

No. 19—King Boongaree
And some of his retainers, are generally the first visitors to every ship on its arrival. His sable majesty, clothed in a gold laced blue coat, with massy epaulets, buttoned up close, to avoid the necessity of a shirt or waistcoat, and wearing a large varnished cocked hat, but neither shoes nor stockings, welcomes the arrival of a stranger with much politeness and many bows, and contrives, if possible to borrow a dump or so, to buy for his 'gin' (wife), who always happens to be ill, some tea, or for himself, who is equally poor, a little of Cooper's drops.[13]

The Australian Aborigines have a rich heritage of oral tradition, but their history is unwritten. As far as we know, Bungaree could not read or write. To tell his story we must rely on eyewitnesses from an alien culture. They were Europeans, with all the inherent attitudes of racial superiority and class and religious bias of the early nineteenth century. Our chief witnesses are the English, Russian and French marine explorers and scientists who visited Port Jackson during their South Pacific voyages. Their evidence is augmented by passing remarks in books and journals by observers who include journalists, artists, army and navy officers, sailors, doctors, ministers of religion, an accountant, a gardener, a pastoralist, a judge advocate and a governor or two.

Not only was Bungaree the most discussed Aborigine of the early nineteenth century, he was just as often sketched or painted. To illustrate Bungaree's story we have a rich gallery of no less than 17 portraits by notable contemporary artists. Some of these are haunting images in which we may look into the eyes of this celebrated 'king' of the

Sydney Aborigines. Artists were attracted to Bungaree like moths to a flame (even after his death). His familiar figure appears as a detail in a further seven works of art. This is extraordinary, because we have only two or three portraits of any Europeans of the period, even the governors of New South Wales.[14]

Australia's First Lithograph

It was an accident of circumstances which brought Augustus Earle, then aged 32, to Sydney. In 1824, while on his way to India from South America, he was stranded for eight months on the remote, rocky and sparsely inhabited island of Tristan da Cunha in the South Atlantic. He was taken off by the *Admiral Cockburn* which was headed for Hobart Town, Van Diemen's Land. Earle may have seen Bungaree for the first time when he arrived in Sydney from Hobart on the brig *Cyprus* on 14 May 1825.[15]

The artist was soon commissioned by a group of emancipated convicts to decorate the dining room of Government House for the farewell banquet given for Governor Sir Thomas Brisbane. In November, the Colony's civil officers (civil servants) paid Earle £50 to paint a striking 2.2 metre high full-length portrait in oils of the governor (now at Government House, Sydney).[16]

Born in London, the son of American portrait painter James Earl (Augustus added the 'e'), Augustus Earle was a versatile and prolific artist whose watercolours, oil paintings and lithographs accurately conveyed the atmosphere and character of the strange people and places he encountered on his journeys.

Sir Thomas Brisbane (1773–1860), an enthusiastic astronomer said by some to be more talented as a star-gazer than as an administrator, brought two lithographic presses to New South Wales in 1821. He planned to use them to print charts of the Southern Hemisphere stars, but none was produced. Augustus Earle obtained one of these presses from Colonial Astronomer James Dunlop. In 1826 the artist used the press for a series of Sydney views and to reproduce several impressions of a portrait of Bungaree which is believed to be the first lithograph ever printed in Australia.[17]

One version (Plate 3), now in the Mitchell Library, Sydney, is thought to be a proof copy. Edward Smith Hall, the crusading editor of the infant *Monitor* newspaper, scarcely three months old, found space to mention Earle's lithographs on 11 August 1826:

> We are much gratified in being able to state, that Mr Earle, the Artist, has at length succeeded in producing several excellent specimens of the well-known Native Chief of Sydney, Bungaree, which, we understand, is intended for sale, and, as usual for Mr Earle, at a very low price. As a first attempt of the kind in the Colony, it has been dedicated to General Darling. The likeness is faithful—and, considering the difficulties, Mr Earle has had to contend with, great credit is due to that gentleman.[18]

In lithography the artist draws directly on a flat stone using greasy ink or a chalk pencil. The stone is immersed in water and then wiped over with printing ink, which is rejected by the wet areas and accepted by the greasy areas. Prints are taken straight from the stone. This was a new technique for Earle, which explains why the words 'KING BUNGAREE' on his subject's breastplate are reversed.

The print has been clumsily hand-coloured in varying shades of brownish sepia. Details are blurry and the stone walls of Fort Macquarie (site of the Sydney Opera House) in the background are shadowy. But here, solidly in the foreground, is Bungaree, right arm raised, holding out his black cocked hat decorated with gold ribbons to greet a stranger. He wears his brass gorget, not with a uniform, but over a rather drab brown suit. His eyes are bright, his expression is friendly and his curly hair is rather untidy. The portrait allows us to see Bungaree as if we had been there ourselves. Having developed this theatrical pose, as stylised as any Byzantine icon, Augustus Earle was to repeat it in his portraits of Bungaree for Burford's panorama, his oil painting and a later lithograph.

A second version of the lithograph, titled in ink, *BUNGAREE! 'King' of the Aborigines of New South Wales* (Plate 4), in the Dixson Library, Sydney, is believed to be the final state as sold to the public.

This print has been skillfully hand-coloured and some additions have been made, probably by Earle himself. The reworking has dulled Bungaree's eyes, twisted his lips into a wry grin and made his skin look softer. Rocks and plants in the foreground are neatly outlined, with a more defined Fort Macquarie, now crowned by a red flag, seen in sharp perspective. The background sky is a redder sepia and the print has been glazed. A shadowy Royal Navy ship, perhaps HMS *Warspite* or *Volage*, is seen below in Sydney Cove. These details must have been added after 17 October 1826 when *Warspite*, *Fly* and *Volage*, from the Royal Navy China Squadron under Commodore Sir James Brisbane, came into Port Jackson.[19]

'The lithographic press is constantly employed by that indefatigable artist MR EARLE,' said the *Sydney Gazette*. 'His Majesty King Bungaree, of Australian renown, has just been produced from the lithographic press. The likeness is admirable. His aboriginal princeship is shewing off at some houses in town to the tune of 50s. Bungaree quite enjoys the sight of him self.'[20]

Augustus Earle's oil painting, *Bungaree, A native of New South Wales* (Plate 6), which now hangs, in its gilt wooden frame, in the Australian National Gallery in Canberra (on long-term loan from the National Library of Australia), again portrays Bungaree in typical pose. In place of the brown suit, Bungaree wears a splendid scarlet jacket with brass buttons and gold lace. We know that Commodore Sir James Brisbane presented Bungaree with 'a full suit of his own uniform, together with a sword, of which he [Bungaree] was not a little vain.'[21] The view dominated by Bungaree is the same, but all three British ships are now seen in Sydney Cove, with another vessel, under full sail, off Fort Macquarie. She resembles the French corvette *Astrolabe*, under frigate captain Jules Dumont d'Urville, which arrived in Sydney on 2 December 1826.[22]

There is an air of genuine nobility in the expression and bearing of Bungaree in this study, one of the earliest oil paintings of an Australian Aborigine. 'In certain respects,' commented Tim Bonyhady in *The Colonial Image* (1987), 'the portrait [King Bungaree] . . . appears as a counterpart to Earle's portrait of Sir Thomas Brisbane since it shows Bungaree dressed and acting as if he were governor.'[23]

On Friday 27 October, the Rev. John McGarvie, Presbyterian Minister of the Ebenezer Church on the Hawkesbury River, travelled to Sydney and wrote in his diary: 'Visited the painting gallery of Mr Earle's. The outline admirable the colouring som[what?] heavy— this is the only exhibition in Sydney.' McGarvie appended a list of the artworks on show, which included: '1. Boongarie chief of the Broken Bay tribe in his common Dress'.[24]

McGarvie did not state which medium the artist used for the portrait. However, in July 1829, reviewing the exhibition in an essay titled 'On the State of the Fine Arts in New South Wales', which appeared in the *Sydney Gazette* under the pseudonym 'A. B. Marramatta', he specifically mentioned a *painting* of Bungaree by Augustus Earle:

No. 1. Bungarie [sic], chief of the Broken Bay tribe of blacks, in his usual dress, a blue surcoat, cocked hat, and brass plate on his breast. A print has been published from this painting. The general resemblance is most striking, and the attitude such as Bungaree [sic] assumes in accosting a stranger. It always seems to us, however, to be too stiff; the arm appearing to be fixed to the body with glue, and a four inch spike.[25]

McGarvie's statement is usually taken to mean that the lithograph portrait of Bungaree was copied from Earle's oil. However, in the oil, Bungaree is wearing a red, not a blue surcoat. Examination of the work by curators of the National Library of Australia does not reveal any overpainting or alteration to the colour of the jacket.[26] It seems likely then that what McGarvie saw at Earle's Gallery was an original watercolour or oil study of Bungaree, perhaps the one sent to London as a model for Robert Burford to include in his panorama.

It was thought as recently as 1987 that no prints of Augustus Earle's lithograph of Bungaree had survived.[27] They were rediscovered in that year by Richard Neville, at present curator, Pictures Research, at the Mitchell Library, State Library of New South Wales, Sydney. Neville, then aged 24, was working on his master's thesis in fine arts at the University of Sydney. By comparing them with Earle's portrait in oils, he realised that the two works (previously attributed to Charles Rodius) were versions of Earle's lithograph. New library cards were issued in June 1987.[28]

A little-known naive watercolour by an unknown artist, titled in ink *KING BONGAREE. Lend me one Dump!* (Plate 11), gives us the figure of Bungaree wearing a blue jacket and gold lace on his collar. It is the only portrait of Bungaree which shows him wearing a jacket with epaulets. His garb follows Burford's printed description, part of which has been pasted over a grassy mound on which Bungaree stands. The figure of Bungaree has been cut out around the outline and pasted to a piece of blank paper. This curious work, about half the size of the lithograph, is classified as a 'collage watercolour'. In its present form, it must be dated after the printing of Burford's catalogue in 1829. Could it have been, when intact, Augustus Earle's original study of Bungaree, or was it merely copied from Burford's exhibition or Earle's lithograph?

Augustus Earle has introduced us to the image of Bungaree in his final years. After his death in 1830, Bungaree's reputation as a mimic, beggar and affable drunkard expanded whenever the story was told. In the passage of the years, the other side of Bungaree, just as fascinating, has almost been forgotten. It was his contact with the last great explorers and map makers of the South Pacific which shaped his early life.

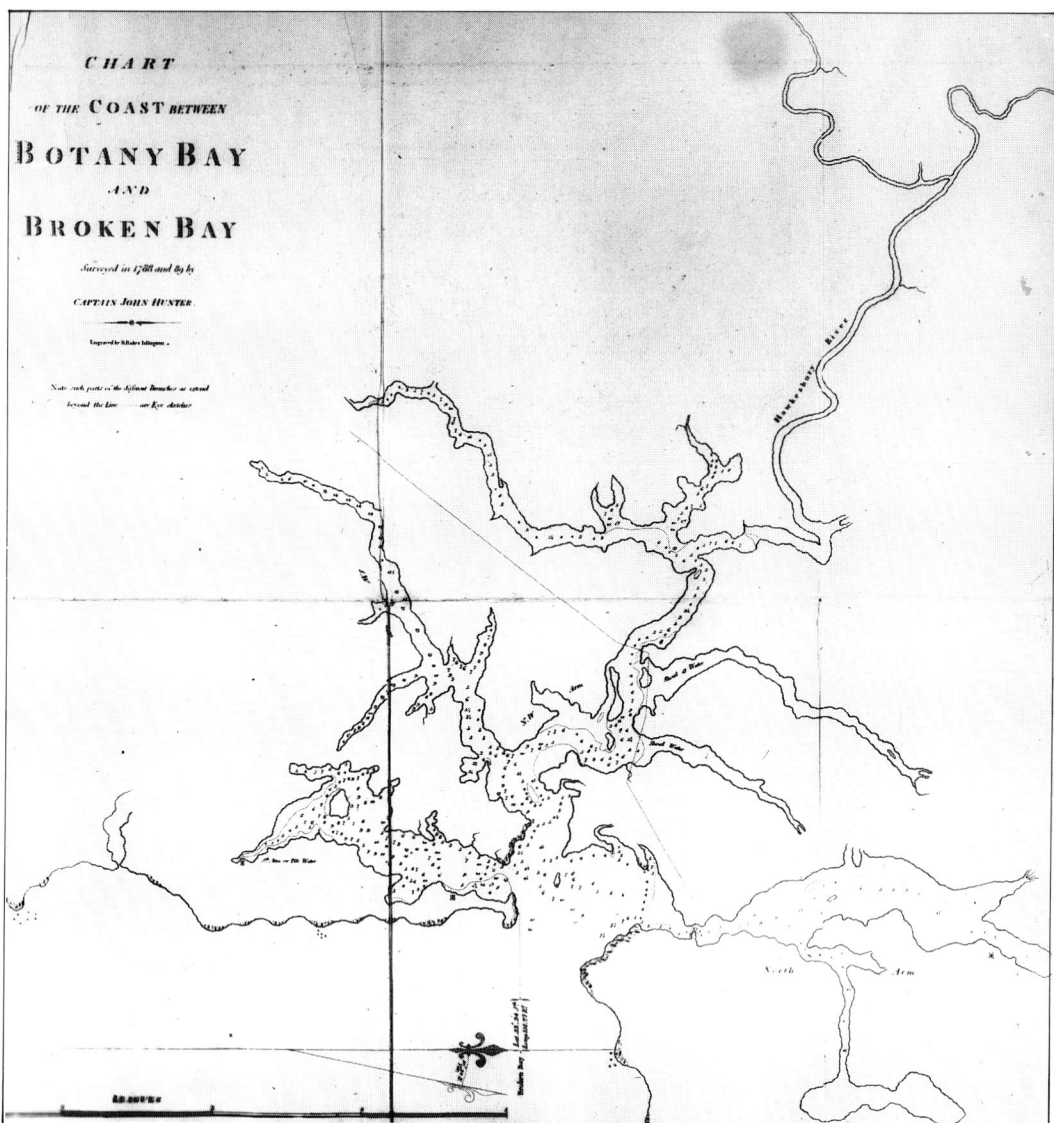

Map 1. *BROKEN BAY*
Detail: 'Chart of the coast between Botany Bay and Broken Bay'. John Hunter, 1788–9.
Hunter, John, *An Historical Journal of the Transactions at Port Jackson and Norfolk Island . . .* London, John Stockdale, 1793.

2 A Boy at Broken Bay

Bungaree's story begins with the sea, which always dominated his life.

At Broken Bay, a wide sheet of shallow blue water bites into the rim of the southeast coastline of the continent we call Australia. Impelled by a line of sandbars off the coast, the white breakers of the Pacific Ocean slap ceaselessly against the steep sandstone headlands.

The English name for the place was written on the charts by Lieutenant James Cook, who spied broken land 'that seemed to form a bay' as HMS *Endeavour* sailed by at sunset on 6 May 1770. If a few sharp-eyed Aboriginal people looked out to sea that evening and saw the ship they might have imagined it was a vision, some gigantic white-winged bird or sea monster, like a dream in their Dreamtime. Cook's ship had sailed from Botany Bay that morning after an eight-day visit during which the wealthy young Lincolnshire botanist Joseph Banks and his colleague Dr Daniel Solander had collected a rich trophy of 3,000 plant specimens. Heading north, *Endeavour* passed another inlet where, said Cook, 'there appears to be a safe anchorage, which I called Port Jackson'.[1] This was the entrance to the harbour around which now sprawls the city of Sydney with its 3.5 million inhabitants and suburbs stretching north along a peninsula of sandy beaches to the southern shores of Broken Bay.

Some 50,000 years ago, groups of Aborigines, the first Australians, began to cross the land bridges from southern Asia and spread out to populate the great island continent. Some may have reached the coastal strip between Broken Bay and Botany Bay during the Ice Age (roughly 35,000 years ago) when the sea, about 100 metres lower than its present level, was further to the east. Geologists believed that 20,000 years ago both Broken Bay and Port Jackson were rocky valleys crisscrossed by small rivers lying 10–15 kilometres inland from the present shore. At the end of the Ice Age, the sea began to rise gradually and reached its present level about 7,000 years ago, flooding the valleys and creating deep harbours. Any traces of Aboriginal coastal life before that time are submerged beneath the waters.[2]

Somehow the Aborigines survived and adapted to these great physical changes. For countless generations they lived as hunters and gatherers around Broken Bay's myriad coves and inlets, trickling creeks, sandbanks, muddy islands, mangrove swamps and rocky ridges crowned by prickly shrubs and forests of eucalyptus trees with silvery trunks and grey-green leaves.

A wide river, which rose in mountain country 530 kilometres away, wound its way north through deep ravines and spectacularly wild gorges, veering sharply to empty into the northern arm of the bay. The Aborigines called the river *Deerubin*.

Our knowledge of the antiquity of Aboriginal settlement comes from the work of archaeologists who have excavated fire hearths beneath rock shelters and 'kitchen' midden heaps of discarded shells along the present coastline. The coastal Aborigines lived in groups of extended families numbering 25–50 men, women and children who shared a common language and territory. They led a nomadic life, never staying long in one place, ranging up and down the coast and further inland, especially in winter when fish became scarce.

Everything they needed to live was provided by nature, chiefly from the sea. Fish in season were plentiful all around the shores of the bay, in creeks and lagoons and along the rocky coast. Birds of all kinds thronged the sandy shallows and mangroves. The flower stalk of the grass tree (*Xanthorrhoea* species), which grew everywhere in the bush, provided shafts for spears as well as the resin used to cement them together. Shields, clubs and axe handles were crafted from branches and tree roots and axe heads and tools were worked from stone.

Men caught fish from the rocks using long fishing spears with four or more hardwood prongs tipped and barbed with sharp fish or animal bones. Lying across their canoes with their faces below the water, they waited patiently, seldom failing to hit their target squarely. Women sat in canoes, fishing by hand with lines made of twine from twisted strands of bark to which they attached shiny crescent-shaped lures ground from shell. A small stone acted as a sinker. The net carrying bags slung over their shoulders were woven from the same bark twine. Often, two or three children crowded into the canoe with their mother, who held the youngest securely in her lap between her knees and crossed ankles. The women talked, sang and laughed together as they fished, chewing mussels and cockles which they spat into the water as a burley to attract fish.

These flimsy canoes were made of a single sheet of bark cut out by stone hatchets and wedges from she-oak or stringybark trees and tied in a bunch at each end. They were clumsy and shallow, only 15–20 centimetres above water at the highest point, but the Aborigines skillfully steered them close to the surf, using a wooden 'pudding stirrer' paddle in each hand. In the bottom of the canoe a small twig fire was kept burning, on a bed of sand or rocks, so that fish could be cooked as soon as they were caught.

Broken Bay was Bungaree's home country. Here he grew up and swam and played with the other boys of his band. Like all young Aborigines, he played at hunting and mock battles using miniature spears and shields and in time became an expert at spearing fish. Here young Bungaree learned the traditional ways of his people and was initiated, becoming a man.

As well as fish, the coastal people ate a rich variety of seafood: mud and rock oysters, cockles, mussels, turbans and pipis, prawns, crabs and lobsters. Discarded seashells were left in heaps on the sandy beaches. People came from far and wide to feast on blubber whenever a whale or dolphin was stranded. In the bush hunters propelled their spears at kangaroos, wallabies and smaller game, harnessing the powerful lever action of the woomerah. This thick wooden shaft was about 60–80 centimetres long. A peg at one end of the shaft slotted into a hole bored into the butt end of the spear. A sharp-edged shell set into the front end doubled as a knife or scraper. Possums were smoked out of hollow trees and killed with a blow from a wooden club. Small game included ducks, birds, snakes, lizards and kangaroo rats. Women foraged with their digging sticks for yams, waterlily and fern roots and collected fruit, berries, birds' eggs, honey, grubs and insects. They made a sweet drink from the nectar of *Banksia* flower heads soaked in water.

In good weather Bungaree's people slept at night on the ground around a small fire, protected sometimes by a semicircular windbreak made of sheets of stringybark. When

NOUVELLE - HOLLANDE : Nouv^{lle} Galles du Sud.

DESSINS EXÉCUTÉS PAR LES NATURELS.

1. Espèce de Murène . 2 . 4 . 5 . Diverses figures du Dieu des Montagnes bleues . 3 . Squale barbu . 6 . Kangaroo . 7 . 8 . 9 . Poissons .

De l'Imprimerie de Langlois .

Fig. 1.

NOUVELLE-HOLLANDE: Nouv^{elle} Galles du Sud.
DESSINS EXÉCUTÉS PAR LES NATURELS
[New Holland: New South Wales
Designs made by the natives]

Plate 33. 'Historique Atlas de MM. Lesueur et Petit', *Voyage de découvertes aux terres Australes.* Seconde édition, Paris, 1824.

it was cold or raining heavily, they huddled in a *gunyah* of flat bark supported on a framework of branches or sheltered under an overhanging rock ledge or in a *gibber gunyah*, a cave warmed by a fire at the entrance.

The black people of the Sydney-Hawkesbury district left an eloquent pictorial record of their culture in hundreds of petroglyphs or rock engravings depicting mythological beings or hunters and their prey, including birds, fish and kangaroos, which were often clan totems. Stencils of hand shapes were also common. This art was associated with the spiritual and ceremonial life of the Aborigines, particularly their initiation ceremonies.[3] Some of the rock engravings around Sydney were sketched in 1801 by French artist Charles Alexandre Lesueur and published in the Atlas of François Peron's *Voyage de Découvertes aux terra Australes* (Fig. 1).

When he was ready for initiation, at about 13 years of age, a boy was taken from his mother to be instructed in tribal laws and sacred lore. Every few years in summer a corroboree was held, attended by *kooringals* (elders) and *koradgees* (clever men), who supervised the dancing, singing and other ritual ceremonies. Separate stages of the manhood rite might be spread over several years. It was usual for boys to have their upper right incisor tooth knocked out. In some places they were painfully circumcised with a sharp stone or shell. Scarification, a row of raised scars on the upper part of the body, was another symbol of initiation. The skin was cut with a shell or sharp stone knife and the wound was filled with ashes so that it healed into a raised welt or cicatrice. Patterns of scars usually covered the arms and upper part of the body. Scars were also cut when men or women were released from food taboos, or to commemorate marriage or other important stages of life. Often young men had a hole pierced through the septum of their noses in which they wore an ornamental bone or nosepeg. Only after initiation could a man take a wife.

We know from later descriptions and one portrait (Fig. 26) that Bungaree bore the outward signs of initiation. His nose was pierced and the pattern of scars on his chest and shoulders was to cause great interest among Aborigines far from Broken Bay. However, there is no indication that his upper front tooth had been knocked out.

First Contact

Even after 200 years, six or seven generations, white Australians who have learned to love their land cannot hope to comprehend the fear and trauma felt by the Aborigines when the first white settlers arrived at Port Jackson in January 1788. 'They thought they was the devil when they landed first, they did not know what to make of them. When they saw them going up the masts they thought they was opossums'. This story was told by Mahroot (also called Boatswain), an Aborigine from Botany Bay, who spoke in 1845 of the lingering memory of the white invasion of his country.[4] The Aborigines must have wondered if these thick-skinned strangers were people from the skies walking on earth or the ghosts of their ancestors.

News of the arrival in Port Jackson of 'monster birds' from which the white 'devils' disgorged like ants, first into small canoes and then over the shore, would have quickly reached the Aborigines at Broken Bay, 34 kilometres to the north. Communications were good; well-worn tracks followed the coast and meandered through the bush between the two deep harbours.[5]

This time the aliens had come to stay. After a voyage lasting eight months and one week, a British convoy of six hired transport ships, three storeships and HMS *Sirius* and *Supply*, came into the harbour on 26 January 1788. Apart from their crews, the ships carried on board some 1,350 persons. About 750 of these, held below decks in chains, were convicted criminals—convicts—of whom 190 were women. Guarding them were 213 Royal Marines, armed with muskets, some of whom were accompanied by their wives and children. The commander of these unwilling colonists was Captain Arthur Phillip (1738–1814), a naval officer with wide experience, who was to be first governor of New South Wales. Phillip made the decision to abandon Botany Bay and chose the site and planned the settlement which grew around a sheltered bay which he named Sydney Cove. Soon the sound of iron axes rang out for the first time, chopping out the thick primeval forest near a small stream where tents were erected for a makeshift camp.

About five weeks after landing at Port Jackson, Phillip led a small expedition in a longboat and cutter along the coast to explore Broken Bay.[6] Excited and curious at seeing white men for the first time, the Aborigines gathered in groups around the arena of high rocky ridges and cliffs as the boats came in from the sea around the sandstone bluff of Barranjoey (meaning a young kangaroo). One native man and five women who had been fishing in three canoes immediately came alongside to welcome the strangers. To avoid them, Phillip in the cutter, with his French butler Bernard de Maliez and others on board, steered over to the north shore of the bay. James Keltie, master of *Sirius*, and Lieutenant William Bradley and their men were in the longboat.

'When the cutter first landed,' wrote Bradley in his journal, 'they were met by a great number of the Natives, Men, Women & Children, the Men were all armed with Spears, Clubs, Stone Hatchets & Wooden Swords, they were all very friendly & when the Longboat landed were without arms.'[7]

Bradley, a naval draughtsman, captured the atmosphere of the first meetings between the blacks and whites in his watercolour, *View in Broken Bay New South Wales, March 1788* (Plate 2). In the foreground red-coated marines and blue-jacketed sailors warmly shake hands with the Aborigines. The two ship's boats can be seen on the water below with eight canoes nearby. In the distance is the rocky island at the entrance to Broken Bay now called Lion Island.

Several Aboriginal women came down with the men when the boats landed and helped the explorers light a fire. They seemed pleased when they were given small ornaments, but soon lost interest and laid them aside. One young woman in a canoe, whom Phillip described as 'very talkative and remarkably cheerful' stood up and sang a song of welcome.[8] Surgeon George Worgan, a music lover who brought the first piano to New South Wales with him on HMS *Sirius*, passed on an anecdote he heard from one of the party (perhaps Phillip himself) about this lively lady to his brother Dick in England. She had taken a liking to the governor's greatcoat, but could not persuade him to give it to her. 'She tried [what] Jumping Capering, and various Wanton Anticks would do, but these not succeeding according to her Wishes, She began to Weep, in a most lamentable strain, put on languishing Looks, in short practised all the Siren's Arts.'[9] This small, pale man with his knee-breeches, greatcoat and strange headdress (a cocked hat), must have been seen as a powerful figure by the Broken Bay Aborigines. Phillip was wise not to part with his coat, because heavy rain fell constantly during the eight days the expedition spent around Broken Bay. The men often spent the night trying to sleep in their open boats or huddled in canvas tents on mangrove islands.

Good relations with the Aborigines continued, apart from a clash with a friendly old man who had at first helped the strangers but later took a spade, for which Phillip gave him 'two or three sharp slaps on the shoulder with the open hand'. Their friendship destroyed, the old man seized a spear and threatened the governor, but then dropped his weapon and left. Phillip was struck by his courage 'for several officers and men were then near me'.[10] In this encounter Phillip showed 'the mixture of calm, courage and wrong-headedness that was to characterise most of his dealings with them', wrote W. E. H. Stanner in *White Man Got No Dreaming*.[11]

The two boats returned to Port Jackson by water, not overland as Phillip had planned, as some of his men were suffering from dysentery.

The natives at Broken Bay, 'tho' very friendly, appeared to be numerous', Governor Phillip reported to Lord Sydney in his first dispatch to London on 15 May 1788. He said the land in general was very high and mostly barren and rocky. Much of the north-west branch of the bay was low and swampy, although there were pelicans and other birds in great numbers. He was most impressed by the extensive south-west branch, which he named Pitt Water in honour of the Prime Minister, Pitt the Younger. It was big enough, said Phillip, 'to contain all the Navy of Great Britain'.[12]

'They met with a vast number of the natives,' Worgan wrote,

> some of w[h] they thought they had seen before at Botany Bay, indeed, it is pretty clear, that they wander up & down the Coast, going to the Northwards in the Winter, and returning to y[e] southward (as we expect to find) in the Summer. The Natives were very friendly to them, offered them Fire & Water, were extremely full of their Fun, laughing, Mimicking & Frisking about.[13]

Their bodies were scarified, chiefly around the breasts and arms, the weals sometimes raised several centimetres from the flesh. Most of them were missing the right front tooth in the upper jaw. 'On my showing them that I wanted a front tooth it occasioned a general clamour, and I thought gave me some little merit in their opinion,' Phillip wrote.[14]

Gal-gal-la

The sudden arrival of more than 1,000 Europeans at Sydney Cove effectively dispossessed the native people of their land and food-gathering territory. At first the Aborigines watched, but wisely kept their distance.

Their comings and goings around Port Jackson were followed by the curious eyes of a core of elite professional officers who noted any interesting events in their journals. These men, some of them destined to be admirals and governors, had served King George in Britain's far-flung outposts and many had seen action in the American War of Independence. They had formed impressions of native people in North America and other parts of the world and compared them to the 'Indians' of New South Wales. John Hunter (1737–1821), captain of Sirius, had been a midshipman at the siege of Quebec; William Bradley (1757–1833), the ship's first lieutenant, fought in the East Indies; Surgeon General John White (1758–1832) had served in India and the West Indies; marine captain Watkin Tench (1758–1833) spent three months as a prisoner in Maryland; and his friend William Dawes (1762–1836) had been wounded in action against the French at Chesapeake Bay in 1781. Judge Advocate David Collins (1756–1810) served in Nova Scotia and was at the Battle of Bunker's Hill (Boston), an experience he shared with naval lieutenant Phillip Gidley King (1758–1808) and Major Robert Ross (1740–1798) who was at Quebec and later captured by the French and exchanged.

When the two races met, a clash of cultures was inevitable. After two convicts were speared to death on 29 May 1788 while gathering rushes to thatch a hut, Governor Phillip and 12 marines set out to search for the murderers. After marching almost to Botany Bay without seeing a single Aborigine, they suddenly came across 50 canoes drawn up on a beach. In the next cove they were met by an armed but peaceful gathering of about 200 men, women and children.[15]

In a dispatch to Lord Sydney dated 18 July 1788, Phillip wrote: 'Their numbers [of natives] in the neighbourhood of this Settlement, that is within Ten Miles to the Northward, and Ten Miles to the Southward, I reckon at fifteen hundred'.[16] Misunderstanding and mistrust began to grow on both sides. By October that year the Aborigines, according to Bradley, were attacking 'almost every person who has met with them that has not had a musquet'.[17]

At the end of December 1788 a strongly built young Aborigine from the north side of Port Jackson was captured on the orders of Governor Phillip. He was brought, trussed with ropes, to Sydney Cove, where his hair was cut short; he was washed and dressed in European clothes. This gentle, quiet man, aged about 30, was at first called Manly, after the place where he was taken. After a while, he told his captors his name was Arabanoo. When taken to the newly built Government House, Arabanoo cried out in surprise when he looked up and saw people leaning out of a window on the top floor. He dined at a side table at the governor's house where he heartily ate fish and ducks, enjoyed bread and drank tea avidly, but refused all liquor.[18]

In April and May 1789 boat crews from the British settlement reported finding bodies of 'Indians' in all the coves and inlets of the harbour. 'On inspection,' recorded Watkin Tench, 'it appeared that all the parties had died a natural death: pustules similar to those occasioned by the small pox, were thickly spread on their bodies.'[19] David Collins said that the numbers of Aborigines swept off by the smallpox epidemic, by their own account, was incredible. So it was that the most devastating impact of the whites upon the black inhabitants of New South Wales was not inflicted by the musket, but by the introduction of disease. Within two years, smallpox had wiped out about half the Aborigines living around Port Jackson.

When Arabanoo was taken by boat to look for his former companions, not one living person could be found. Appalled by the sight of decaying bodies huddled in rock shelters all around the harbour, he cried out 'All dead! All dead!', then hung his head in mourning and said little more. A few days later, said Collins, it was learned that the few Aborigines who had survived had 'fled up the harbours to avoid the pestilence that so dreadfully raged'.[20]

Four Aborigines suffering from smallpox were brought in for treatment by Surgeon John White. Two elderly men died. They were survived by a boy about eight years old named Nanbaree and Abaroo or Boorong, a girl about 13 years old. Arabanoo nursed the children back to health, but then became the next victim of the disease. He died on 18 May 1789 and was buried in Governor Phillip's garden.[21]

The governor set off for a second excursion to Broken Bay early on Saturday 6 June 1789 with a party including Captain John Hunter, David Collins, George Johnston, Surgeon Worgan, Midshipman Newton Fowell and two others. Carrying their own provisions, water, arms and ammunition, they marched north, along sandy beaches and through thick woods, often falling in with well-trodden Aboriginal paths.

They arrived at Pitt Water that afternoon and found the boats sent around to meet them. One of the boat crews discovered a naked young Aboriginal woman hiding in the grass not far from their tents. She was very much frightened, but unable to flee from them because she was weak and lame after an attack of smallpox. They lit a fire nearby and comforted her, using a few expressions they had learned from 'poor Ara-ban-oo while he was alive'.[22]

On this expedition the explorers discovered the Deerubin River of the Aborigines which they named the Hawkesbury, and rowed 20 miles along the freshwater stream before turning back because of short supplies. They returned overland and met the boats again at Manly Cove on Monday 15 June. Hunter wrote: 'In our Journey, we fell in with several dead bodies who had probably falled by the Small Pox, but they were mere Skelletons so that it was impossible to say of what disease they died.'[23]

Phillip made a further journey by boat from Port Jackson on 26 June. Two boats followed the course of the river for 60–70 miles until they were stopped by a waterfall near Richmond Hill (at the junction of the Grose and Nepean Rivers). Here they saw several natives along the river banks who were suffering from smallpox.[24] Strangely, no Europeans in the settlement at Sydney Cove caught the contagious disease, although many had visited Aborigines suffering from it. The only casualty was a North American Indian, a sailor from the *Supply*, who contracted smallpox and died. David Collins commented:

> To this disorder they also gave a name, Gal-gal-la; and that it was small-pox there was scarcely a doubt; for the person seized with it was affected exactly as Europeans are who have that disorder; and on many that had recovered from it we saw the traces, in some of the ravages of it on the face.[25]

So perished hundreds of Aborigines from the Botany Bay, Port Jackson and Broken Bay areas. Smallpox wiped out most of the Bidjigal, who lived in the inland area between Parramatta and the Nepean River. The Cadigal, whose territory stretched from South Head (*Cadi*) south to Botany Bay, were reduced from a band of 50 or 60 people in 1788 to only three in 1791, including the boy Nanbaree and his kinsman Coleby. These three

Fig. 2.

[Aboriginal woman and child at Broken Bay]
Engraving. From a sketch by John Hunter.
Title page: Hunter, John, *An Historical Journal of the*

Transactions at Port Jackson and Norfolk Island . . . London, John Stockdale, 1793.

were forced to unite with another tribe to ensure their survival. Measles, influenza and alcohol, as well as clashes with the white invaders, were to account for many more deaths.

Time and Place

It was William Collins, first judge advocate of New South Wales, who specifically stated in 1799 that Bungaree was a native of the north side of Broken Bay.[26] Bungaree's patron, Governor Lachlan Macquarie, was ambivalent about this. In 1815 Macquarie designated Bungaree 'Chief of the Broken Bay Tribe',[27] but in 1822 he described him as chief of the 'Pitt Water Tribe'.[28] Pittwater is the southern branch of Broken Bay.

An educated guess would place Bungaree's birthplace somewhere in Broken Bay, perhaps at Patonga, across from the bush-clad West Head (Ku-ring-gai National Park), or in today's Brisbane Water, the bay's northern branch.

A rough picture of the social organisation of coastal Aborigines north of Sydney in

Black Swans.
of
New South Wales.

Fig. 3.

Black Swans of New South Wales
(View on Reed's Mistake River, N.S.W.)
Engraved by William Preston after an original by James Wallis, 1819.

Plate VII: Wallis, James, *An Historical Account of the Colony of New South Wales* . . . London, 1821.

1788 can be pieced together from the observations of First Fleet journal keepers, early settlers, historians, linguists and anthropologists. The Aborigines had no written language, so the way their names were written down varies from one witness to another.

Collins noted that the native people at Port Jackson were divided into family groups:

> Each family has a particular place of residence, from which is derived its distinguishing name. This is formed by adding the monosyllable Gal to the name of the place: thus the southern shore of Botany Bay is called Gwea, and the people who inhabit it style themselves Gweagal. Those who live on the north shore of Port Jackson are called Cam-mer-ray-gal, that part of the harbour being distinguished by the name of Cam-mer-ray.[29]

These bands or clans of family members were called 'tribes' by the First Fleet observers. The Aborigines at Broken Bay belonged to the Ku-ring-gai (singular *kuri* or *koori*) language group, spread widely along the Pacific shores from the north side of Port Jackson to below Lake Macquarie. The Rev. Lancelot Threlkeld, a missionary who was the first person to seriously study Aboriginal languages, told the New South Wales Legislative Council in 1838:

> The native languages throughout New South Wales are, I feel persuaded, based upon the same origin; but I have found the dialects of various tribes differ from those which occupy the country around Lake Macquarie, that is to say, of those tribes occupying the limits bounded by the North head of Port Jackson, on the south, and Hunter's River on the north, and extending inland about 60 miles , all of which speak the same dialect.[30]

If the word 'language' is substituted for 'dialect', modern scholars are in broad agreement with Threlkeld about the boundaries of the Ku-ring-gai speakers. They agree also that a different language was spoken by the people living from South Head to Botany Bay who have come to be known as the Eora. This may have been a dialect of Dharug, the language of the inland or 'woods tribes', who populated the Cumberland Plains west to the foot of the Blue Mountains. South of Botany Bay to the Shoalhaven River the native language was Dharawal (which gave its name to Thirroul, N.S.W.), closely related to Dharug.[31]

'It is not possible to determine the exact position of the Central Coast from which Bungary and his family came,' wrote local historian Frederick Charles Bennett in *The Story of the Aboriginal People of the Central Coast of New South Wales* (1968), 'it is more probable that they came from the Patonga area but it is still possible that they were the family group whose hunting grounds were in the vicinity of the area near Bungary Norah.'[32] There is some confusion over the location of Bungary Norah, which Bennett says means 'Bungaree's grinding stone'. It is usually taken to be Norah Head, where a road has been named after Bungaree in more recent times. However, Captain James Wallis, writing in 1821, said 'Bunjaree's Norah' was the name given by the Aborigines to the 'river' at 'Reed's Mistake', a small harbour 18 miles south of Newcastle', in other words at the entrance to Lake Macquarie.[33] Reed's Mistake got its name in 1800 when Captain William Reid (or Reed) in the 30-ton schooner *Martha* sailed into the entrance of Lake Macquarie believing it was Hunter's River.

In his book, *An Historical Account of the Colony of new South Wales* (1821), Wallis presented an engraving, *Black Swans of New South Wales* (Fig. 3), subtitled *View on Reed's Mistake River, N.S.W.* 'The scenery on this river, called by the natives Bunjarees Norah, is rich, luxuriant, and picturesque,' he wrote. 'Kangaroos are found here in abundance, as well as wild fowl: the natives are a very friendly tribe, and excellent fishermen.'

It seems unlikely that Bungaree was born as far north as Bungary Norah, because in 1801 he was not able to communicate with Budgery Dick, an Aboriginal he met at Reed's Mistake, who presumably spoke Awaba, the language of the people then living around today's Lake Macquarie and Newcastle.[34]

Modern historians have identified six bands of the Ku-ring-gai language nation in the area bounded by Port Jackson, Broken Bay and the Lane Cove River. The most numerous and powerful was the Cammeraigal (Gammarigal), occupying the land east of the Lane Cove River and north to Middle Harbour, whose warriors acted as *Koradgees* (Collins' *Carrahdys*) during initiation ceremonies at Farm Cove and other places. The Sydney suburb of Cammeray is named after them. Other Ku-ring-gai-speaking bands were the Carigal (West Head), Terramerragal (Turramurra), Kayimai (Manly harbour), Cannangal (Manly coast) and Goruagal (Fig Tree Point).[35]

It is impossible to determine the year of Bungaree's birth. Sentimentalists would like him to have been born in 1770, the year James Cook passed Broken Bay in *Endeavour*. Bungaree may have been born as early as 1765, if he was 'about 55 years of age', an estimate by Captain Bellingshausen in 1820 [36]; or in 1772, if he was about 45 years of age in 1817 as stated by Phillip Parker King.[37] A birth date as late as 1778–80 is possible. Bungaree would then have been a young boy during Governor Phillip's first visits to Broken Bay and about 19 or 20 years old when he signed on with Matthew Flinders on HMS *Norfolk* in 1799.

After the disruption of Aboriginal life and culture which followed the smallpox outbreak, the survivors combined to form new social groups, known to Europeans by such names as the 'Botany Bay Tribe', the 'Kissing Point Tribe' (Ryde) and the 'Womerah Tribe' (Rushcutters Bay). One such group of people, which included Bungaree, was called the 'Broken Bay Tribe'.

3 Sailing with Matthew Flinders

At the other side of the world on another eastern seaboard, the low-lying Lincolnshire fens border The Wash, a muddy inlet of the sombre North Sea.

The fens, said outsiders, were as flat as a writing slate or a page in a schoolbook, but to a sharp-eyed native of Lincolnshire, like young Matthew Flinders, there were as many peaks and troughs as the ocean. The countryside around the market town of Donington, where Flinders lived, seemed like a giant patchwork of intensely green squares, the sunken fields where farmers grew corn, barley, spinach, celery and potatoes. Donington was also a centre for flax and hemp crops to supply sails and ropes for the Royal Navy. The fields were edged with blue ribbons of swift-flowing dikes higher than a boy's head and creaking timber windmills constantly pumping up flumes of water. Dominating the landscape of flat fields was the Gothic tower of St Botolph's church at Boston which locals called 'The Stump'.

Once the fenlanders lived like amphibians in the oozy mud and rushes in cottages thatched with reeds on river islands which almost sank beneath the water in winter. From small boats they trapped eels and netted wild geese and ducks. Many Lincolnshire men went to sea as fishermen or sailors. Some kept cattle and Lincoln sheep and strapped on stilts to guide their animals through the marshes to pasture. They dug peat turf for fires and made baskets from willows growing along the river banks. The fenlanders despised upland folk who spent their lives on dry ground.

In those days villages like Donington, Spilsby, Revesby, Boston and Partney were islands surrounded by swamps. Then in the seventeenth century, the Earls of Bedford sent for Cornelius Vermuyden, a Dutch engineer, who brought his men from the Low Countries over the North Sea to cut canals and build windmills and water pumps to drain the saturated fens. Like a sponge squeezed out, the earth shrank and the land dropped 12 feet below the level of the dikes.[1] The fens had been tamed, but not the fenlanders.

Everywhere in the fens water raced towards the sea. After school and at weekends small boys spent their free time fishing and mucking about in boats. Visiting Boston, a lively port, Flinders would see ships loading at the warehouses on the Witham River quays. From the third-floor attic of his family's brick house he could trace the thin streams emptying into wider canals which flowed to the sea walls at the muddy black edges of the Wash 9 miles away. They say that one day Matthew Flinders felt that impulse and followed a run of water until the sea mists rolled in like a dark blanket and he was lost. The church bells sounded and a search party soon found him and took him home to a warm fire.[2]

Matthew Flinders, who was to become Australia's greatest maritime explorer, was born in Donington on 16 March 1774, the son of Matthew Flinders (1750–1802), a surgeon and apothecary.[3] The name Flinders suggests a Flemish origin, which has been traced to Thomas of Flanders, a sixteenth-century Nottingham stocking weaver. Matthew's great-grandfather, John Flinders (1682–1741), who settled in Donington about 1700, was the first of three generations of surgeons.[4]

His father expected young Matthew to follow him as a surgeon, but by the age of 14 the boy had made up his mind to become a mariner. Shortly before his death Flinders told the *Naval Chronicle* that he was 'induced to go to sea against the wishes of friends from reading *Robinson Crusoe*'.[5] Matthew's uncle John Flinders, whose son John was a naval lieutenant, urged him to study Euclid and navigation. Matthew spent a year doggedly learning mathematics and navigation from John Robertson's *Elements of Navigation* and Hamilton Moore's *Practical Navigator*.[6] The next year he joined the Royal Navy as a junior midshipman, which at that time meant an officer's servant. He was posted to HMS *Alert*, a depot ship based at Chatham, where he trained on the spars and rigging and 'learned the ropes'. Matthew spent the next year on HMS *Bellerophon*, commanded by his patron Captain Thomas Pasley.[7]

At the age of 17, Matthew Flinders sailed as a midshipman on HMS *Providence* on 2 August 1791 with William Bligh (after the famous mutiny on the *Bounty*) on the second and successful voyage to bring breadfruit trees from Tahiti to the West Indies. He is said to have learned the practical skills of navigation, marine surveying and charting directly from Bligh, who in turn learned from James Cook while sailing master on HMS *Resolution*. During this voyage Flinders had his first taste of the tropics and the South Seas. They touched at Adventure Bay in Van Diemen's Land and returned through the dangerous coral maze of Torres Strait.[8]

Two years later, when *Providence* returned to England on 7 August 1793, Matthew Flinders made the acquaintance of Sir Joseph Banks in dealings between the great man of science and the ship's botanist James Wiles.[9] He rejoined *Bellerophon* and took part in the Battle of Brest on 'the glorious first of June' in which Pasley, then a rear admiral, lost a leg to cannon fire.

After shore leave and a visit to his family and relatives in Lincolnshire, Matthew Flinders enlisted as master's mate on HMS *Reliance*, which sailed for Port Jackson in company with HMS *Supply* on 25 February 1795, bringing Captain John Hunter to Sydney as second governor of New South Wales. Also on board was Matthew's younger brother, Samuel Ward Flinders, a midshipman, Captain Henry Waterhouse, who had served with Flinders on *Bellerophon*, Lieutenant John Shortland and Bennelong, the Aborigine from Port Jackson who came to England with Governor Arthur Phillip.[10]

After the death of Arabanoo, Bennelong and Coleby, two Camaraigal men from Manly, were captured at the governor's orders in November 1789. Coleby escaped, but Bennelong soon adopted European dress and customs, including a fondness for wine and brandy.[11] When they arrived in London in 1793, Bennelong and his companion Yemmerrawannie, a young Aborigine who had been taught to wait at table, were lionised by society and Bennelong was presented to King George at St James' Palace.[12] Following Yemmerrawannie's death in England in 1794, Bennelong became ill. He was nursed back to health during the voyage by the ship's surgeon George Bass. In return, Bennelong instructed Bass in the language of the Sydney Aborigines.

George Bass, 32 years old, 6 feet tall and the son of a farmer born in Aswarby near Sleaford in Lincolnshire, and Matthew Flinders, 5 feet 6 inches and just 21 years old, became close friends. They shared a love of the sea and decided to complete the exploration of the east coast of New Holland together.[13]

Reliance arrived at Port Jackson on 7 September 1795. A few weeks later (26 October), Bass and Flinders, with William Martin, the surgeon's boy servant, set out on a nine-day expedition in the *Tom Thumb*, a small single-masted boat only 8 feet long. They steered out of Sydney Heads and through the turbulent Pacific Ocean swell to Botany Bay, then explored the winding George's River for 20 miles above its mouth. They were encouraged in their exploration by Governor Hunter, who had sailed as captain of HMS *Sirius* in the First Fleet and was the first to survey Botany Bay, Port Jackson and Broken Bay.[14]

In January 1796 Bass and Flinders sailed with *Reliance* to Norfolk Island. On their return to Sydney Cove in March 1796, the two men took a larger boat, also called *Tom Thumb*, and explored the coast south of Botany Bay. They spent the first three nights at sea, dropping a stone as anchor. They then rowed up a small stream where they met a large group of hostile Aborigines whom Flinders pacified by clipping their hair and beards with a large pair of scissors while Bass spread their sea-sodden gunpowder on the rocks to dry in the sun. Another night was spent running before a storm through breaking waves. While Flinders steered with an oar, Bass wrestled with the sail and Martin bailed water for dear life. Running close to the surf, they pulled down their mast and found the boat suddenly becalmed behind a reef at Wattamolla, now part of the Royal National Park. After exploring Port Hacking, *Tom Thumb* returned to her anchorage beside *Reliance* in Port Jackson on 2 April.[15]

In September 1796, Flinders sailed from Sydney to the convict settlement at Norfolk Island on *Reliance*, commanded by Henry Waterhouse. During a stormy passage, the leaky old ship then circumnavigated the world via Cape Horn and the Cape of Good Hope, returning in June 1797 with cattle for the starving colony—26 cows, 3 bulls and 60 head of sheep.[16]

While Flinders was busy in Port Jackson with repairs to *Reliance*, Bass was able to continue his 'part-time' exploration. At the end of 1797 in a voyage of 1,200 miles, in

Fig. 4.

The Tom Thumb *in Difficulties*
Cassell's *Picturesque Australasia* (1889).

a 28-foot open whaleboat with six oarsmen, Bass rounded Wilson's Promontory and discovered Western Port (Westernport, Victoria). He returned to Sydney in February 1798 convinced that there was a wide opening between Van Diemen's Land and the continent. The same month, Governor Hunter sent Flinders to the Furneaux Islands in the schooner *Francis* to pick up crew and some of the cargo from the wreck of the merchant ship *Sydney Cove*.[17]

After another trip to Norfolk Island in the *Reliance*, Governor Hunter gave Matthew Flinders command of the colonial-built decked 25-ton vessel *Norfolk*. The three-month voyage which followed was the greatest achievement of Bass and Flinders as a team. With a crew of eight volunteer seamen, they sailed south from Sydney Cove on 7 October 1798. The little ship steered westward through the passage later called Bass Strait by way of the Furneaux Islands and made the first circumnavigation of Van Diemen's Land.

They entered and partly surveyed the estuary of the River Tamar, where Launceston now stands. *Norfolk* returned to Port Jackson on 12 January 1799 after a voyage of 14 weeks. In time, this discovery shortened the voyage from the Cape of Good Hope to Sydney by at least a week.[18]

On 27 May 1799 Flinders said goodbye to his friend George Bass who sailed for England via China on the *Nautilus*. On his next voyage, Bass set sail for Chile on the brig *Venus*, and was never seen again.[19]

Governor Hunter wrote a personal letter on 1 June 1799 to Sir Joseph Banks, who was destined to play a major role in Flinders' career, advising him of the discovery of Bass Strait.[20] Flinders' reports and accurate charts were sent to England and published in the *Naval Chronicle*.

The Little Sloop

The tiny *Norfolk* which Flinders and Bass sailed around Van Diemen's Land was built in 1797 on Norfolk Island from Norfolk pine at the direction of Captain John Townson of the New South Wales Corps. She arrived at Port Jackson in June 1798. Cramped and leaking, but with a covered deck, a mast and bowsprit and two pumps, she was superior to the open whaleboat.[21] Flinders said of the *Norfolk*: 'Upon the whole she performed wonderfully; seas that were apparently determined to swallow her up she rode over with all the ease and majesty of an old experienced petrel'.

In May 1770, when HMS *Endeavour* passed Stradbroke Island, an acute observer on board, none other than Joseph Banks, noticed the sudden 'dirty clay colour' of the sea and was 'led to conclude that the bottom of the bay might open into a large river'.[22] James Cook disagreed. 'It was a point that could not be cleared up, as we had the wind,' Cook wrote, 'but should anyone be desirous of doing it that may come after me, this place may always be found by three hills [the Glass Houses] which lay to the northward of it.'

Sailing a league (about 4.5 kilometres) out to sea, Cook took Moreton Island to be the mainland coast and marked a bay on his map as a wide indentation facing the ocean between Point Lookout and Cape Moreton. He named this Morton Bay (now Moreton Bay) after James Douglas, the fourteenth Earl of Morton, President of the Royal Society. The expanse of water which he glimpsed behind the cape, Cook named Glass House

Bay after the strange conical hills nearby which he called the Glass Houses because their shape reminded him of the glass kilns of his native Yorkshire.[23]

On 4 July 1799, Governor Hunter added a postscript to a letter he had begun writing to Sir Joseph Banks on 1 June: 'I am just fitting out the little Sloop to send Lt. Flinders to the Northward to look into Harvey Bay, which I have conceivd from the largeness of the opening may shew us a large & extensive Sea within, or perhaps a navigable river which may leed us some distance into the interior of the Country.' The suggestion for this expedition had come from Matthew Flinders.[24] Years later, Flinders wrote in his book *Terra Australis* (1814):

> His Excellency accepted a proposition to explore *Glass-house* and Hervey's Bays, two large openings to the northwards, of which the entrances only were known . . . The sloop Norfolk was again allotted to us, with nearly the same volunteer crew as before; and I was accompanied by Mr W. S . [Samuel] Flinders, a midshipman of the *Reliance*, and by *Bongaree*, a native, whose good disposition and manly conduct had attracted my esteem.[25]

Matthew Flinders, who had known Bungaree long enough to form an opinion of his character, had found his Man Friday. During six weeks of exploration, Bungaree was his constant companion in the ship's boat. Flinders, now aged 25, valued Bungaree's friendship and came to rely on his skill as a go-between with the coastal Aborigines.[26]

In *Terra Australis* Flinders gives only a brief account of the voyage 'almost confined to nautical subjects'. He directed readers desiring more information on the places visited and their inhabitants to his personal journal, given to Governor Hunter. The journal, published in Vol. II of *An Account of the English Colony in New South Wales* by David Collins (1802), contains the first references to Bungaree in historical records. Collins writes as if he is also familiar with Bungaree (spelt Bongaree by Flinders and Bong-ree by Collins): 'The vessel was manned with volunteers from the two king's ships, and Lieutenant Flinders was accompanied by Bong-ree, a native of the northside of Broken Bay, who had been noted for his good disposition, and open and manly conduct'.

The *Norfolk* took on provisions for 11 weeks. She sailed out of Port Jackson into the Pacific Ocean on 8 July 1799 and turned northwards, sighting the coast next morning to the north of Port Stephens. A day later, the little sloop sprang a leak. She let in 'as much water as kept one pump constantly going' and the pumps were frequently choked with maize from her former cargo.

On Thursday 11 July, Flinders explored a large shallow bay, which he called Shoal Bay, a name he said was 'but too well merited'. The next day about noon they landed on the south headland of the bay to observe the latitude. They spent an hour examining three nearby Aboriginal huts which were circular and about 8 feet in diameter. The huts had frames made of strong vines tied together with wiry grass and were roofed with soft bark. One was a double hut with two recesses, large enough for 12 or 15 people. 'How much superior in contrivance to those about Port Jackson, or in Van Diemen's Island,' Collins commented in a footnote:

> Bong-ree readily admitted that they were much superior to any huts of the natives which he had before seen. He brought away a small hand basket, made of some kind of leaf, capable of containing five or six pints of water, and very nearly resembling those used at Coupang [Kupang] in the island of Timor for carrying toddy [palm wine], which Mr Flinders had noticed there.

After examining a palm tree with edible nuts, Flinders concluded that 'as Bong-ree . . . never saw or heard of it before', Shoal Bay was probably one of the most southerly places in which the tree could be found. They did not find the entrance to the Clarence River.

On Saturday 13 July, *Norfolk* passed Cape Byron and Mount Warning and rounded Cape Moreton, dropping anchor at the entrance to Cook's Glass House Bay that night. Ranging within 1 mile of the shore next day they saw a group of about 10 Aborigines waving a green branch. 'They appeared to be friendly, using nearly the same word in calling our people that would have been made use of by a Port Jackson native,' said Flinders.

Skirmish Over a Hat

As day broke on Tuesday 16 July, Flinders was searching for a place to repair the ship's leak. Baffled by a maze of shallow water channels and sandbanks, he was forced to leave *Norfolk* anchored 5 miles offshore. After breakfast he steered the ship's boat towards a sandy point of land, taking Bungaree with him. A few dogs came down to the beach and soon a few Aborigines appeared, some carrying fishing nets over their shoulders. The sailors rested on their oars while they conversed with the natives by signs and by repeating the words they used. 'As they seemed to be friendly, Bong-ree wished to make them a visit; and seeing nothing among them but pieces of firewood which the natives usually carry with them, the boat was backed in, and he jumped on shore, naked, and as unarmed as they themselves appeared.'

Bungaree quickly exchanged the yarn band he wore around his waist for a fillet (a narrow band or ribbon) of kangaroo hair. The English sailors kept their muskets at the ready, but everything went well; in fact the natives seemed shy. Matthew Flinders, who was wearing a splendid cabbage tree hat, joined Bungaree, taking his gun with him. He put down the gun and held out a woollen cap which one man took from him. When Flinders made signs that he expected the man's net bag in exchange, the Aborigine gave him to understand that he must first give him his own hat. 'This hat was made of the white filaments of the cabbage-tree, and it seemed to excite the attention and wishes of the whole party.' As Flinders did not offer his hat in return, the man threw the cap on the bank behind him and came forward. He seemed anxious to have the hat or the gun, or both.

Flinders and Bungaree retreated slowly towards the boat, but turned around when they found the Aborigines right behind them. One of the men, laughing and talking to Flinders, tried to remove the hat from his head with a long stick. This provoked a ripple of laughter. Another man stretched out his arm to take the hat, but was afraid to come close enough to reach it.

When Flinders and Bungaree got into the boat, the Aboriginal fishermen tried to persuade them to land again. When this failed, one of them threw a piece of firewood at the boat, but it fell short. The incident was treated as a joke and raised a laugh. Another man ran into the water and hurled his piece of wood, which also fell short. He then took the stick and slipped off its hook to reveal a spear. Running up to his waist in the water, he hurled the spear which passed half a metre over the the centre of the boat, but touched no-one.

This 'impudent and unprovoked attack' (in Collins' opinion) was a serious turn of events.

Flinders picked up his musket, loaded with buckshot, and twice attempted to fire at the spear thrower, but the flint was wet and it misfired. Ignorant of the effect of firearms, the Aborigines showed no concern. At the third attempt the gun went off. The man in the water instantly fell flat, while those on shore jumped up and scrambled towards the sandbank behind them, some upright and some crawling on all fours. One of the sailors fired his gun among the Aborigines, who at first fell flat on their faces, but then ran into the bush.

The man in the water stood up and ran off, but more slowly than the rest. Obviously wounded, he stooped, holding one hand behind him and looking over his shoulder as if expecting to see a spear in his back. He was the first victim of the white man's 'thunder-stick' in this part of Australia. Bungaree later said another Aborigine had his arm broken by the second shot from the boat.

Matthew Flinders decided it was time to give these 'black savages' a lesson, to ensure the future safety of himself and his men. He loaded two musket balls into his gun and fired at an Aborigine 200 yards away who was looking out from the trees. One ball hit the edge of the bank in front of the man, while the other flew over his head. They could not see whether the shots had had any effect. Flinders, Bungaree and one of the boat crew landed on the beach to take away the fishing nets, which it was assumed the natives had abandoned in their flight. Climbing the bank, Flinders saw several men running in different directions among the trees. Suspecting they were preparing an attack, he directed Bungaree and the sailor to return to the boat. Later Bungaree 'whose eyes were better than those of Mr Flinders' said he believed they were running to conceal themselves. They did not leave their nets.

Fifteen years later in *Terra Australis*, Flinders explained this 'unfortunate occurrence' in a few words: 'There was a party of natives on the point, and our communication was at first friendly, but after receiving presents they made an attack, and one of them was wounded by our fire'. There was no mention of his cabbage tree hat. This first contact between the exploring party and the inhabitants of what is now Bribie Island was an echo of a similar incident in which James Cook fired his musket at two Aborigines who resisted his landing at Botany Bay in 1770. Sadly, these encounters set the pattern for continuing conflict between the white settlers and the black people of Australia. At the first sign of trouble, Flinders had fallen back on firearms. He had handled this meeting with the Aboriginal fishermen badly and his inexperience had led him to misinterpret their intentions. Bungaree's presence and knowledge of Aboriginal protocol may have helped to avert more bloodshed on both sides.

Flinders gave the name Point Skirmish (now Skirmish Point) to the flat, sandy beach at the lower end of Bribie Island where this brief clash took place. Close by today is the small seaside resort of Boongaree, joined to the Queensland mainland by a long timber bridge. This town, its post office and caravan park carry the name of the brave Aborigine from Broken Bay.

The *Norfolk* was brought around Skirmish Point to an opening 1 mile wide which Flinders, 'from the quantity of pumice stone on its borders', named the Pumice-stone River (now Pumicestone Passage). 'It led towards the remarkable peaks called the Glass Houses, which were now suspected to be volcanic, and excited my curiosity,' he wrote. Unable to make much headway against the outgoing tide, the ship's party landed on a beach on the eastern shore. They inspected a group of five or six empty huts, with roofs like archways, 12–15 feet in length, similar to those at Shoal Bay. They found a shield and a fishing net in the huts.

Returning to the sloop, Flinders was told that the leak had been caused by a plank coming away near the keel. Very little water came in after caulking with oakum (teased hemp rope) from the inside. They left the wide channel and Glass Houses for future examination and turned the sloop into the bay on the afternoon tide.

Next day they anchored off Red-cliff (Redcliff) Point, named because of the colour of the rocks, tinged red by iron, then pulled over to a green headland (Woody Point). Flinders was intrigued by a strong twined fishing net 14 fathoms (25 metres) long with large mesh holes found in a hut nearby. The net was taken 'as proof of the superior ingenuity of these over the natives of Port Jackson'. Flinders left behind a hatchet to console the owners for the loss of their handiwork. They noticed a rotting stringybark canoe and saw traces of dogs, kangaroos and emus on the beach.

The following morning the explorers passed several bushy islands. Heading to the third of these, their attention was attracted by a group of about 20 Aborigines who seemed to be standing up in canoes, using all their strength to paddle with long poles or spears, shifting their hands in unison 'in the manner of the South Sea islanders'. Flinders ordered the sloop to be put under easy sail, pistols and muskets were prepared and the decks were cleared for possible action: 'what was their surprise in discovering, that, instead of advancing in canoes to attack them, they were standing upon a large flat [sandbank], that surrounded the third island, driving fish into their nets, and that they had but two canoes among them'. The fishermen stood in a line, splashing the water with long sticks, first on one side, then on the other. 'Thus this hostile array turned out to be a few peaceable fishermen: peaceable indeed; for on the approach of the vessel they sunk their canoes upon the flat, and retreated to the island, where they made their fires.'

They continued to explore the bay by boat, landing on Friday 19 July on an island covered with mangroves, palms and a kind of pine. There were traces of fireplaces and abundant bird life. 'The black and white cockatoo, the beautiful lilac-headed parroquet, and the bald-headed mocking bird of Port Jackson [kookaburra], were seen here.' Flinders returned to the *Norfolk*, planning to run into Pumice-stone River to look for a place to repair the sloop and visit the Glass Houses. They spent all day Saturday trying to get into the channel, finally anchoring near the entrance at sunset.

Early on Sunday Flinders went to examine the channel. On approaching Point Skirmish, 'five or six natives came down to the boat unarmed, and, by friendly gestures and offers of their girdles and small nets, endeavoured to persuade him to land'. Flinders, however, suspected their motives and decided not to trust them.

The passage was intricate, but there was enough water to allow the sloop to enter. They saw many pelicans and were soon greeted with 'the creaking note of the swan'. Before leaving they had shot and killed eight of the birds. As they were about to leave, two Aborigines came down to the beach and gestured to the party to land. The boat was run ashore on dry sand, out of reach of possible spears, but when Flinders aimed his gun at two red-billed birds, the natives ran into the bush. When Bungaree went towards them they returned and exchanged their hair fillets and belts for a white woollen cap. They came to the boat for a piece of white cloth and some biscuit 'to make the exchange equal'. All this time, Flinders was on shore with his gun, to cover Bungaree 'in case their behaviour should be unfriendly'. When he advanced towards them, the Aborigines were 'very vociferous' for him to stay back and would not allow him to approach without laying down the musket. 'This place was about six miles from Point Skirmish,' wrote David Collins, 'but it was evident that the fame and dread of their fire-arms had reached thus far, and were most probably increased by the shooting of the swans, which they must have witnessed.'

Trim the Cat

In a biographical tribute to his cat Trim, written 10 years later on the Ile de France (Mauritius), Matthew Flinders mentioned the affection between Bungaree and Trim which began during the voyage of the *Norfolk*:

> In an expedition made to examine the northern parts of New South Wales, Trim presented a request to be one of the party, promising to take upon himself the defence of our bread bags, and his services were accepted. Bongaree, an intelligent native of Port Jackson, was also on board our little sloop; and with him Trim formed an intimate acquaintance. If he had occasion to drink, he mewed to Bongaree and leaped up to the water cask; if to eat, he called him down below and went straight to his kid [kit], where there was generally a remnant of black swan. In short, Bongaree was his great resource, and his kindness was repaid with caresses.[27]

This memory of his friendship with the ship's cat shows an unexpected side of Bungaree's nature. Although he may have preferred to sleep on deck, Bungaree kept his kit bag below. He seems to have courageously adapted to life at sea, which must have been daunting to most Aborigines.

Trim had been born on *Reliance* between Cape Town and Port Jackson. Flinders, who called his cat 'the most affectionate of friends', described him as 'clear black', with four white feet, a white underlip and a blaze of white on his chest. He was plump and playful, a good swimmer, and leapt up the rigging to the topmast quicker than any sailor.

Song and Dance

On Monday 22 July, working through 'an infinity of shoals', *Norfolk* again got into the channel. She was emptied and brought ashore on a small beach on the mainland, 5 miles above Point Skirmish. Next day the leak was plugged by filling up the seams with oakum, nailing back the loose plank and 'covering the whole with tarred canvas and some sheet lead'. Later, while waiting for the tide to rise, Flinders tried unsuccessfully to shoot some more black swans. He spotted 'several large fish, or, animals, that came to the surface of the water to blow, in the manner of a porpoise, or rather of a seal'. These were probably the seagrass-feeding dugong, still occasionally seen in Moreton Bay. He fired three musket balls into one and Bungaree threw a spear into another, but both sank and were not seen again.

While they were preparing the sails, which had been loosened to dry, three unarmed Aborigines appeared on the beach near the sloop. 'Bong-ree went up to them in his usual undaunted manner,' wrote Collins, 'but they would not suffer Mr Flinders or any of his party to approach them, without first laying down their muskets.' The men were given presents of yarn caps, pork and biscuit and made signs to Bungaree to go with them to receive headbands and arm fillets.

These three men then began 'dancing and singing in concert in a pleasing manner'—but when the number of white men in their audience had increased to eight, they became alarmed and suspicious. Seeing this, Flinders removed his shot belt and gave it to one of his men to take away. 'By this shot belt they seemed to recognise Mr Flinders as the person who had fired upon them before.' The Aborigines still insisted that Flinders should stay further away from them than the others.

In return for this impromptu entertainment, three of the Scots sailors were asked to dance a reel, 'but, for want of music they made a very bad performance, which was contemplated by the natives without much amusement or curiosity'. The Aborigines could not be persuaded to visit the sloop, but they parted company in a friendly manner. There was to be another such concert a few days later.

The following day *Norfolk* sailed 2 miles through divided channels fringed by mangrove islets and muddy flats. Next morning Flinders, Bungaree and two sailors took the ship's boat as far as possible, then landed and set out towards the beckoning Glass Houses. After trudging through swamps and rocky country for 9 miles, they reached the top of a stony mount only 4 miles from the highest Glass House peak. Matthew Flinders wrote later: 'On the 27th, we reached the foot of the nearest Glass House, a flat-topped peak, one mile and a half north of the stony mount. It was impossible to ascend this almost perpendicular rock; and finding no marks of volcanic eruption, we returned to the boat, and to the sloop the same evening.' They crossed a broad stream and walked 3 miles back to the river, where the waiting sailors gave Flinders a black swan they had just caught, 'ready for satisfying the appetites of his party', said Collins, 'which were not trifling, for a more laborious and tiresome walk of the same length would seldom be experienced'.

On Sunday 28 July the little sloop turned back down the passage. Groups of Aborigines followed them along the bank, keeping abreast, dancing and singing to attract attention. *Norfolk* berthed near the entrance, and three more black swans were caught. Soon after, Flinders took some of the crew ashore with axes to cut down a pine log so the timber could be evaluated at Port Jackson. Bungaree was talking to several Aborigines nearby when the tree fell. They were greatly startled by the crash and report. 'The gallant and unsuspecting native, Bong-ree, made them a present of one of his spears, and a throwing stick [woomerah], of which he showed them the use, for they appeared to be wholly ignorant of the latter, and their weapons of the former kind were inferior to his.'

Strong southerly winds and squalls kept the sloop at anchor for two days until 31 July. During this time, Aborigines came down both sides of the passage to visit them, once again singing and dancing, though their voices were almost lost in the wind. No spears were seen among them. Flinders took the opportunity to watch the Aboriginal method of fishing which was 'perfectly new to his companion Bong-ree'. Those camped on the east shore, near the *Norfolk*, went out at daylight each morning with nets slung over their shoulders. When a fish was spotted, the fisherman 'by some dexterous manoeuvre, gets at the back of it, and spreads his scoop net'. Others prevented the fish escaping at the sides and it was 'almost infallibly caught' in one of the nets. Sometimes the men ran up to their stomachs in the water. Soon they built a fire near the beach, so 'their fish was no sooner out of the water than it was on the fire'.

When the rain stopped on Tuesday afternoon (30 July), a party from the sloop went to the eastern side for firewood and to take up an invitation to visit the Aborigines. Seeing their approach, some of the natives carried their nets into the bush. Three men who remained allowed the foreigners to come near without putting down their muskets. Though still timid, they were encouraged by signs to sing:

> They began a song in concert, which actually was musical and pleasing, and not merely in the diatonic scale, descending by thirds, as at Port Jackson: the descent of this was waving, in rather a melancholy soothing strain. The song of Bong-ree, which he gave them at the conclusion of theirs, sounded barbarous and grating to the ear; for Bong-ree was an indifferent songster, even amongst his own countrymen.

While singing, the natives slowly moved their limbs and bodies, 'their hands being held up in a supplicating posture, and the tone and manner of their song and gestures seemed to bespeak the good will and forbearance of their auditors'.

Each singer then selected a partner from the strangers, placing his mouth close to the other's ear, 'as if to produce a greater effect, or, it might be, to teach them the song'. They were pleased when given worsted caps and a pair of old blanket trousers. Several other men appeared (probably those who had removed the fishing nets) and joined in the general song and dance. Three of these new arrivals had unusually large heads and one with a ferocious expression was described as having 'more the appearance of a baboon than of a human being'. His large mouth was set with teeth 'of every hue between black, white, green and yellow'.

Among other friendly exchanges, the Aborigines learned the white men's names. Matthew Flinders they called 'Mid-ger Plindah' and his brother Samuel they named 'Dam-well'. Three of the Aborigines were named Yel-yel-bah, Ye-woo and Bo-ma-ri-go. The new arrivals were introduced and their names were spoken and repeated until the British mariners could pronounce them. 'This ceremony was reciprocal, and accorded with what Captain Cook had said before of an inhabitant of Endeavour river, "he introduced the strangers by name, a ceremony which upon such occasions was never omitted".'

Traditionally, most Aborigines have several names and such an exchange of names denoted a special relationship. To show his regard for Governor Phillip, Bennelong had given him one of his own names, Wolawaree. He also called Phillip Been-èn-a (father), adopting for himself the name Governor. 'This interchange,' said Watkin Tench, 'we found is a constant symbol of friendship among them.'[28]

Flinders attributed the friendly relations with the local people to the superior force of his firearms. His participation in these happy sessions of singing and dancing and the solemn name-exchange ceremony contrasted with his bluster at the first meeting with the Aborigines, a result of Bungaree's willing services as an intermediary.

In *Robinson Crusoe*, the book which had so much influence on Matthew Flinders' life, Crusoe, seeking to allay Friday's fears, loads his gun and fires at a parrot (which he had taken to be a hawk) which drops to the ground. After the name-exchange ceremony, Matthew Flinders decided to demonstrate the power of firearms. His new friends watched nervously as he removed the buckshot from his musket and loaded a charge of small shot. They seemed to be on the point of running away, so he placed them behind the sailors. Flinders took aim and fired at the hawk, but the shot broke only its leg and the bird flew away. In Collins' account, Flinders is moved to recall how ineffectual his attempts to impress the natives had been: 'Bong-ree, his musician, had annoyed his auditors with his barbarous sounds, and the clumsy exhibition of his Scotch dancers unaccompanied with the aid of music, had been viewed by them without wonder or gratification'.

'These people were evidently of the same race as those at Port Jackson, though speaking a language that Bongaree cold not understand,' Flinders wrote in *Terra Australis* about the Aborigines at Bribie Island and Moreton Bay. 'They fish almost wholly with cast and setting nets, live more in society than the natives to the southward, and are much better lodged. Their spears are of solid wood, and used without the throwing stick.'

In his fuller journal, edited by David Collins, Flinders was more specific in his observations of their way of life. He noted that the natives were smaller than Englishmen and generally resembled the Port Jackson Aborigines in their features and physique, particularly in the curve of the thigh and the small calf of the leg, but added: 'there was not one in all this group, whose countenance had so little of the savage, or the symmetry of whose limbs expressed strength and agility, so much, as those of their companion Bong-ree'.

Apart from the fillets they wore around their waists, heads and upper arms, the Aborigines around Bribie Island went naked. These fillets were made of hair twisted into threads and woven into net like 'bandages'. Flinders was impressed by their fishing nets, especially one seine net 80 feet long, and the fact that they carried their possessions in bags hung around their necks. He thought their method of obtaining food would result in a difference in manners and perhaps in disposition compared to natives who mostly depended on the spear or fiz-gig—'fish-gigs', long spears ending in a fork with prongs to which sharp serrated bones were fastened. The cooperation of two or more people was needed to use fishing nets, he reasoned, whereas the solitary spearman, like those at Port Jackson, 'prowls along, a gloomy, unsettled, and unsocial being'. The fishing net, appearing to be a more certain source of food, made a change of place less necessary, as would the difficulty of carrying a large net from one place to another, which would require a more permanent residence. He supposed the use of nets arose from the shallow waters of the bay.

It is probable that the Aboriginal fishermen encountered by Flinders' expedition were Undanbi people of the Turubul language group, spoken throughout the territory ranging from the coastal strip along Coolum Beach and Moreton Bay and from Noosa Heads south to the mouth of the Brisbane River and including the Glass House mountains and Bribie Island.

Flinders had spent more than 16 days meticulously charting Glass House Bay, but, hampered by the leaking sloop, he failed to find the mouth of the Brisbane River, which was screened by the muddy, mangrove-covered Fisherman's Island. However, he established that the land Cook had seen was in fact two islands, Stradbroke and Moreton, which sheltered the 50-kilometre shoreline of the shallow bay from the ocean.

'On more than one occasion have I traversed every inch of [Flinders'] journey in Moreton Bay, not alone from Bribie, where the sloop "Norfolk" was repaired, but across the marshy flats right to the foot of the mountain he did not climb,' wrote Thomas Welsby in his preface to 'A Glimpse of Moreton Bay' in *The Discoverers of the Brisbane River* (1913). Welsby identified the islands visited by Flinders as Mud, St Helena, Peel, Coochie Mudlow, Green and Macleay.[29]

No further gunshots were to disturb the peace of the Moreton Bay fishermen for nearly 25 years. In 1824 soldiers and convicts from Sydney set up camp at Red-cliff Point. The settlement was abandoned soon after and moved to a site on the Brisbane River which became the cruel convict outpost of Moreton Bay, later known as Brisbane.

On Wednesday 31 July 1799 *Norfolk* finally beat out of Pumicestone Passage with the tide. The crew saw a large turtle asleep in the water and speculated that the long Aboriginal nets might be used to catch them. They reached Hervey Bay within two days, passing Wide Bay on 1 August and Sandy Cape the next day.

Flinders' party remained in Hervey Bay until 7 August, searching the deep, extensive harbour without finding any trace of an opening which might lead to a river. They landed at a sandy inlet where they found three wooden spears and a small shield. They met no Aborigines, but saw numerous 'smokes' from their fires around the bay. On 8 August *Norfolk* cleared Break Sea Spit and turned south towards Port Jackson, which was reached on 20 August 1799.

Ambitious Plans

Early in 1800 John Hunter returned to England with Captain Henry Waterhouse on *Reliance*. Matthew Flinders rejoined his old ship, which left Port Jackson on 3 March 1800. The worn-out craft was barely seaworthy. Kept afloat by the pumps, she made a tedious voyage via Cape Town, where Flinders passed a naval examination which confirmed his rank as lieutenant. *Reliance* sailed around Cape Horn, touched at the island of St Helena and docked at Plymouth on 26 August in such bad condition that she was taking in 9–10 inches of water per hour.[30]

Lieutenant Governor Colonel William Paterson sent a box of seeds and specimens to London with Waterhouse for Sir Joseph Banks (1743–1820), the influential president of the Royal Society.[31] Banks had made his name as a botanist and explorer in the epic voyage of the *Endeavour* with James Cook. He was considered to be an expert on New South Wales and had played a leading role in the establishment of the colony. He had the ear of his friend First Lord of the Admiralty Earl Spencer and was a confidant of King George III, for whom he unofficially directed the Royal Gardens at Kew. Sir Joseph's hunger for plants and natural history never waned. He kept up a large correspondence with men of science all around the world. He promoted and coordinated scientific expeditions, employed artists, botanists and gardeners and persuaded army and navy officers (and even governors) to act as amateur artists and collectors on his behalf. He helped to develop Australia's wool-growing industry.[32]

Though Matthew Flinders had been away for five and a half years and had just spent nearly six months at sea, he did not hurry home to Donington. On 6 September, still on board ship at Spithead, he sat down in his cabin to write a letter to Banks, seeking the great man's support to complete the investigation of the coast of the land he called Terra Australis. 'It cannot be doubted, but that a very great part of this still extensive country remains either totally unknown, or has been partially examined at a time when navigation was much less advanced than at present,' he wrote. 'The interests of geography and natural history in general, and of the British nation in particular, seem to require, that this only remaining considerable part of the globe should be thoroughly explored.'

Flinders offered his services as commander of such an expedition, for which, he said, two ships would be needed. He planned to go to London at the first opportunity to call on Sir Joseph and to deliver his charts to the Admiralty. As a part-time explorer in small boats and ships, Flinders had achieved a great deal. His first-hand knowledge of the south-eastern and eastern coastline of New Holland was unique and his detailed charts were to win him esteem.[33]

Though still a junior officer, he had precisely the right combination of experience, vision and ambition to lead a voyage of discovery which would fill in the blanks and complete the unfinished map of New Holland. In the miniature portrait (Plate 7) painted about this time, Matthew Flinders appears as a clean-shaven, dark-haired young man. The wistful, rather dreamy look about his eyes is balanced by a sombre, determined expression.

Banks, aged 57 in 1800, soon became Flinders' patron. He was impressed by the young man's chart-making skills, which he already knew from the reports of Hunter and Bass. He also knew that Flinders came from Lincolnshire, not far from his own estates at Revesby Abbey, near Boston. The letter was timely. In June 1800, the French Republic had applied for a passport for two ships, *Géographe* and *Naturaliste*, under Captain Nicolas Baudin, for a voyage of discovery in the South Seas which would include the southern coastline of New Holland. Baudin's expedition set out in October that year.

With Sir Joseph Banks as his backer, Matthew Flinders achieved his ambition. On 12 December 1800, he was ordered by the Admiralty to prepare for the voyage. His pamphlet, *Observations on the Coast of Van Diemen's Land, on Bass's Strait And its Islands*, dedicated to Banks, had been published earlier that year. On 16 February 1801, the 26-year-old Flinders was made commander of HMS *Investigator*, formerly HMS *Xenophon* and before that the *Fram*, a North Sea cat or collier. She was 100 feet 4 inches long and 25 feet 5 inches broad.[34] Flinders described *Investigator*:

> A north country built ship, of three hundred and thirty-four tons; and, in form, nearly resembled the description by Captain Cook as best calculated for voyages of discovery. She had been purchased some years before into His Majesty's service; and having been newly coppered and repaired was considered to be the best vessel which could, at that time, be spared for the projected voyage to Terra Australis.[35]

Flinders had leapt, in one bound, from the post of a junior officer of a 25-ton sloop with a crew of eight to the command of a 334-ton sloop with a complement of 88 persons; the best vessel that could be spared while Britain was at war with France.

On 15 April 1801, Flinders went home to Lincolnshire to meet his sweetheart Ann Chappell, daughter of a sailor and step-daughter of the Reverend William Tyler, rector of Brothertoft. They were married two days later at Partney. Flinders planned to take Ann with him to Port Jackson, where she could stay 'under some friendly roof' while he completed the most dangerous part of the survey. Ann came on board *Investigator* on 27 April and remained there several weeks.[36]

However, Sir Joseph Banks did not approve of either the marriage or the arrangement and on 21 May gave Flinders an ultimatum by letter. Two days later, Flinders told Sir Joseph by letter, 'I will give up the wife for the voyage of discovery'.[37] Ann left the ship and remained in Britain with her relations. She prepared for a long, lonely period of waiting for her husband to return from his voyage of exploration. It was to be tragically longer than either anticipated.

To the Coal River

Nearly two years after the expedition to Moreton Bay with Matthew Flinders, Bungaree's services were again called on by the authorities of New South Wales. In 1801 and 1804 he played a minor role in the foundation of the convict settlement at the mouth of the Hunter River, 160 kilometres north of Sydney, which was, in time, to become the city of Newcastle.

Plate 1. Detail: *PANORAMA OF SYDNEY N.S.W. in the Year 1829, as painted by Robert Burford and Exhibited in Leicester-square, LONDON.*
Robert Burford, 1829.
Hand-coloured engraving.
Frontispiece: *Description of a View of the Town of Sydney, New South Wales . . .* Bartholomew Close (London), J. & C. Adlard, 1829.
Dixson Galleries, Sydney.

Plate 2. *View in Broken Bay, New South Wales, March 1788*
William Bradley, 1788.
Watercolour (signed 'W.B.').
A Voyage to New South Wales, manuscript journal of Lieutenant William Bradley, Mitchell Library, Sydney.

Plate 3. *'BUNGAREE.'*
Augustus Earle, 1826 (previously atttributed to Charles Rodius).
Hand-coloured lithograph, 25 x 40 cm.
Mitchell Library, Sydney.

Plate 4. *'BUNGAREE!'*
'King' of the Aborigines of New South Wales
Augustus Earle, 1826 (previously attributed to Charles Rodius).
Hand-coloured lithograph, 25.4 x 40 cm.
Dixson Library, Sydney.

Plate 5. *Vue de George's Street à Sydney*
(Nouvelles Galles du Sud)
(View of George Street, Sydney [New South Wales])
Louis Auguste de Sainson, 1826.
Coloured lithograph by Alexis Nöel, 1830, 21 x 31.8 cm.
Plate 32: Atlas Historique. D'Urville, Jules Dumont, *Voyage de la Corvette l'Astrolabe . . .* Paris, J. Tartu, 1833.
Rex Nan Kivell Collection, National Library of Australia, Canberra.

Plate 6. *Bungaree,*
A Native of New South Wales
Augustus Earle, 1826.
Oil on canvas, 68.5 x 50.6 cm.
Rex Nan Kivell Collection, National Library of Australia, Canberra (on loan to Australian National Gallery, Canberra).

Plate 7. *Matthew Flinders*
Unknown artist, 1801.
Miniature, watercolour on ivory, oval, 6 x 4.9 cm.
(Framed with a lock of hair at the back)
Mitchell Library, Sydney.

Personal relics of Matthew Flinders
Presented by his grandson, Sir Matthew Flinders Petrie.
Photographs, 1991. Mitchell Library, Sydney.

Plate 8. Matthew Flinders' cocked hat, c. 1800
Black velour, black braid, black leather cockade, ribbon and button.

Plate 9. Matthew Flinders' sextant
Made by Watkins, London.

Plate 10. Set of French chessmen brought from Mauritius, 1810.
Shaving brush, glass dish, mirror and ink bottle in box.
Box owned by Mrs Ann Flinders containing locks of Matthew Flinders' hair.

Plate 11. *Sydney.*
KING BONGAREE.
Lend me one Dump!
Artist unknown, c. 1830.
Collage watercolour.
A. W. Fuller Collection, Dixson Library, Sydney.

8. St. James Church.
9. Botany Bay.
10. Cooper's Distillery.
11. Road to Paramatta.
12. New Court House.
13. Market.
14 Mr Barnet Levys.

15 School of Industry.
16 Natives.
17 Entrance to Government Gardens.
18 Genl Darling & Col Dumaresq.
19 King Bongaree.
20 Bank of New South.
21 Military Barracks.

22 Land Board Office.
23 Sir John Jamieson's.
24 Colonial Treasurer's.
25 Scotch Kirk.
26 Cockle Bay.
27 St Phillips.
28 Sydney Hotel.

Plate 1.

Plate 2.

Plate 3.

BUNGAREE. *Chief of the Aborigines of New South Wales*

Plate 4.

VUE DE GEORGE'S STREET A SYDNEY

(Nouvelle Galles du Sud.)

Plate 5.

Plate 6.

Plate 7.

Plate 11.

Plate 8.

Plate 9.

Plate 10.

In March 1791 Cornish-born convicts William and Mary Bryant, with their two small children and seven other convicts, stole Governor Arthur Phillip's six-oared cutter and slipped out of Sydney Cove by night. Starving and lashed by storms the fugitives sailed 3,254 miles through treacherous coral reefs in less than 10 weeks to the Dutch outpost of Coupang (Kupang) on the island of Timor. Their feat of navigation is comparable to Captain William Bligh's six week voyage with 18 of his men in a 23-foot long open launch across 3,618 miles of the Pacific Ocean from Tonga to Coupang after the mutiny on HMS *Bounty* in 1789.[38] After two days the escaped convicts reached 'a little creek' to the north of Port Jackson where they found a 'quantity of fine burning coal', one of the survivors, James Martin, wrote later while in Newgate Gaol.[39]

While unsuccessfully pursuing Irish convict 'bolters' who had seized the schooner *Cumberland* in September 1797, Lieutenant John Shortland in a whaleboat passed a rocky islet, crossed a dangerous sand bar, and entered a river which he named Hunter's River after the Governor. 'In the harbour was found a very considerable quantity of coal of a very good sort and lying so near the water side as to be conveniently shipped,' David Collins recorded. Coal seams in the cliffs could be clearly seen from the sea.[40]

The Lady Nelson & Frances Schooner entering Hunters or Coal River.

Fig. 5.

The Lady Nelson & Frances Schooner entering Hunters or Coal River
Engraving by S. I. Neele after James Grant, 1801.

Grant, James, *The Narrative of a Voyage of Discovery . . .* London, 1803.

In June 1801, the new governor of New South Wales, Phillip Gidley King, a veteran of the First Fleet voyage of 1788, sent a party in the sloop HMS *Lady Nelson*, commanded by Lieutenant James Grant, a 28-year-old Scot, to examine and survey the entrance to Hunter's River, which had become known as 'Coal River' or 'Coal Harbour'. The expedition was led by William Paterson, a keen botanist. He was accompanied by Surgeon John Harris of the New South Wales Corps; surveyor Francis Barrallier, a French-born ensign in the New South Wales Corps; botanist George Caley; and artist and naturalist John William Lewin. Like the governor, Paterson was a protégé of Sir Joseph Banks. Grant had been nominated by Banks, Caley was employed by him to collect plants and Banks had arranged for Lewin to collect insects in New Holland. John Platt, a miner, and several workmen and labourers were sent to cut and store timber and dig and load coal.

'With us likewise,' Grant noted, 'went one of the natives, named Bangaree.'[41]

Lady Nelson, 60 tons and 52 feet long, was built at Deptford on the Thames in 1799. This unusual craft, intended for surveying inshore waters, was fitted with three sliding keels or centreboards, the invention of Captain John Schanck, a former commissioner of the Transport Board. When the keels were raised she could enter water as shallow as 6 feet. Snub-nosed and square of stern, *Lady Nelson* was considered unsafe by her crew, who dubbed her 'His Majesty's Tinder Box'. She carried enough timber on board to build another ship of the same size. The sloop, with a crew of 15 press-ganged men under Grant, left London in January 1800 and was the first ship from England to sail through Bass Strait.

She arrived at Port Jackson on 16 December 1800 and moored off Garden Island, where vegetables were grown for her new crew, mostly convicts. Though her main and after keels had been lost in rough weather on the maiden voyage, Grant reported that the *Lady Nelson* was 'equal to any as a sea boat'.[42]

Budgerie Dick

Lady Nelson set sail from Port Jackson for the Hunter River on 10 June 1801. She was accompanied by the 41-ton schooner *Francis*, which was to be loaded with coal. At noon the next day they passed Broken Bay. Due to the error of a pilot on board who mistook the entrance for the Hunter River, the ship put in at Reed's Mistake on 12 June.

Surgeon Harris went ashore to reconnoitre but could not find any river. He returned with an Aborigine who ran down to the boat, crying out 'Whale Boat!' and 'Budgerie Dick!' (budgerie or boodgery meaning 'good'). It was supposed the name was given to him by sailors pursuing the convicts who seized the *Norfolk* at Broken Bay in October 1800 and ran her aground. 'This man had some fish with him, which he threw into the boat first, and then jumped into it himself, without the least hesitation,' wrote Grant:

> Our new acquaintance Dick, as soon as he got on board, continued his cries of Whale Boat! and in order to discover what he meant by them, I introduced him to Bangaree, with directions to the latter to question him on the subject. Bangaree pointed to him to sit down, which, I have observed before, implied that a stranger was received with friendship. It was in vain for me to desire Bangaree to proceed in his enquiries, there was another etiquette, which could not be omitted, and this was a continuance in profound silence. This lasted for about 20 minutes, at the expiration of which time they by degrees entered into discourse, drawing near to each other, as they began to talk. We received, however, little information from Dick, whether it was that Bangaree did not well understand him; and I am inclined to think so, for some

of our people, who were best acquainted with the language spoken by the natives around Sydney, were at the same loss.

The ship took Budgerie Dick to the Hunter River. Grant hoisted a flag on the island (now Nobbys Head) to indicate the entrance of the river. The next day Dick left as the party explored the bush. Two days later, said Grant, Dick reappeared with two companions. One of them had visited Sydney and was known to Colonel Paterson, so 'a kind of conversation was kept up'.[43]

After landing, Bungaree also ran off and was sorely missed. Surgeon Harris and Paterson both mentioned him in their letters sent from the Hunter River to Governor King in Sydney on the same day, 25 June 1801. Harris blamed Grant for mistaking the entrance of the river and added:

> The Natives here are remarkably shy. I am afraid they have been badly used by the White people Here some time since—
> We have notwithstanding caught two of them in the Woods, treated them kindly and let them go About their business. I hope it may have a good effect. The Native which we brought . . . with us, Bonjary ran off after we reached the River and has not since returned—.[44]

Paterson wrote:

> We have not yet had any communication with the natives. We have seen them at a distance, but remarkably shy. Yesterday, the 22nd, Mr. Barrallier and Bowen fell in with one by accident and brought him on board, but as Bungery had left us we could make nothing of him.[45]

The *Francis* returned to Port Jackson with 75 tons of coal which was exchanged with the master of the ship *Marquis Cornwallis* for nails and iron, 'articles that were much wanted', wrote David Collins, 'thus, for the first time, making the natural produce of the country contribute to its wants'. The coal, Australia's first export cargo, was taken to Bengal to be sold.[46]

On 4 July Grant reported to King that he had found 'a strata of coal four feet in thickness and of an excellent kind . . . The miner informed me they were equal to any bed of coals he had even seen in England.' Grant left for Sydney on 22 July 1801 and arrived three days later. Shortly afterwards, he resigned his post and returned to England. Governor King appointed John Murray, former master's mate of the *Porpoise*, to command *Lady Nelson* which afterwards resumed the survey of Bass Strait.[47]

There is no mention of whether or not Bungaree returned to the exploring party at the Coal River. He may have rejoined his people at Broken Bay or gone back to Sydney on foot.

The engraved plates in Grant's book are thought to be based on originals by J. W. Lewin, who also painted a watercolour titled *A sketch . . . on the banks of the Paterson's River, New South Wales*, showing Colonel Paterson resting in a makeshift bark shelter.[48] Lewin, a natural-history painter and naturalist, arrived in Port Jackson aboard the *Minerva* on 11 January 1800. He had an undertaking to collect insects for Dru Drury, a friend of Sir Joseph Banks who owned a fine collection of insects.

In November 1801 King sent 12 prisoners to work in mines at the Coal River, which was at first called King's Town after the governor, but was later renamed Newcastle. There was one magistrate and a corporal and eight private soldiers to guard the miners. The settlement was abandoned about June 1802 after unspecified misconduct by its superintendent, Major Martin Mason.[49]

Fig 6.

Model of HMS *Investigator*   South Australian Maritime Museum, Port Adelaide.
Photograph 1992   © Copyright S.A. Maritime Museum.

4 Voyage of the Investigator

The refitting and provisioning of *Investigator*, watched over by Sir Joseph Banks, was almost complete by 27 March 1801 and she was moved from Sheerness to the Nore in the Thames Estuary. However, England and France, ever the best of enemies, were again at war and her sailing orders were delayed pending the arrival of a 'safe passage' passport from the French government.

On top of the usual rations of beef, pork and biscuits, the sloop carried lemon and lime juice, sauerkraut, vinegar, essence of malt and 'portable soup', all intended to ward off scurvy. Pieces of iron, pocket knives, looking glasses, combs, beads and earrings were loaded to trade with the natives of New Holland. An officer's library in the captain's cabin included a copy of Sir Joseph Banks' journal and a set of the *Encyclopaedia Britannica*, both presented by Banks. The East India Company donated 600 as 'table money' for the officer's mess.[1]

On 26 May the ship was ordered to Spithead, but winds delayed her arrival until 2 June. The French passport, signed in Paris by the Ministers of the Marine and Colonies on 23 May, did not reach Flinders until 17 July. It instructed French officers not to interfere with *Investigator* or her officers and to give assistance if required.[2] The sailing orders, which arrived the same day, instructed Matthew Flinders to visit Madeira and the Cape of Good Hope and then proceed to the coast of New Holland and to call at King George's Sound on the west coast to refresh if needed. He was to make a rough survey of the southern coastline as far as Bass's Strait, using his 'best endeavours to discover such harbours as there may be in those parts'. He was to sail to Port Jackson to refit the ship and rest the crew and consult the governor of New South Wales 'upon the best means of carrying on the survey of the coast'. He was then to explore and chart the north-west coast, the Gulf of Carpentaria and Torres Strait (between New Holland and New Guinea). The *Lady Nelson* would accompany *Investigator* as tender and could be used to explore rivers and details of the coast.[3]

Sir Joseph Banks had selected a team of distinguished 'scientific gentlemen' to take part in the expedition. These were Robert Brown (naturalist), Ferdinand Lukas Bauer (natural-history painter), William Westall (landscape and figure painter), John Crossley (astronomer), Peter Good (gardener) and John Allen (miner).

Brown, a surgeon's mate, aged 27, was appointed when African explorer Mungo Park declined the post of botanist. At the age of 18 Brown had contributed notes on Scottish flora to the Natural History Society of Edinburgh. He was to be paid £420 per annum. Bauer, aged 41, was an experienced botanist, draughtsman and natural-history painter from Vienna. His field trip to Greece and the Mediterranean islands with Oxford botanist Dr.

HMS *Investigator*

Sloop, 334 tons, previously HMS *Xenophon* (1798) and before that the *Fram* (1795), a North Sea cat or collier.
Left Spithead, 18 July 1801.
Moored at Port Jackson as a hulk, 21 July 1803.
Refitted. Returned to Britain October 1805.
Arms: Two 18-pounder, six 12-pounder carronades, two six-pounder long guns, two swivels.
Boats: Launch, two cutters, gig.
Anchors: Six bower, two stream and two kedge anchors.
Crew: 88 men, including officers and scientists.
Deaths: 19.

Commander: Matthew Flinders, frigate captain.
Lieutenants: Robert Fowler, Samuel Ward Flinders.
Master: John Thistle, died at Cape Catastrophe, 21 February 1802. Replaced by John Aken.
Midshipmen: John Franklin (seven others).
Surgeon: Hugh Bell.
Surgeon's Assistant: Robert Purdie.
Naturalist: Robert Brown.
Natural-history painter: Ferdinand Bauer.
Landscape painter: William Westall.
Astronomer: John Crossley (left ship at Cape).
Miner: John Allen.
Gardener: Peter Good, died at Port Jackson, 6 November 1803.
Supernumaries: Bungaree, Nanbaree (returned on *Lady Nelson*, 18 October 1802).

John Sibthorpe in 1786–7 brought forth the magnificent plant paintings for *Flora Graeca*, published 1806–40. In 1790 Bauer had been appointed a botanical artist at Kew Gardens. Westall, aged 19, a landscape and figure painter, trained as an artist under his brother Richard, then studied at the Royal Academy in London. The two artists were to be paid £315 each.

Good, who had been sent to India to bring back plants collected by botanist Christopher Smith, was a foreman at the Royal Gardens at Kew. He was tempted by Banks to leave his position as gardener at Weymess Castle near Kilmarnock, Scotland. Little is known about John Allen, but he was to receive £105, the same salary as Peter Good. The astronomer Crossley became ill and left the ship at the Cape of Good Hope.

First Lieutenant Robert Fowler had served on the ship when she was the *Xenophon*. Matthew's brother Samuel Ward Flinders was promoted to second lieutenant and John Franklin, their young relative from Spilsby, Lincolnshire, was one of the eight midshipmen. In later years Franklin became governor of Van Diemen's Land and a famous Arctic explorer. He was to perish in an attempt to find the Arctic North-West Passage. The ship's surgeon was Hugh Bell and the master John Thistle, who had served Bass in the whaleboat and Flinders on *Norfolk*.[4]

Investigator raised anchor and finally left Spithead on 18 July 1801. Beneath her copper-sheathing skin, rot had begun to creep through her timbers. While still in the English Channel she was found to be leaking at the rate of 3 inches an hour.[5]

Baudin in *Géographe*, accompanied by *Naturaliste* under Emmanuel Hamelin, had reached the south-west coast of New Holland near Cape Leeuwin on 27 May 1801. The French ships sailed up the western coast, already mapped by the Dutch, and remained in Timor for 56 days.[6] During this time, *Investigator* traversed 12,000 miles across the vast seas, stopping at Funchal in Madeira and at the Cape of Good Hope to caulk the ship's planks. The leak was reduced to 2 inches per hour.

Investigator sighted Cape Leeuwin on Sunday 6 December 1801. She came to anchor in King George Sound (site of present day Albany) on the evening of 8 December. In three busy weeks, Brown, Bauer and Good collected 500 species of plants, Westall made several sketches and the seamen cut timber and refilled the ship's water casks. They met many local Aborigines and shortly before they left, Flinders brought the Marines ashore to stage a parade which delighted the natives so much that they created a corroboree mimicking their drill and marching.[7]

On Tuesday 5 January 1802, *Investigator* sailed east along the barren Great Australian Bight towards the previously 'unknown coast', stretching 1,000 miles roughly along the coastline of modern South Australia, which Flinders was the first to survey. He landed frequently and explored the bays and harbours he would later name after members of his crew and villages in his native Lincolnshire. On Sunday 21 February, John Thistle, midshipman William Taylor and six seamen were drowned when a cutter overturned near Cape Catastrophe. Their bodies were not recovered.[8]

Returning south from Timor, Baudin had anchored in the D'Entrecasteaux Channel on the south coast of Van Diemen's Land, where he stayed, according to Lieutenant Louis de Freycinet, 'picking up shells and catching butterflies' from January to March 1802. Baudin made for Bass Strait and sailed west from Western Port to Otway and Cape Banks, then on 8 April *Géographe* met *Investigator* in Encounter Bay within sight of Kangaroo Island.[9] Flinders and Robert Brown went on board the ship, which had been separated from *Naturaliste* during a gale in Bass Strait, and had a friendly conversation with Baudin.[10]

On 26 April Flinders entered and examined an extensive harbour which he believed he had discovered. In fact, only 10 weeks earlier, John Murray in the *Lady Nelson* had been the first European to cross the difficult bar to enter the bay Governor King named Port Phillip.[11]

Investigator entered Port Jackson on 9 May 1802 after a voyage lasting nine months and nine days. In the harbour Flinders found *Naturaliste* at anchor, also HMS *Porpoise* and *Lady Nelson*. The ship was allotted a berth at Cattle Point (Bennelong Point) to refit for the second leg of the voyage. During 12 weeks in port the masts were rerigged, the seams caulked inside and out, the ship was painted and a plant cabin was constructed.

Matthew Flinders immediately went ashore to make an official call on Governor Philip Gidley King from whom he received generous hospitality, both official and social.[12]

On 18 May *Naturaliste* sailed north, bound for the Ile de France, so she was not in Port Jackson on 20 June when *Géographe* came through the Heads after several days beating against the winds offshore. Baudin's crew were so ill with scurvy that only 12 out of 170 men could work the ship. Governor King sent a longboat from *Investigator* to help bring the French ship into port at Neutral Bay. The French expedition remained in Sydney for five months (*Naturaliste* was forced to return there on 3 July). Their tents were set up next to those of the *Investigator* and the colony was put on short rations to supply food to the sick French sailors in hospital.[13]

Sydney Town

It is supposed that some time about the year 1800, Bungaree, in the words of anthropologist Dr Frederick McCarthy, 'came with the remnant of his Broken Bay group to settle in Sydney'.[14] It may have been after Bungaree's voyage aboard *Norfolk* in late 1799, or after he 'ran off' from the Hunter River about June 1801.

Aborigines commonly frequented the town at this time and they appeared on the whole

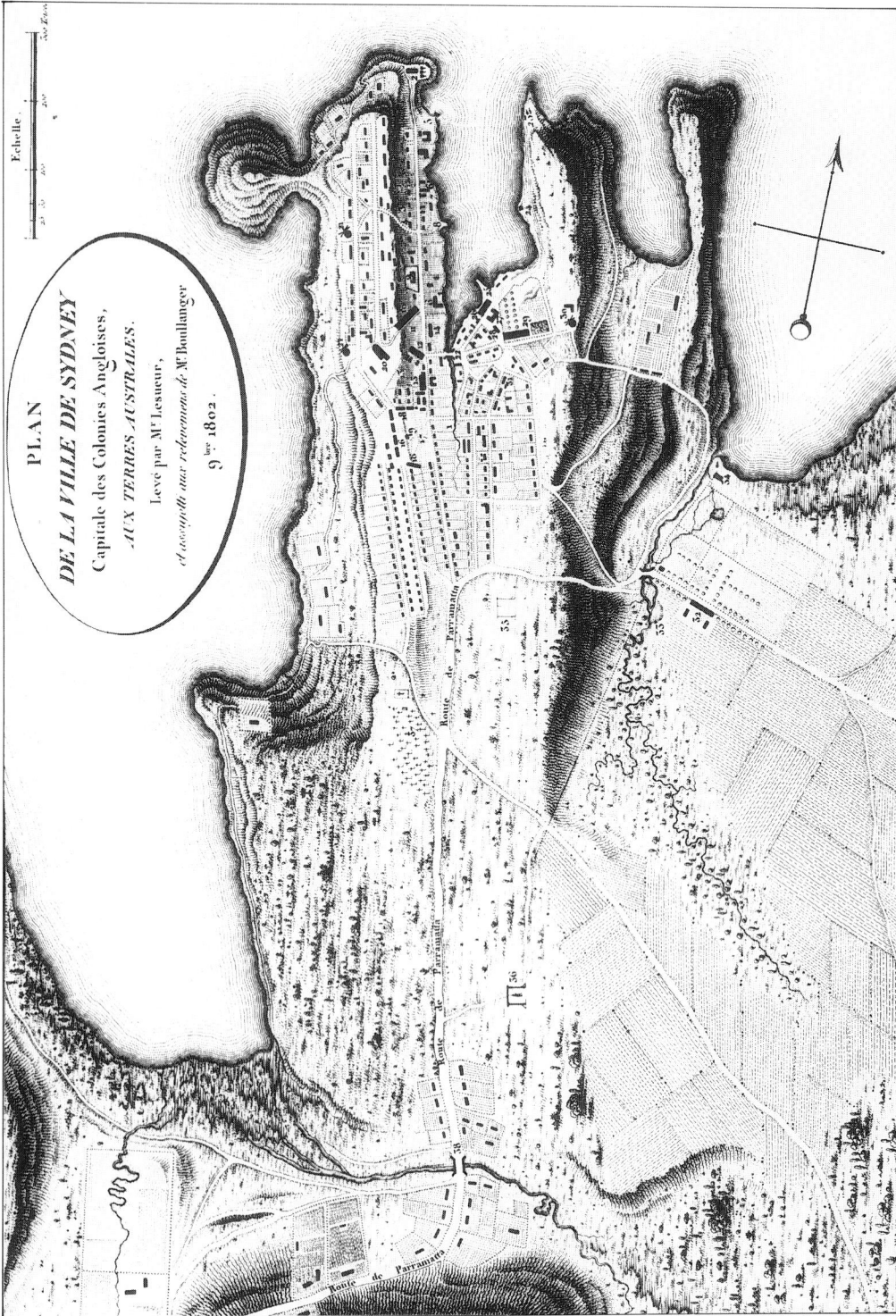

PLAN
DE LA VILLE DE SYDNEY
Capitale des Colonies Angloises,
AUX TERRES AUSTRALES.
Levé par Mr Lesueur,
et construit aux relevemens de Mr Boullanger
9bre 1802.

NOUVELLE-HOLLANDE : Colonies Angloises.

1. Bâterie du Pavillon des Signaux.
2. Batterie de l'Hôpital.
3. Bâtimens de l'Hôpital.
4. Hôpital transporté d'Europe.
5. Magasin de Mr Campbell.
6. Chantier de Construction.
7. Chaloupe de Mr Bass.
8. Celle de l'Hôpital.
9. Prison.
10. Magasin des Infirmes; portes et des Infirmiers.

12. Maison du Lieutenant-gouverneur.
13. Jardin du Lieutenant-gouverneur.
14. Maison d'Education publique.
15. Magasin de tirans et Legumes Secs.
16. Casernes des Soldats.
17. Place des Casernes.
18. Logemens des Officiers.
19. Magasin à Poudre.
20. Eglise.
21. Moulin à vent.
22. Pont.

23. Celle du Gouvernement.
24. Magasin général de Meubles, d'Instrumens &c.
25. Magasin d'Habillemens, de Cordages &c.
26. Atelier Public.
27. Maison et Jardin du Gouvernement.
28. Moulin et Boulangerie du Gouvernement.
29. Imprimerie du Gouvernement, et de la

32. Habitation
33. Briqueterie
34. Chantier
35. 1er Potence établie sur la Nouvelle-Hollande (France)
36. Potence en activité
37. Cimetière
38. I^{ier} étage de Brick ; field où se trouvent plu-
     sieurs fabriques de Tuiles, de Poteries, &c.

} de Mr Palmer.

to live at peace with the white settlers. There were many places that Bungaree and his people could camp close to the township, on the rugged north shore of the harbour, still virgin bushland, at Wooloomooloo, or near Farm Cove (Woccanmagully), a traditional site for initiation ceremonies, corroborees and ritual battles.

Naturalist George Suttor recalled his arrival in Sydney on the *Porpoise* in November 1800, bringing cuttings of grape vines, lemons, hops and apples given to him by Sir Joseph Banks. Suttor was particularly impressed by the 'novel sight' as they sailed up the harbour of 'several bark canoes of the natives, generally with one or two native women fishing'. He thought:

> The town of Sydney had then more the appearance of a camp than a town, mixed with stumps and dead trees. The New South Wales Corps occupied a large part, living in huts; generally the houses were thatched, the walls mostly of wattle and plaster, white washed within and without, a few were glazed, but most were not.[15]

Less than two years later, in May 1802, arriving after nine months at sea in the *Investigator*, Peter Good, the gardener, found most things about Sydney Cove to be, in a word, snug. He described the 'fine Spacious Harbour . . . a number of fine Snug Coves and inlets . . . all as Smooth as a mill Pond'. The south and east shores, he said, were 'mostly cleared with pretty Snug houses & Gardens' and the town was 'seated at the end of a Snug Cove'. Good noticed the shingled roofs 'covered with wood cut in the form of Tiles which very much resemble Slate'. Several of the principal houses, he said, were 'built of Brik and white washed others with wood painted'. With the eye of a landscape gardener, he wrote in his journal: 'Art or even imagination can scarce form anything more grand than the various windings of the harbour'.[16]

In a letter his sister in Lincolnshire, young John Franklin remarked: 'The town is near the size of Spalding, but the houses are built very stragling, and chiefly wood, some as the Governor &c are stone . . . the trees and rubbish are much cleared away'.[17]

Samuel Smith, a 30-year-old ordinary seaman on the *Investigator*, entered some remarks in his journal about the natives he saw around 'Sidney': 'The Natives here upon Acct of their frequent intercourse with the English are more civiliz'd than any where upon the Coast, their languidge differs, greatly, in 40 Miles, they are Detrimental to the White people in going through the country from Sidney to Parramatta.'[18]

The lively scene which Sydney Cove presented in 1802 is seen in *Vue de la partie méridionale de la Ville de SYDNEY* (Fig. 7), engraved from the original pencil and pen-and-ink drawing by the French draughtsman Charles Alexandre Lesueur. The tiny whitewashed and shingle-roofed cottages which Peter Good described are seen dotted around the V-shaped head of Sydney Cove and crowding the slopes and cliffs on the western side, the raffish area called The Rocks. A timber bridge crosses the Tank Stream, the town's vital source of water, trickling at low tide over sand flats into the cove. The frame of the brig *Portland* lies on the sand close by. On the skyline at left is the square stone clock tower and

Map 2. *PLAN DE LA VILLE DE SYDNEY*
Capital des Colonies Angloises, AUX TERRES AUSTRALES
['Plan of the Town of Sydney, Capital of the English Settlement, in the South Lands']
Engraved from a watercolour by Charles Alexandre Lesueur, 1802.
Plate 17: 'Historique Atlas de MM. Lesueur et Petit', *Voyage de découvertes aux terres Australes*, seconde édition. Paris, 1824.

weathervane of St Phillip's church, which was used as an observatory. Next to it on a knoll stands the military windmill; the disused first government windmill is further to the right near a prominent tree trunk. Below the tower is the new stone gaol and on the waterside, the Hospital Wharf and the Naval Dockyard with many small boats pulled up on the beach. At right, before Dawes Point, is the unfinished wharf and storehouse of shipping merchant Robert Campbell. Next door, protected by a shady verandah, is Campbell's home, Wharf House.

At Bennelong Point in the foreground is the French encampment, with coopers and sailmakers busily repairing casks and sails around the ship's tents, with *Naturaliste* and *Géographe* at anchor. The ship at right without sails (seen stern-on) is probably *Investigator*. The vessel scudding along under full sail further to the right, resembling Grant's drawing of *Lady Nelson* (Fig. 8), does not appear in Lesueur's original sketch, but has been added by the engraver. Other ships in port at the time included a privateer brig and two whaling ships, *Britannia* and *Venus*, which brought the welcome news in May 1802 that peace had been concluded between France and Britain at the Treaty of Amiens in October the previous year.

While in port, François Péron (1775–1810), a naturalist and zoologist on board the *Géographe*, found time to spy out Sydney's defences. In his report to the French Admiralty, Péron recommended an invasion but concluded that Sydney Cove was too difficult to attack directly (he suggested a landing at Broken Bay). Péron painted a rosy picture of the international maritime activity of the seaport: ships loading coal for India and the Cape of Good Hope, convict transports setting out for China, whalers bound for New Zealand, sealers for Bass's Strait, traders for the South Seas and even a gun-runner taking arms to South America. 'At the same time,' Péron added, 'the intrepid Captain Flinders,

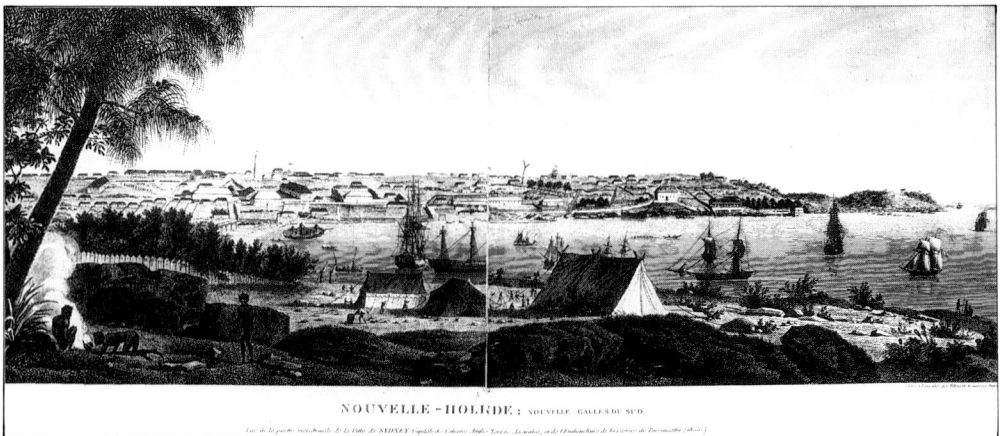

Fig 7.

NOUVELLE-HOLLANDE: NOUVELLE GALLES DU SUD.
    Vue de la partie méridionale de la Ville de SYDNEY Capitale des Colonies Anglais aux Terres Australes, et de l'Embouchure de la rivière de Parramatta . . .
[View of the southern part of the town of Sydney, capital of the English colonies in Terra Australis, and of the mouth of the Parramatta River . . .]

Engraved from a drawing by Charles Alexandre Lesueur, 1802.
Plate 19: Historique Atlas de MM. Lesueur et Petit. *Voyage de découvertes aux terres Australes.* Seconde édition. Paris, 1824.

after effecting a junction with his companion ship, the *Lady Nelson*, was getting ready to continue his grand voyage round New Holland.'[19]

The worthy and brave fellow

On 10 May 1802, nine days after arriving in Sydney, Matthew Flinders wrote a formal letter to Governor King, asking that he be allowed to enlist two volunteer 'natives of this country' to be carried as supernumaries on the books of the *Investigator*.[20] His suggestion was officially adopted three days later. Flinders wrote in *Terra Australis*:

> I had before experienced much advantage from the presence of a native of Port Jackson, in bringing about a friendly intercourse with the inhabitants of other parts of the coast; and on representing this to the governor, he authorised me to receive two on board. *Bongaree*, the worthy and brave fellow who had sailed with me on the Norfolk, now volunteered again; the other was *Nanbaree*, a good-natured lad, of whom colonel Collins has made mention in his *Account of New South Wales*.[21]

Bungaree and Nanbaree, now aged about 20, joined nine seamen and five convicts who came on board to replace the boat crew lost at Spencer Gulf and two men discharged at Port Jackson.

Fig. 8.

H. M. Sloop Lady Nelson, on the Thames
Engraving by S. I. Neele after James Grant, 1801.
Frontispiece: Grant, James: *The Narrative of a Voyage,*

Performed in His Majesty's Vessel The Lady Nelson of Sixty Tons Burthen, With sliding keels, in the years 1800, 1801, and 1802 . . . London, 1803.

HM Sloop Lady Nelson

Sloop, rigged as a brig, 60 tons, built at Deptford on the Thames, 1799. Purchased 1800.

Fitted with three sliding keels or centreboards, the invention of Captain John Schanck. Draught with keels raised less than 6 feet.

Left Port Jackson in company with HMS *Investigator*, 22 July 1802.

Lost two of her three anchors, and parts of two sliding keels after twice running aground.

Sent back to Port Jackson from Cumberland Islands, Great Barrier Reef (with Nanbaree on board), 18 October 1802.

As a 'Colonial Marine' vessel, *Lady Nelson* carried cargo between Port Jackson and Newcastle. She was taken by Timor pirates who killed her crew and scuttled the wreck at Babar Island, north-east of Timor, 1825.

Dimensions: 52 feet long.

Arms: 6 guns.

Crew: 15 men.

Deaths: None.

Commander: Lieutenant John Murray.

First mate: Henry Hacking.

Second mate: John Johnson (Jorgen Jorgensen).

After his recovery from smallpox in 1789, Nanbaree had been adopted by Surgeon John White, who gave him a string of European names: Andrew Sneap Hammond Douglas White. The boy became White's 'gamekeeper'.[22] All the same, he quickly returned to his own people when White left the colony in December 1794 and was initiated at the *Yoo-lahng-erah-ba-diahng* ceremony at Farm Cove in January 1795 described by Judge Advocate David Collins. An illustration in Collins' *An Account of the English Colony in New South Wales*, shows Nanbaree with others having his front tooth removed. In the following figure (Fig. 9), his relative Coleby is seen applying a cooked fish to quell the pain in Nanbaree's gum 'which suffered from the stroke more than any others'.[23] Nanbaree served as a seaman on HMS *Reliance* from 1795 until he joined the *Investigator* in 1802.

Matthew Flinders wrote to Sir Joseph Banks from Port Jackson on 20 May reporting on his discoveries to date and set to work to complete his charts, which he left with Governor King.[24] He wrote to his wife Ann on 31 May, telling her, regretfully: 'Thou wouldst have been situated as comfortably here as I hoped, and told thee. Two better or more agreeable women than Mrs King and Mrs Paterson are not easily found; these would have been thy choicest friends.' In the same letter he told Ann: 'Trim, like his master, is becoming grey; he is at present fat and frisky, and takes meat from our forks with his former dexterity. He is commonly my bedfellow.'[25]

Lady Nelson was now commanded by Lieutenant John Murray and her first mate was Henry Hacking, the Port Jackson pilot. The second mate was a colourful character, born Jorgen Jorgensen, who signed on as John Johnson. This Danish sailor, author, explorer and botanist remained in the crew until 1804.

The two ships sailed out of Sydney Heads on 22 July 1802. Passing the entrance to Broken Bay 9 miles out to sea, *Investigator* headed north along the Pacific coast towards Moreton and Hervey Bays, explored by Flinders and Bungaree three years earlier in the little sloop *Norfolk*, then on through the Great Barrier Reef, rounding Cape York into Torres Strait and the Gulf of Carpentaria.

The Sand Island

On Friday 30 July, *Investigator* got across the dangerous sandbar at Breaksea Spit and anchored at Sandy Cape, the northern tip of Great Sandy Island (now Fraser Island) on Hervey Bay to allow botanist Robert Brown to spend some time on shore collecting plants.

Yoo-long Erah-ba-diang .e.

Fig. 9.

Yoo-long-Erah ba-diang [No. 8]
Engraving by J. Nagle after Thomas Watling.

Collins, David. *An Account of the English Colony in New South Wales* London, T. Cadell Jun. and W. Davies, 1798.

Next morning, the ship anchored close to shore with armed boats attached to grapnel hooks to protect the landing parties who came ashore with Bungaree in one boat and Nanbaree in the other. Brown's party of six people walked along the shore to the upper reaches of the bay, while Murray's party went to cut wood for fuel.

Flinders's group, also of six people 'including my native friend *Bungaree*', walked towards Sandy Cape. He later described how Bungaree, despite his ignorance of the local language, managed to establish peaceful relations with some Aboriginal warriors who were waving tree branches and gesturing to the whites to return to the ship:

> Bungaree stripped off his clothes and laid aside his spear, as inducements for them to wait for him; but finding they did not understand his language, the poor fellow, in the simplicity of his heart, addressed them in broken English, hoping to succeed better. At length they suffered him to come up, and by degrees our whole party joined; and after receiving some presents, twenty of them returned with us to the boats, and were feasted upon the blubber of two porpoises, which had been brought on shore purposely for them.[26]

The porpoise blubber took the fancy of the Aborigines, said Samuel Smith: 'it being given to them, they eat it raw with satisfaction & an eager Appetite; the Captn gave them red caps, Tommy hawks &c. in order to create Friendship with them'.[27]

Peter Good, accompanying Brown and Bauer, looked about the world's largest sand island, so starkly different to his moist green Scottish homeland, and remarked: 'it is astonishing to see what Vegetation is produced from Sand, here were Banksia latifolia some Cassuarina & other Trees of considerable size—'[28] Not far from the beach, the naturalists found about a dozen fishing nets belonging to the Aborigines which they obtained by exchanging them for hatchets and night caps.

'On our joining the Captns party we found many of the natives along with them,' wrote Robert Brown. 'I learned that they had had intercourse with them soon after we left them . . . brought about by Bongare the Port Jackson native who boldly went up to a considerable party of them arm'd with spears'.[29]

Both Brown and Flinders noticed that the island's natives resembled those at Port Jackson, but they were 'more fleshy'. Flinders attributed this to their ability to obtain a better food supply using their scoop nets.[30] Surgeon Bell observed that the fishermens' wrists were calloused on the outer knuckle, probably from using these fishing nets. 'This was even the case with the youngest of the party a lad about 14 or 13 years,' said Brown.[31]

Flinders commented:

> Our native did not understand a word of their language, nor did they seem to know the use of his womerah or throwing stick; for one of them being invited to imitate Bongaree, who lanced a spear with it very dexterously, and to a great distance, he, in the most awkward manner, threw both womerah and spear together.[32]

'They appeared sorry when we went into the Boat,' wrote Peter Good, 'some came into the water after us & appeared to wish to accompany us.'[33]

Investigator sailed on to explore Hervey Bay and later Bustard Bay. On 13 September, near Port Curtis (Gladstone), where they spent four days, *Lady Nelson* grounded on a shoal and lost her main sliding keel. Brown and Flinders went on board the following day to inspect the damage.

Robert Brown, though a clever and methodical botanist, was a poor journal-keeper. His handwriting wavers between neat copperplate script and illegibility and he often omits punctuation marks. Brown, who was sparing in his references to Bungaree (which he spelt as Bongare, Bonjare and Bongaree), mentions two incidents involving Nanbaree (also Nanberry or Nanbury).

While attempting to climb a hill in the Port Curtis area, the botanist's party was 'saluted with a shower of stones' by Aborigines: 'We ascended the hill & the natives retird in about a quarter of an hour some of the party among them Nanberry the native of Port Jackson having straggled a little from the rest were attacked by the natives & obligd to retreat. The attack was made with a war woop and a discharge of stones.' The Aborigines 'scampered off' when Brown discharged 'my own pocket pistol' and others fired muskets. Brown put a small adze in a canoe and left behind a red nightcap in exchange for baskets taken by Flinders the previous day.[34]

On Sunday 8 August Flinders recorded: 'Fish seemed to be plentiful, and some were speared by Bongaree, who was a constant attendant in my boat; and yet our efforts with the seine were altogether unsuccessful'.[35]

Next day the ships anchored in Keppel Bay, where they remained for nine days. Flinders discovered the passage from Kepple Bay behind Curtis Island to Port Curtis on 13 August. Here the natives were friendly. One morning they appeared at the ship with two lost seamen whom they had treated kindly and fed on ducks. Flinders and his men spent a week exploring Shoalwater Bay, where they met more Aborigines and killed a huge goanna 2 or 3 feet long.

Peter Good wrote in his journal for 30 August:

> On landing we found a Canoe on the Beach & saw some Natives who fled on our approach— after being near an hour in the woods we fell in with a party of Natives who met us resolutely being well armed with Spears & Helemans [shields]—it was some time before we could get them to parly.—We had a Native of Port Jackson with us but he could not understand their language.

Once again the Aborigines were astonished to see Bungaree throwing his spear with a woomerah. Their own spears were strong and heavy.[36]

That same day Brown took part in a naming ceremony with the Shoalwater Bay people. 'They introduced each other to us & the introductions seem[ed] . . . almost a harangue probably on the merits of the person introduced, who during its continuance was mostly silent.' Their canoes were shorter, deeper and stronger than those seen previously on the coast. In each canoe there was a 'Turtle peg' (a kind of harpoon) and some string or cord. 'They expresd admiration at Nanbury's dexterity with the spear, but were terrified at the report of a musket which we fird on purpose to shew them the spirit of fire arms.' Only one of the Aborigines had the courage to examine the musket which he did 'with evident symptoms of fear'.[37] On another day Brown watched whales playing around the ship 'in considerable numbers'.[38]

Lady Nelson twice ran aground in treacherous waters near Broad Sound, losing part of her after sliding keel and breaking off a part of the new main keel. She had now lost two of her three anchors and found it difficult to keep up with the *Investigator*.

A New Creation

Flinders began to search for possible openings to break out of the enclosing reefs and islands of the Great Barrier Reef. He was fascinated by the beauty of the coral formations. One afternoon (9 October) Flinders and Brown went on the reef with a party.

> . . . the water being very clear round the edges, a new creation, as it was to us, but imitative of the old, was there presented to our view. We had wheat sheaves, mushrooms, stagshorns, cabbage leaves, and a variety of other forms, glowing under water with vivid tints of every shade betwixt green, purple, brown, and white: equalling in beauty and excelling in grandeur the most favourite parterre of the curious florist. These were different species of coral and fungus, growing, as it were, out of the solid rock and each had its peculiar form and shade of colouring.

But, he added, whilst contemplating the richness of the scene, 'we could not long forget with what destruction it was pregnant'.[39] When a promising exit appeared in the reefs off the Cumberland Islands on 18 October 1802 Flinders ordered *Lady Nelson* to return to Sydney. Nanbaree was not to be among the circumnavigators. 'Nanbarre, one of the two natives, having expressed a wish to go back to Port Jackson, was sent to the Lady Nelson in the morning, with two seamen exchanged for the same number of that vessel's crew'.[40]

Matthew Flinders took the opportunity to send a tender note to his wife Ann, addressed to 'My dearest love'. 'Amidst my various and constant occupations,' he wrote, 'thou art not one day forgotten. Be happy my beloved, rest assured of my faith, and trust that I will return safely to sooth thy distress, and repay thee for all thy anxieties concerning me.' He signed the letter 'Thy own, Matthw. Flinders'.[41]

A lone ship in the maze of treacherous coral outcrops, *Investigator* steered east through Flinders Passage, north-east of present day Townsville, 'threading the needle' to the open sea. Flinders warned navigators who would follow:

> The commander who proposes to make the experiment must not, however, be one who throws his ship's head around in a hurry, so soon as breakers are announced from aloft; if he do not feel his nerves strong enough to thread the needle, as it is called, amongst the reefs, whilst he directs the steerage from the mast head, I would strongly recommend him not to approach this part of New South Wales.[42]

The ship's course, reckoned by the trial and error of visual sighting, lay northwards outside the Great Barrier Reef. In 1770 Cook in the *Endeavour* had sailed between the reef and the mainland, until she ran aground on the coral south of today's Cooktown.

On 29 October Flinders brought his ship to anchor off the Murray Islands, still outside the reef, at the entrance to Torres Strait. Soon three long canoes appeared, manned by 50 islanders. Flinders was wary, recalling the attacks made on the *Providence* and *Assistant* in the area in 1792 when three of Bligh's men were wounded by arrows, one dying later. He ordered armed marines to stand by and the ship's guns were primed and ready to fire, but the natives bartered peacefully that day and the next, trading coconuts, plantain, pearl oyster shell, necklaces of cowries and bows and arrows for hatchets and pieces of iron, which they called *toree*.

These islanders were not Aborigines but Melanesians. Flinders described them as active, muscular men, 'dark chocolate' in colour. Apart from shell ornaments and plaited fibres of bark worn around their waists, necks and ankles they were naked. 'Our friend Bongaree could not understand any thing of their language, nor did they pay much attention to him; he seemed, indeed, to feel his own inferiority, and made but a poor figure among them.' This was a contrast to the previous voyage when Flinders had praised Bungaree's physique in comparison to the Aborigines in Moreton Bay.[43]

Investigator steered to the west, passing Cape York on 31 October, sailing between Prince of Wales and Wednesday Islands into the broad waters of the Gulf of Carpentaria. She took only three days to find a safe passage through the shallows and sharp coral of Torres Strait. With this discovery ships sailing from the Pacific to Java, India or the Cape of Good Hope would be able to clip nearly 40 days off the length of their voyage.

In four months, during which *Investigator* had survived many dangers on her way north through the Great Barrier Reef and Torres Strait, the ship's timbers had been rotting. She began to leak badly while off Prince of Wales Island and was soon taking in from 10 to 14 inches of water per hour.[44]

The last Europeans known to have explored the Gulf of Carpentaria were the Dutch under Abel Tasman in 1644. On Sunday 7 November 1802 the whaleboat was lowered to allow the botanists to collect plants from land near a small inlet on the east coast of the gulf. Once more Bungaree went ashore, 'naked and unarmed' to meet a group of Aborigines, but they retreated from him. Flinders considered it unsafe to land, so the botanical gentlemen were rowed higher up the river, but after hearing voices in the woods they returned to their first landing place.[45]

On 10 November they reached Cape Keer-Weer or 'Turn-again', named by Captain Willem Jansz of the *Duyfken* to mark the point where he turned back in 1606 after a crewman was speared and killed. A week later the low-lying Sweers Island (near Normanton) was chosen to careen *Investigator* to caulk her seams. 'Two planks were found to be rotten, and the timber underneath was in no better state,' the carpenter reported. 'The botanists and myself find useful employment for a few days, whilst the deficiencies were repairing,' Flinders noted. More rotten boards were found a few days later.[46]

On 20 November, Flinders in one of the ship's boats met some Aboriginal men on a small island who were dragging rafts made of mangrove roots. He exchanged red worsted caps, fillets, a hatchet and an adze with them for two spears and a woomerah with nearly the same form as those used at Port Jackson. He named the place Horseshoe Island for its shape.

The new ship's master John Aken and carpenter Russell Mart submitted an official report to Flinders on 26 November, concluding: 'From the state to which the ship now seems to be advanced, it is our joint opinion, that in twelve months there will scarcely be a sound timber in her; but that if she remain in fine weather and happen no accident, she may run six months longer without much risk'.[47]

Matthew Flinders realised with 'surprise and sorrow' that he could not hope to complete his detailed survey and would have to return to Port Jackson as quickly as possible. The monsoon season, with its sticky heat and rainstorms, was fast approaching, but Flinders decided to push his rotten ship and continue charting the gulf. By 28 November they had repaired as much of the damage as possible. Before leaving, some sailors carved the name *Investigator* on a tree at Sweers Island.[48] The tree was blown down by a cyclone in 1887 and is now in the Queensland Museum in Brisbane.

The crew were able to add fresh meat to their rations of salt pork and ship's biscuits after catching 46 green turtles, each weighing about 300 pounds, at Bountiful Island. Mornington Island was named on 7 December. Flinders spent Christmas Day 1802 in a boat taking his bearings among the Sir Edward Pellew Group of islands.

Mysterious traces of foreign visitors, including skulls, recently felled trees, a piece of teak and an earthenware pot, were seen at Sweers and Bentinck Islands. On one of the Pellew Islands Flinders found intricate fireplaces with the remains of charcoal fires, earthen jars and boat's rudders, seemingly of Asiatic origin. The local Aborigines seemed to be avoiding contact.

It was hot and humid and the monsoon squalls had begun. All on board were plagued by black flies and 'musketoes'.

They reached Groote Eylandt on 5 January 1803 and spent two weeks circling the island and collecting new plants on shore. On nearby Chasm Island a gallery of Aboriginal rock paintings was discovered in caves and shelters. 'In the cavern we found some specimens of native art, in drawings of people, turtles, kangaroos, and a hand. The porpoises were about two feet long and had had some trouble bestowed upon them. They were done with something like red paint upon the whitish ground of the rock, and variegated with some scratches of black.'[49] William Westall copied some of the paintings. Dr Frederick D. McCarthy recorded some 900 Aboriginal rock paintings at 27 sites when he visited Chasm Island in 1948.[50]

A seaman, William Murray, had accidentally drowned on New Year's Day. More tragedies followed. On 21 January at Morgan's Island in Blue Mud Bay, north-west of Groote Eylandt, a master's mate named Whitewood was speared four times when he reached out to take a spear from one man while talking to a group of Aborigines. A boat's crew under Aken fired on the natives, killing one.

Flinders was upset by the incident and sent a boat to recover the man's body.[51] William Westall made a sketch of the dead man (Fig. 10) and handed his body to Surgeon Bell. 'He was dissected and his head put in spirits,' noted Peter Good.[52] Flinders named the island where this incident took place after Thomas Morgan, a seaman who died of sunstroke that day.

Further north, in a wide, deep inlet later named Caledon Bay, Lieutenant Fowler, Surgeon Bell and Bungaree went ashore on 3 February in the whaleboat to search for fresh water. They spoke to several Aborigines on the beach, said Brown, and 'by means of Bongaree the Native of Port Jackson soon came to a friendly intercourse with the natives'. There were 12 men, several armed with fishing spears and some with woomerahs which were decorated at one end with a kind of mop made of human hair. 'Some of the natives were prevailed upon to enter the boat & these seemd so much at their ease that as to show some opposition to theft they were not allowd however to retain anything they laid hold of in this manner notwithstanding which they parted from the boat crew in an amicable way.'[53]

In the passage recording this meeting and also in an earlier reference at Port Lincoln printed in *Terra Australis* (1814), Flinders called the indigenous people 'Australians', two of the earliest known instances of the use of the name. He did not use this term in his 1802–3 journals.

'They staid to receive him,' Flinders wrote, 'without showing the timidity so usual with the Australians; and after a friendly intercourse in which mutual presents were made, Mr Fowler returned with the information that fresh water was plentiful.'

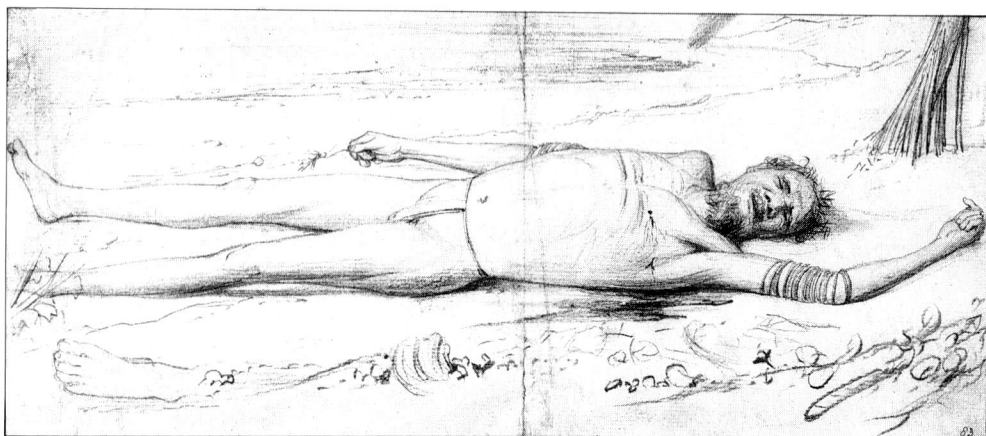

Fig.10.

Blue Mud Bay   Pencil, 15.2 x 35 cm.
Native shot on Morgan's Island   National Library of Australia, Canberra.
William Westall, 1803.

Woga is Captured

The next day, Friday 4 February, Flinders went ashore at Point Alexander in Caledon Bay. 'I landed with the botanical gentlemen; the natives running from their night residence to meet us. There were twelve middle-aged and young men, all of whom expressed much joy, especially at seeing Bongaree, our good-natured Indian from Port Jackson.'

When two other ship's boats arrived the Aborigines retired to the shrub, except for two men who helped to haul in the seine net. The others came back slowly and were given some of the catch. Tents were put up and Flinders went into the bush towards some sandhills to take his bearings. While doing this he twice heard the sound of Aborigines running through the bush and calling to each other. When a musket was fired, Flinders returned to the tents 'with all expedition'.

Some Aborigines had followed the botanists' party. One of them snatched a hatchet from Westall's servant and ran off. 'Each of our party had a native with him, walking arm in arm, and Mr Brown's servant had two, who paid him particular attention; so much so, that whilst one held him by the arm, the other snatched the musket off his shoulder, and they all again ran off.' Bauer fired his musket after the thief with no effect and the botanists returned to the tents.

After a parley with two Aborigines the musket was returned with its ram-rod missing and its stock broken. A hatchet was given in return. After this the Aborigines again came to the tents. Next day an Aborigine called Yehangeree ran off with a wooding axe and Flinders decided to put a stop to the thieving. A marine corporal and private suffered sunstroke when they ran after him without their hats. They were almost delirious when taken on board the ship, but soon recovered. 'Finding these people so determinately bent upon stealing every thing within their reach,' said Flinders, 'I ordered lieutenant Fowler to watch an opportunity of seizing two of them; and after a while to release one, making him understand that the other would be carried away in the ship, if the stolen axe were not returned.' A similar tactic had been employed by Captain James Cook, not always with favourable results.

On Monday morning two of the Aborigines came to the tents bringing fruit. Being invited to eat some fish they sat down and were immediately seized. The older man was released and the other, a boy of about 14 year of age named Woga or Woogah (Fig. 11), was taken as hostage for the axe. A six-pound gun was loaded with grapeshot and kept ready in case of trouble. That evening Flinders, accompanied by Bungaree, rowed ashore with Woga to a place where the Aborigines had gathered and many were hiding behind bushes. 'Two came forward, bringing a young girl in their arms; and by expressive signs they offered her to Bongaree, in order to entice him on shore, for the purpose, apparently, of seizing him by way of retaliation.'[54]

In Peter Good's words, the Aborigines 'presented a young woman, called Bungery & gave him to understand he might have her if he would land'.[55] This strategy was not successful (possibly to Bungaree's disappointment). Flinders demanded the return of the axe but the Aborigines replied that they had beaten the thief Yehangeree and he had gone away.

Woga was carried on board the *Investigator* 'through a great deal of crying, intreating, threatening, and struggling on his part. He there ate heartily, laughed, sometimes cried, and noticed every thing; frequently expressing admiration at what he saw, and especially

Fig. 11.

Caledon Bay
WOOGAH, *a native*
William Westall, 1803.
Pencil, 15.2 x 15.9 cm.
National Library of Australia, Canberra.

at the sheep, hogs and cats'. After breakfast next morning Flinders took Woga to the tents, but he tried to escape as the boat neared the shore and was tied up again. 'He struggled much, calling upon Bongaree to assist him; but after a while, became quiet, and I left him bound to a tree, eating rice and fish.'

Later that day the scientific party was threatened by a band of Aborigines who closed in on them with spears poised. The aggressors fled and disappeared after a volley of buckshot was fired. Flinders said he would have been glad to keep Woga, 'for he was a sprightly lad', but he was concerned that the hostility of the Aborigines might endanger later white visitors, particularly Baudin, who was expected soon in the gulf. Poor Woga begged to be released, 'promising, with tears in his eyes, to bring back the axe'. He was given some clothing and presents and then 'took to his heels with all his might' and was not seen again.[56] Woga, said Peter Good, 'endeavoured to prevail upon Bungery to go with him'.[57] The axe was not returned.

Although Robert Brown's plant-collecting had been somewhat hampered by the interference of the Aborigines at Caledon Bay, he managed to compile a vocabulary of 50 words of the local dialect. Flinders speculated on the different Aboriginal languages in *Terra Australis*:

> The language of Caledon Bay may . . . be totally different to what is spoken on the East and South Coasts, and yet the inhabitants have one common origin; but I do not think that the language is absolutely and wholly different, though it certainly was no better understood by Bongaree than by ourselves. In three instances I found a similarity: the personal pronoun of Port Jackson, *gni-a* (I) was used here, and apparently in the same sense; when inquiry was made after the axe, the natives replied '*Yehangeree py*,' making signs of beating; and *py* signifies to beat, in the Port Jackson language; the third instance was of the lad Woga calling to Bongaree in the boat, which after he had done several times without being answered, he became angry and exclaimed *Bongaree-gah*! in a vehement manner, as Bongaree himself would have done in a similar case.[58]

At dawn on 10 February 1803 *Investigator* left Caledon Bay, steering north. Next day Flinders sighted the eastern tip of the west coast of the Gulf of Carpentaria, which he named Cape Arnhem. A week later, riding at anchor off Cape Wilberforce at the north-west corner of Arnhem Land, the expedition's survey of the coastline of the gulf was completed.

Rounding the Cape on 17 February they discovered 'six vessels covered over like hulks, as if laid up for the bad season'. When Samuel Flinders took an armed boat to investigate he found they were 'Malay' prows (proas) from Macassar (today's South Sulawesi), fishing for trepang (*bêche-de-mer* or sea slug) which they cured and sold to Chinese traders in Timor. Five more prows arrived the next day and Flinders, with the help of his Malay cook, talked to their elderly chief Pobasso (or Probasso), who told him the boats were part of a fleet of 60 owned by the Rajah of Boni. Pobasso said that with the aid of a pocket compass he had made six or seven similar voyages over a period of 26 years. The trepang, prized by the Chinese as an aphrodisiac, was dried in the sun and then smoked over charcoal fires. This explained the fireplaces, jars and other Asian implements seen earlier at Sweers and Bentinck Islands.[59]

Fig. 12.

Probasso, a Malay Chief
William Westall, 1803.
Pencil, 17.6 x 27.7 cm.
National Library of Australia, Canberra.

William Westall sketched '*Probasso, Mallay*' (Fig. 12) and the prows in the anchorage, which Flinders named Malay Road.

To satisfy themselves about the object of the fleet's voyage, Flinders and Robert Brown went on board Pobasso's prow the next morning. 'The old man received us on deck,' wrote Brown. 'He did not seem very anxious to shew his vessel below & we only looked from the stern. Every thing below seemd at least in as much confusion as on the Deck.'[60] The trepang fleet sailed for the Gulf of Carpentaria on 19 February while *Investigator* headed west to resume her survey. The botanists made their last plant collection on the north coast at Arnhem Bay.

Dividing the Mullet

On his first visit to Broken Bay in March 1788, Captain Arthur Phillip observed that fish was the chief food of the people there. 'The shark, I believe they never eat,' he added.[61]

Matthew Flinders in *Terra Australis* mentioned this taboo in a story which says more about Bungaree's manners and his friendship with Flinders than about his prowess at fishing. At daylight on 25 February in the English Company's Islands Flinders was taking bearings from a low point to the south-west while Bungaree speared a few fish:

> Bongaree was busily employed preparing his fish, when my bearings were concluded. The natives of Port Jackson have a prejudice against all fish of the ray kind [stingrays] as well as against sharks; and whilst they devour with eager avidity the blubber of a whale or porpoise, a piece of skate would excite disgust. Our good natured Indian had been ridiculed by the sailors for this unaccountable whim, but he had not been cured; and it so happened, that the fish he had speared this morning were three small rays and a mullet. This last, being the most delicate, he presented to Mr Westall and me, so soon as it was cooked; and then went to saunter by the water side, whilst the boats' crew should cook and eat the rays, although, having had nothing since the morning before, it may be supposed he did not want appetite. I noticed this in silence till the whole were prepared, and then had him called up to take his portion of the mullet; but it was with much difficulty that his modesty and forbearance could be overcome, for these qualities, so seldom expected in a savage, formed leading features in the character of my humble friend. But there was one of the sailors also, who preferred hunger to ray-eating! It might be supposed he had an eye to the mullet; but this was not the case. He had been seven or eight years with me, mostly in New South Wales, had learned many of the native habits, and even imbibed this ridiculous notion respecting rays and sharks; though he could not allege, as Bongaree did, that 'they might be very good for white men, but would kill him.' The mullet accordingly underwent a further division; and Mr Westall and myself, having no prejudice against rays, made up our proportion of this scanty repast from one of them.[62]

On 6 March Flinders decided to run for Coupang (Kupang) on the island of Timor, then a Dutch port. Many of the crew had come down with scurvy or dysentery and Flinders' feet were so ulcerated that he could not take his usual place at the masthead. On 31 March 1803, Brown wrote: 'About 4 PM anchord in Coepang Road about half a mile from the fort nearly abreast of it'. Next day Brown and Flinders called on the Dutch governor.[63]

Investigator spent a week in Coupang taking on provisions and making emergency repairs. The water casks were filled and she sailed again on 8 April, leaving behind the Malay cook and 'a youth from Port Jackson' who did not return on time.[64] They returned to Sydney via the west coast, stopping only at Middle Island in the Recherche Archipelago, where two anchors were cut adrift to prevent the ship being driven ashore. During the harrowing voyage of two months, scurvy and contagious dysentery ravaged the crew and six seamen died. Many on board, including Robert Brown, were seriously ill when *Investigator* anchored in Port Jackson on 9 June 1803 after the first circumnavigation of Australia. Because Flinders and his crew were all British, Bungaree became, by default, the first Australian to sail around the continent.

The sick men were landed at Garden Island, but four more were to die. The first was Peter Good the Scots gardener, who died on Friday 10 June 1803 and was laid to rest in his final snug haven near St Phillip's on Church Hill. Flinders called Good 'a zealous, worthy man'.[65]

The voyage of *Investigator* was completed and Bungaree and the rest of her crew were discharged. To recuperate from his illness, Matthew Flinders spent a few weeks at the Hawkesbury River settlement north of Sydney, close to the foot of the Blue Mountains. He enjoyed the change, remarking, 'the fresh air there, with a vegetable diet and medical care, soon made a great alteration in the scorbutic sores which had disabled me for months; and in the beginning of July I returned to the ship, nearly recovered'.[66]

Preparing to leave, Matthew Flinders recorded his impressions of Port Jackson and the Colony of New South Wales in 1803:

> The number of inhabitants was increasing rapidly; and that energetic spirit of enterprize which characterises Britain's children, seemed to be throwing out vigorous shoots in the new world . . . all this . . . made the fine harbour of Port Jackson a lively scene of business, highly interesting to the contemplator of the rise of nations. In Sydney and Parramatta, houses of stone and brick were taking place of wood and plaster; a neat church was built in the latter; and one commenced in the former place; wharfs were constructing or repairing,—a stone bridge over the stream which runs through the town of Sydney was nearly finished . . . In the interior the forests were giving way before the axe, and their places becoming every year more extensively occupied by wheat, barley, oats, maize, and the vegetables and fruits of southern Europe.[67]

One more farewell had to be made. The worn-out *Investigator* was considered to be so rotten that a hard gale would have sent her to the bottom. She was condemned as unseaworthy and unfit for further service. Determined to complete his survey of the western coast, Flinders decided to return to England to find a suitable ship. As a service to the colony, Flinders and his crew put down two extra moorings in Sydney Cove. 'That done, we left the ship as a storehouse hulk on the 21st, and prepared for our voyage to England.'[68] *Investigator* was moored alongside the hulk of HMS *Supply*.

Before the voyage of Matthew Flinders on the *Investigator*, knowledge of the geography of 'New Holland' was fragmentary. Flinders filled in the blanks of the uncharted coasts and established that the country, which he wished to call Australia, was one great island continent. In the process he became our greatest maritime explorer and chart maker. After the daily risks and hazards at sea, Flinders must have looked forward to the rewards. He could expect to return home to England to be welcomed as a hero, to be feted, promoted and reunited with his loving wife. Events did not follow this normal course.

Wreck Reef to the Ile de France

The scientists Brown and Bauer decided to remain in New South Wales to complete the classification and painting of their animal and plant collection. Bauer had made 350 sketches during the voyage and collected 100 specimens of animals between King George Sound and Port Jackson.

Matthew Flinders left Sydney on 10 August 1803 as a passenger aboard *Porpoise*, commanded by Lieutenant Robert Fowler. The ship was accompanied by *Bridgewater* and *Cato*, East Indiamen whose captains were keen to try the route through Torres Strait.

Tragedy struck eight days later when both *Porpoise* and *Cato* ran aground at night on an unchartered coral outcrop later called Wreck Reef. Three men were drowned and *Bridgewater* abandoned the castaways and sailed off north where she later disappeared at sea. The survivors sheltered in sailcloth tents rigged up on a low-lying sandbank called Providential Bank. Flinders' faithful companion Trim, also on *Porpoise*, swam safely to the bank and set up his quarters in the provision tent.

Taking 12 men in the six-oared ship's cutter *Hope*, Flinders returned 740 miles to Port Jackson in 13 days and nights. Tired and unshaven, he arrived at Government House in Sydney at 3.30 p.m. on 8 September 1803 to acquaint the startled Governor King with the news of his misfortunes. He was given command of *Cumberland*, a small, leaky colonial schooner of 29 tons, and returned to Wreck Reef just six weeks after the shipwreck.

Four days after relieving his shipmates, Flinders set out in the *Cumberland* for the Cape of Good Hope. Samuel Flinders, John Franklin and Robert Fowler boarded the merchant ship *Rolla* for their return journey. Trim was reunited with his master.

Short of water and provisions, with his crew exhausted from long hours at the pumps following a storm in the Indian Ocean early in December, Flinders decided to put in for repairs at the Ile de France (Mauritius), a French possession. He was unaware that the Treaty of Amiens had been broken and that England and France were once again at war. *Cumberland* arrived off the south coast of the island and was taken under pilot to Port Louis on 17 September 1803. The next day, Matthew Flinders was arrested by General Charles Mathieu Isadore Decaen (1769–1832), Napoleon's commander on the island, and confined to a room in the Café Marengo. Flinders did not know that Captain Nicolas Baudin of *Géographe*, returning from his expedition, had died at Ile de France the previous day. Decaen, who had recently read François Péron's report suggesting an attack on Port Jackson, thought Flinders was a spy.

Decaen could not believe that Flinders did not know war had broken out again, or that anyone would attempt such a long voyage in such a small ship. He considered that Flinders' French government passport was only valid for *Investigator*, and not for *Cumberland* or for Flinders himself.[69]

5 'The Most Intelligent of that Race'

Shiploads of Irish political prisoners were transported to New South Wales following the Irish Rebellion of 1798, which included the Battle of Vinegar Hill in County Wexford.

Rumours of an impending convict rebellion swept through Sydney in 1800 and 1802. The next year, 15 convicts escaped from the Government Farm at Castle Hill, 5 miles north of Parramatta, and raided farms. Finally, on the Sunday evening of 4 March 1804, a band of 250 mostly Irish convicts from Castle Hill broke out and set fire to a cottage. Seizing muskets, pitchforks, scythes and axes, they subdued the guards, burnt down the guardhouse, gave the official flogger a taste of his own medicine and marched off towards Green Hills (Windsor).

It was a short-lived uprising. Warned by a horseman who reached Sydney late that night, Governor King sent Major George Johnston with a detachment of redcoats from the New South Wales Corps. They marched through the night and confronted the rebels at Vinegar Hill, near the present Rouse Hill, at 11 a.m. the next day.[1]

The scene which followed was reminiscent of the slaying of Wat Tyler in front of his peasant army by the Lord Mayor of London as he parleyed with the 'boy king' Richard II at Smithfield (London) in 1381.[2] Under a flag of truce, rebel leaders Phillip Cunningham and William Johnston, both former soldiers, stepped forward to negotiate with Johnston and Quartermaster Thomas Laycock. A contemporary print shows Cunningham, refusing to surrender, crying 'Death or Liberty, Major'. Major Johnston, on horseback, claps a cocked pistol to Cunningham's head and replies: 'You scoundrel. I'll liberate you.'[3] The soldiers and armed settlers opened fire on the mob, who fled into the bush. Cunningham was shot and later that day was hanged from a staircase of the Public Store in Windsor which he had boasted he would plunder. Nine rebels were killed and 26 captured during the battle.

Philip Gidley King, a Protestant Loyalist, came down hard on the Irish rebels. Five, including William Johnston, were hanged. Nine others were flogged and 37 men involved in the uprising were sentenced to hard labour in the Hunter River coal mines.[4]

King ordered the reopening of the abandoned penal settlement at Hunter River to accommodate the recaptured convicts. A 'fleet' of three ships, *Lady Nelson*, the cutter *Resource* and the sloop *James*, left Port Jackson on 28 March 1804. On board *Lady Nelson* were the commandant, Lieutenant Charles Menzies, Ferdinand Bauer, the natural-history painter from the *Investigator*, John Millam (or Mileham) the surgeon, John Tucker, storekeeper, one overseer, two carpenters, three sawyers, a gardener, a salt boiler and 16 convicts.

Aboard *Resource* were superintendent of convicts Mr Knight and 12 convicts, while *James*, owned by merchant seaman Thomas Reiby, carried naturalist George Caley, two miners, a sergeant and four privates, with tools and stores for six months.[5] It is likely that Bungaree also accompanied the soldiers and convicts.

Lady Nelson and *Resource* returned to Sydney laden with coal and cedar, but *James* and her cargo were dashed to pieces on a beach on the northern side of Broken Bay.[6]

Three months later, the governor sent Bungaree in *Resource* to escort a party of Aborigines who had been visiting Sydney back to their home country near the Hunter's River settlement. King wrote to Menzies on 24 May 1804: 'Six Natives of your neighbourhood having come here soon after you Settled, they now return with Bongaru in the Resource'. They were each given six days rations, a jacket, cap, blanket and 4 pounds of tobacco. King expressed the hope that the Aborigines would tell their friends what they had seen in Sydney. He was pleased that Menzies was on 'such good footing' with the local tribes, but advised him to be wary of allowing more than one or two 'strange natives' into the settlement at a time.[7]

Writing to the governor from 'King's Town' on 1 July 1804, Lieutenant Menzies, then aged 21, praised Bungaree as an intermediary between blacks and whites, put him on the rations, and gave him a glowing character reference.

> We have always been and still continue on the most friendly terms with the numerous Natives here, to preserve which I have directed the Storekeeper to victual Boungaree. He is the most intelligent of that race I have as yet Seen and Should a misunderstanding unfortunately take place he will be Sure to reconcile them; and I have given Strict directions to the crews of all Vessels going up the river to treat them in a friendly manner, as I know they have frequently been very ill used by some who are neither guided by principal or humanity.[8]

Menzies (1783–1866), later Sir Charles, was in charge of a detachment of marines at the convict uprising at Vinegar Hill. He later served Britain with distinction in the Napoleonic Wars, became Queen Victoria's aide-de-camp in 1852 and was promoted to the rank of general in 1857.

Caley returned to Port Jackson in August with 47 pages of notes describing plants in the Hunter's River area.

Francis brought news to Port Jackson on 5 September that 'the Native Bungary' had been sent to track a runaway convict cedar-cutter who escaped into the bush soon after landing. The *Sydney Gazette* was confident that Bungaree 'would doubtless overtake him before he could proceed to any very considerable distance'. The prisoner was caught soon after.[9]

The Returning Boomerang

'It is not allowed to meddle with their [the natives'] affairs, as they settle their own affairs in a Very Severe Manner by Spears,' wrote Samuel Smith while the *Investigator* was in port at Sydney Cove in the Southern Hemisphere winter of 1802.[10]

One such trial by ordeal or ritual combat, 'the most malignant that has been witnessed', according to the *Sydney Gazette*, took place at Farm Cove on Sunday morning 16 December 1804 to punish 'the heroic *Willamannan*', an Aborigine who had taken the name of the ship *William and Ann*.[11] After avoiding 'an immense number of spears', Willamannan was wounded in the hand by a spear which passed through his shield.

. . . the wound brought on a stubborn conflict which for nearly an hour was general; during which time the white spectators were justly astonished at the dexterity and incredible force with which a bent, edged waddy resembling slightly a Turkish scyemetar [scimitar] was thrown by Bungary, a native distinguished by his remarkable courtesy. The weapon, thrown at 20 or 30 yards distance, twirled round in the air with astonishing velocity, and alighting on the right arm of one of his opponents, actually rebounded to a distance not less than 70 or 80 yards, leaving a horrible contusion behind, and exciting universal admiration .[12]

Bungaree was the first Aborigine ever seen by Europeans throwing a returning boomerang in the area around Sydney and it is likely he introduced the weapon to Port Jackson.

The boomerang, a crescent-shaped piece of timber which whirs through the air, is the best known and celebrated invention of the Australian Aborigines. It probably developed from a simple throwing stick used to kill birds and small animals. There are two main types. The large, heavy and accurate non-returning boomerang, used for hunting and fighting, is usually thrown just above ground level and travels almost in a straight line to its target. The thinner, flatter and lighter returning boomerang, shaped like a crescent moon (or scimitar), spins and slices to great heights and distances, making a whizzing noise, then comes back to the feet of the skillful thrower.

Wooden artefacts rot in the ground and are rarely found, but the antiquity of the boomerang was firmly established in 1974 when a collection of wooden implements, including complete boomerangs and digging sticks, was dug up from the Wyrie Swamp, a peat quarry formed about 10,000 years ago near Millicent, South Australia.[13] Anthropologists believe the boomerang was not in universal use throughout Australia and that the majority were non-returning types. The returning boomerang was mainly used in eastern and western Australia.

On his first day in Botany Bay in 1770, Joseph Banks on board *Endeavour* noticed the 'crooked' wooden weapons 'about 2 1/2 feet long, in shape much resembling a scymetar' brandished by Aborigines, which were probably boomerangs.[14]

None of the First Fleet journal keepers ever recorded seeing any type of boomerang. However, weapons described as 'wooden swords' illustrated in *Implements of New South Wales* in Surgeon John White's *Journal of a Voyage to New South Wales* (1790)[15] and the figure 'A Wooden Sword' in *The Voyage of Governor Phillip to Botany Bay* (1789)[16] appear to be non-returning boomerangs. In *A Narrative of the Expedition to Botany Bay* (1789) Captain Watkin Tench mentioned 'long wooden swords, shaped like a sabre, capable of inflicting a mortal wound'.[17] The purpose of the weapon was clearly not understood by the settlers. Stencils of the slender non-returning boomerangs are found in rock shelters in the Sydney and Hawkesbury districts.

On the returning boomerang, the silence of the Europeans is deafening. They would certainly have described such an interesting weapon if they had seen it being thrown. We can only presume that it was not known by the coastal bands they encountered between Botany Bay in the south and Broken Bay in the north.

The first written record of the returning boomerang in Australia was made in 1802 by Francis Louis Barrallier, a French-born ensign in the New South Wales Corps, during an attempt to find a way across the Blue Mountains west of Sydney. His remarks were merely a footnote in his journal, written in French, for 12 November 1802:

The natives of this part of the country make use of a weapon which is not employed by, and is even unknown to, the natives of Sydney. It is composed of a piece of wood in the form of a half circle which they make as sharp as a sabre on both edges, and pointed at each end. They throw it on the ground or in the air, making it revolve on itself, and with such a velocity that one cannot see it returning towards the ground; only the whizzing of it is heard. When they throw it along the ground it is exactly like a cannon-ball, knocking down everything in its passage.[18]

It will be recalled that Barrallier, a trained surveyor and engineer, was one of the party, which included Bungaree, sent to the Hunter River by Governor King on *Lady Nelson* in 1801. At the time of Barrallier's inland expedition, Bungaree was on board the leaking *Investigator*, far to the north in the Gulf of Carpentaria.

It is possible that Bungaree may have seen the returning boomerang in flight during the voyage with Matthew Flinders, or obtained one from the Aborigines he met in the Hunter River district in 1801 and 1804. The word boomerang is derived from a Dharug word *bumarang*, from the Georges River area south of Sydney, but it may be connected to *boomori*, the Aboriginal word for wind around the Hunter River.[19] Perhaps Barrallier or his guide Cogy (Gogy), who came from the Cow Pastures (Appin) area, told Bungaree about the boomerang following his return to Sydney in June 1803 aboard *Investigator*?

Bungaree had become an agent of change, helping in the transfer of skill and technology from one place and people to another, a process which ethnologists call acculturisation. During his two voyages with Matthew Flinders, Bungaree also introduced the woomerah or spear-thrower to coastal Aborigines in the north of Australia who did not know it.

1805–14: The Missing Years

After December 1804, when he was seen throwing the returning boomerang in Sydney, Bungaree disappears 'off the map' for almost 10 years. This decade of his life has not been documented and any ideas about his activities or whereabouts are purely speculation.

In all that time, Bungaree is mentioned only once in print—in a passing reference in a murder report in the *Sydney Gazette* (6 November 1808)—which points to the possibility that he remained at King's Town (Newcastle), either in the settlement or on its fringes.

Two sailors from the *Halcyon* went by boat with a European boy and an Aborigine known as Port Stephens Robert to see the ship *Dundee*, wrecked opposite King's Town. As they were walking on the beach, Robert suddenly turned and speared John Bosch, one of the sailors. Bosch was wounded, but escaped by diving into the water and swimming out to sea. The Aborigine then clubbed and killed the other man John Spillers with a *nulla nulla* (club) and mutilated his body. When the boy's body was found later his head had been scalped. Describing Port Stephens Robert, the newspaper said: 'His visage is rendered remarkable, by a cut which he received from Bungary that has occasioned an indentation nearly in the centre of his forehead'. Those are the bare facts. We have no idea where or when Bungaree left his mark on Port Stephens Robert.[20]

Now for the theories. In his book *Bribie—The Basket Maker* (1937), in which he devoted a chapter to 'Bongaree, THE NATIVE', Thomas Welsby indulges in a few speculations which are easily disproved. Welsby conjectured that Bungaree left Sydney with Matthew Flinders on the *Porpoise* in August 1802, bound for England. He says Bungaree's name was mentioned while the cutter *Hope* was making its voyage back to Sydney to aid the stranded crews of *Porpoise* and *Cato* at Wreck Reef.[21] This is true, but Flinders mentioned Bungaree only in connection with how far south the pandanus palm grew.[22]

Finally, says Welsby: 'I really do think he was in the *Cumberland* when Flinders sailed on his last and sadly eventful trip to England, the day of leaving Sydney being Wednesday 21st September, 1803. Bungaree must have reached the "Old Country", as the first mention of his name again is not dated until he settled at Georges Head, the year given as 1815.'[23] Obviously Welsby was unable to consult the *Sydney Gazette*, in which he would have read of Bungaree tracking escaped convicts from King's Town (9 September 1804) and his boomerang demonstration at Farm Cove (23 December 1804); or *The Historical Records of Australia*, which reprinted Governor King's and Lieutenant Menzies' letters about Bungaree, the dates being 24 May and 1 July 1804.

In his booklet, *The Story of the Aboriginal People of the Central Coast* (1968), Frederick Charles Bennett, who was a member of the Brisbane Water and Wyong Historical Societies, placed Bungaree with his family on the Central Coast of New South Wales during the missing years:

> Bungary was, in 1804, sent to Lieutenant Menzies at the newly re-established penal settlement at Newcastle to help him with the local natives. Unfortunately, some of the prisoners soon absconded, made their way back to Sydney through the Central Coast, and killed Bungary's father on the way. They were captured and returned but could not be punished for lack of acceptable evidence.[24]

Bungaree, said Bennett, then returned to his family group, of which he then became the elder.[25]

This seems perfectly feasible. However, there is no existing historical reference to the death of Bungaree's father (whose name is not known). If Bungaree had settled down on the Central Coast after tracking convicts in September 1804, what was he doing in Sydney in December that year? Unfortunately, Bennett cannot be relied upon. He has Bungaree aboard HMS *Porpoise* in 1799 instead of the *Norfolk* and also says that Nanbaree circumnavigated Australia, when in fact he returned to Port Jackson in *Lady Nelson* from a point less than halfway around the continent.[26]

It is possible that Bungaree spent the years 1805 to 1814 at Broken Bay or in Sydney, living a life much like the one which is so well documented from 1815 to 1830. He may have gone on one or more voyages with the sealing and whaling ships which operated from Port Jackson and Broken Bay and which often took Aborigines on as full crew members. Again, this is pure speculation.

The little colony spreading out from Sydney Town to the Hawkesbury River was often in turmoil following the *coup* against Governor William Bligh. Directed by the wealthy pastoralist John Macarthur, 'Rum Corps' troops occupied Government House at Sydney on the hot night of 26 January 1808, the twentieth anniversary of the foundation of New South Wales. Order began to return with the arrival of Lachlan Macquarie, who assumed office as governor on 1 January 1810.

A Prisoner on a Tropic Isle

One European of note during those years was able to find ample time to spare some thought for Bungaree and to write nostalgically about him. Far across the Indian Ocean, Matthew Flinders, who had seen so many islands, languished from late in 1803 on the Ile de France.

Here Flinders was detained for more than six years and 'treated as a spy' by the French commander General Decaen.[27] Historian Manning Clark summed up the period as the 'agony at Mauritius', during which Flinders 'rotted away as a prisoner of war those years which should have been the years of recognition'.[28]

The scorbutic sores which had plagued Flinders were healed by February 1804, although he was still physically weak a month later. His health quickly recovered when he was permitted to leave the confined quarters of the *Café Marengo* in April and was able to live more comfortably at the *Maison Despeaux* or Garden Prison. For company, Flinders had his servant John Elder, who had been a carpenter on *Porpoise*. He had access to all his books and papers except his log covering the voyage from Port Jackson to the Ile de France. He spent his time copying and revising his charts, which were sent to the Admiralty in London. Decaen eventually released *Cumberland* and her crew.

In August 1805, after 20 months of detention, Flinders was allowed to lodge with the family of Madame Delphine D'Arifat and her daughters on the 305-metre high plateau at Whilhelm's Plains in the centre of the island. For the next five years he lived in a garden pavilion surrounded by fruit trees on the D'Arifat's plantation. Here he worked long hours each day on his charts and journals and on the major portion of his book, *A Voyage to Terra Australis*.[29]

No solitary hermit, Matthew Flinders shared the family life of his hosts and was able to receive visitors. Each day he read books and wrote his journal, walked a little, learned French and taught English to the D'Arifat girls, Delphine and Sophie. After dinner, they sometimes sang or played cards or music (he played the flute). Flinders explored the mountains with his friend Thomas Pitot, who smuggled out his letters. Intimidated perhaps by the mountain peaks, Flinders, born in the low-lying fens, felt himself to be 'a prisoner on a mountainous island'.[30]

In March 1806 Napoleon sent an order to release Flinders, but the document did not reach General Decaen until July 1807. Even then Decaen continued to detain him, fearing now that Flinders knew too much about the island's defences.

In a letter to his brother Samuel in December 1806, Flinders described the plateau as a land 'gemmed with flowers' with 'charming gardens shaded by mango and other fruit trees, cool fish ponds, splashing cascades and tumbling waterfalls, coffee and clove plantations, breathing out a spicy, natural fragrance'.[31] Bernadin de Saint Pierre's *Paul et Virginie*, a romantic French tale in the style of *Robinson Crusoe*, about a young man and woman shipwrecked on a tropic island, was written at nearby Pamplemousses.

With despair Flinders learnt from a copy of the *Moniteur* in 1809 that the previously unknown coast near Spencer Gulf had been mapped as *Terre Napolean* and that 'French names were given to all my discoveries'.

Sometime in 1809, he wrote a moving tribute to Trim, his companion in so many adventures, who had cheered him in the early days of his detention. He feared his pet had been taken and eaten in 1804 by negro slaves. 'Thus perished my faithful intelligent Trim! The sporting, affectionate and useful companion of my voyages during four years,' he wrote.[32] In remembering Trim, Flinders must have also recalled Bungaree, who had fed Trim and was 'repaid with caresses'.

Matthew Flinders makes many sentimental references to Bungaree in *A Voyage to Terra Australis*, his account of the voyage of *Investigator*, published in London in 1814. In print Flinders, who rarely embroidered the action for publication, invariably spoke of Bungaree with greater affection and gratitude than he did in his original journal. These are examples of just one day's events.

Journal on HMS Investigator (1801–3)	Terra Australis (1814)
31 July 1802	
. . . the party with me consisted of six, including the native Bongaree.	. . . the party with me, also, of six persons, including my native friend Bongaree.
Through the medium of our native, who went to them singly, unarmed, and naked, a communication was brought on.	Bongaree stripped off his clothes and laid aside his spear . . . the poor fellow, in the simplicity of his heart.
Our native could not understand any word of their language, certainly; nor did they seem to know the use of his throwing stick; for on one of them being asked to use it, he threw the stick and spear together.	Our native did not understand a word of their language, nor did they seem to know the use of his womerah or throwing stick, for one of them being invited to imitate Bongaree.

A Brief Freedom

In June 1809 a fleet of British ships blockaded the Ile de France.

His French captors officially informed Flinders of his release in March 1810. They returned his sword when he signed a parole promising not to act against France in the current war. He finally left his island prison aboard the *Harriet*, bound for Bengal, but transferred to HMS *Otter* which took him to the Cape of Good Hope on 13 June 1810. The British forces attacked and captured Ile de France in December that year.

On 23 October 1810 Matthew Flinders was 'home' at Spithead. He had been away from Britain and separated from his wife Ann for nine years and three months. The 'real' Robinson Crusoe, Alexander Selkirk, was marooned on the island of Juan Fernandez for only four years and four months.

Sadly, neither Matthew Flinders' new-found freedom nor his life were to last very long. Aged 36, but plagued by illness, he already looked like an old man. The Admiralty, somewhat reluctantly, promoted him to post captain, dated only to his release from Ile de France. Matthew and Ann were forced to live frugally in a series of London lodging houses while he prepared the manuscript of *Terra Australis* for publication.

There was one joyous event, the birth of their daughter Anne on 1 April 1812. Soon Flinders' health failed again. Suffering great pain from his old kidney and bladder complaints, Flinders corrected proofs and completed his book shortly before his death on 18 June 1814.[33]

In *My Love Must Wait* (1941), her moving novel about Matthew Flinders, Ernestine Hill imagines the visions which swirled through the navigator's mind on his deathbed. In one dream he sees, rising up before him, the figure of 'Boongaree, naked and black, grinning his fidelity'.[34]

6 Macquarie's Favourite

Born on the windswept isle of Ulva near Mull in the Hebrides Islands off the west coast of Scotland, Lachlan Macquarie joined the army at the age of 15 and served as a lieutenant during the American War of Independence. He advanced his military career and fortune in India in active service against Tippo Sahib, Sultan of Mysore, and during the capture of Ceylon (Sri Lanka) from the Dutch. He arrived in Sydney on 28 December 1809 aboard HMS *Dromedary* as lieutenant colonel of the 73rd (Highland) Regiment of Foot and officially assumed office as the fifth governor of New South Wales on 1 January 1810. With the governor was his second wife, Elizabeth Henrietta Macquarie.[1]

Macquarie found a famine-stricken colony, insecure still after the overthrow of Governor William Bligh two years earlier. With great energy he immediately began to implement reforms aimed at restoring order and morale. He disbanded the Rum Corps and used the government monopoly on spirits to build the 'Rum' Hospital (now Parliament House and the Mint in Macquarie Street, Sydney).[2] Macquarie set about the task of transforming Sydney into an orderly town with wide streets and fine Georgian buildings designed by convict architect Francis Greenway, to whom he granted a pardon.[3]

The new governor put a stop to the cruel and indiscriminate flogging of convicts and encouraged emancipated convicts and small free settlers to the ire of the 'pure merinos', an elite of wealthy sheep farmers and wool exporters led by John Macarthur. Macquarie encouraged exploration, built roads, established country towns and set up the first bank. Throughout the Napoleonic Wars, Britain had been busy making guns and bullets. The result was that little coinage or 'small change' was minted. In New South Wales a paper currency sprang up, with notes and IOUs for as little as threepence in circulation. In 1812, £10,000 worth of Spanish silver dollar coins was shipped to Sydney from India. The canny Macquarie had the centre stamped out of each coin to make a 'dump' worth 15 pence (one shilling and threepence). The remaining outer ring, nicknamed the 'holey dollar', retained the coin's original value of five shillings.[4]

Shortly after his arrival in Port Jackson, Macquarie met an Aborigine for the first time. According to Ensign Alexander Huey of the 73rd Regiment, there was a native on board the pilot boat which met the *Dromedary* inside the Heads at 9 o'clock on 28 December. From the ship at 11 o'clock that evening Huey could see a group of Aborigines around a fire, singing songs and beating time on a shield. On Sunday, the last day of 1809, Huey wrote in his journal, that Aborigines assembled 'from the Hawkesbury and many miles around' to fight 'a regular battle in honour of the new Governor'.[5]

Joseph Arnold (1782–1818), a surgeon on HMS *Hindustan*, which accompanied *Dromedary*, was surprised by the size and appearance of the town. 'I expected to find a small collection of irregularly built cottages,' he wrote in a letter to Edward Crowfoot, 'but instead of that, are long and spacious streets, in many places having lofty and magnificent stone buildings.'[6]

Arnold, who was collecting curios, told his brother in a letter:

We can only get things cheap from the savages, who bring coral, shells. etc., and are glad to take old cloaths, biscuits, or wine, for them. We often also take one or two of these fellows with us into the woods and make them carry our things, for they will do anything for rum . . . Most of them that live around Sidney speak as good English as we do. But they all live in the open air among the bushes, and they eat nothing but shell fish and such wild animals as they can catch.[7]

Utterly convinced of the superiority and benefits of British culture, Lachlan Macquarie took a genuine fatherly interest in the Aborigines of New South Wales. He gave them presents and cultivated their friendship. He wished to restore peaceful relations and found it difficult to come to terms with their hostility towards the white settlers who occupied their lands. To this end he made plans for conciliation and issued frequent florid proclamations—scattered liberally with capitalised words—often addressed to the Aborigines, not one of whom could read them.

The Corn Raids

Macquarie's first troubles with the native inhabitants of New South Wales came during a severe drought in 1814 in the outlying districts of Appin and Airds, known as the Cow Pastures. Violence broke out when the 'mountain tribes', the Gandangara from beyond the Burragorang Valley, joined with fierce warriors from Jervis Bay and swept down to help themselves to the ripening ears of maize (sweet corn) on the settler's farms. The peaceful 'Cow Pastures Tribe', Dharug-speaking people, did not take part.

On Saturday 7 May 1814 at Milehouse's farm in Appin three privates of the Veteran's Company militia (made up of retired New South Wales Corps troops) fired on a large group of Aborigines feasting on corn and killed one native boy. The Aborigines replied with a shower of spears and fled after killing a veteran trooper named Isaac Eustace, whose hand they cut off.

At the next-door farm, Butcher's, the militia fired at another group of Aborigines, who also fled, 'leaving a woman and two children behind them, dead', the *Sydney Gazette* reported.[8] Next day the vengeful warriors attacked a hut at nearby Camden on the property run by Elizabeth Macarthur, whose husband was in England. They speared and killed the stock-keeper William Baker and his de facto wife Mary Sullivan.[9]

In a dispatch to Colonial Secretary Earl Bathurst in London, Macquarie blamed these clashes on 'idle and ill disposed Europeans' who, he said, had taken liberties with the native women and had also 'treacherously attacked and killed a Woman and her two children whilst Sleeping, and this unprovoked cruelty produced that retaliation whereby Persons perfectly innocent of the Crime lost their lives'. Macquarie believed that after taking their revenge, the Aborigines would not attack the settlers again unless further provoked by insults and cruelty.[10]

However 'hordes of natives' continued to show themselves around the Cow Pastures, causing great alarm among the settlers, who formed a *corps de garde* to keep a night watch.

Cogy, the Cow Pastures's chief, who had been Francis Barrallier's mountain guide in 1802, fled to Broken Bay 'from a personal wish to maintain a friendly footing with us'. The chief alleged that the mountain tribes were cannibals.[11]

In April and May 1814 the Gandangara made several attacks on labourers at the properties of Edward and George Cox at Mulgoa, who defended themselves with muskets. At Emu Ford (Penrith) not far from Mulgoa, grazier and road-builder William Cox was beginning to assemble work gangs of mostly convict tradesmen and labourers to start work carving a 12-foot-wide bullock cart road over the Blue Mountains and down to the plains on the far side.[12]

Governor Macquarie proclaimed a General Order, dated 18 June 1814, which was published in the *Sydney Gazette* and read at churches on the last Sundays in June and July. He regretted 'the unhappy Conflicts which have lately taken place between the Settlers in the remote Districts of Bringelly, Airds, and Appin, and the natives of the Mountains adjoining those Districts'. He said a legal investigation heard before a bench of magistrates had shown there was enough evidence to 'convince any unprejudiced Man' that the first personal attacks were made by the settlers and their servants. 'It appears, however, that the Natives have lately shown a Disposition to help themselves to a Portion of the Maize and other Grain belonging to the Settlers in these Districts, in a Manner very different from their former Habits'.

Macquarie warned the settlers against taking the law into their own hands again or committing any 'wanton Acts of Oppression and Cruelty against the Natives', who, he wrote, were entitled to the protection of British laws 'so long as they conduct themselves conformably to them'. He promised 'the most exemplary Punishment' to formentors of hostilities on either side.[13]

In an editorial the *Sydney Gazette* took up the governor's theme, saying the native attackers might have been driven by hunger. If settlers allowed them to enter their fields and gave them a few corn cobs, they would go on to the next farm.[14] Just two weeks after Macquarie's proclamation, a further 'unhappy instance of the dreadful effects of warfare with the natives of the interior' took place at Mulgoa, the official newspaper reported:

> Yesterday sennight [15 July] the wife of a person named [James] Daly at Mulgowy, having only 3 days lain in, was alarmed by the noise and shouts of a number of natives unexpectedly, and rising from bed fired a musket towards them, to intimidate them—which had the contrary effect: the poor woman immediately deserted the house, leaving 2 fine children, beside the infant that was in bed: and on her return had the wretchedness to behold the two eldest lifeless on the floor, and the little infant tumbled out of bed, which they had stripped, but the child otherwise unharmed.[15]

James Daly left his farm, while the mountain tribes, for the moment, faded away into the cliffs and gullies of their wild homeland. The governor held five mountain tribesmen responsible for the bloodshed: Bitugally, Goondel, Murrah, Yallaman and Wallah.[16]

An Experiment in Civilisation

Macquarie's orders showed that despite the many clashes on the frontiers of settlement during 1814, he continued to play the role of a conciliator seeking a permanent state of peace between blacks and whites.

On 8 October 1814, in a lengthy dispatch to Colonial Secretary Bathurst, the governor outlined his 'Reflections' on the Aborigines and submitted proposals for an 'Experiment towards the Civilization of these Natives'. He had given considerable thought to a series of measures aimed at converting 'this Uncultivated race' from a liability into an asset:

> Scarcely emerged from the remotest State of rude and Uncivilized Nature, these People appear to possess some Qualities, which, if properly Cultivated and Encouraged, Might render them not only less wretched and destitute by Reason of their Wild wanderings and Unsettled Habits, but progressively Useful to the Country According to their Capabilities either as Labourers in Agricultural Employ or among the lower Class of Mechanics.

Although subject to 'great Indolence', the Aborigines were of 'free open and favourable Dispositions, honestly Inclined'. The principal part of their lives, he said, was 'Wasted in Wandering thro' their Native Woods, in Small tribes of between 20 and 50, in Quest of the immediate Means of Subsistence, Making Opossums, Kangaroos, Grub Worms, and such Animals and Fish, as the Country and its Coasts Afford, the Objects of their Fare'. The introduction of herds and flocks had not tempted them to alter their mode of living, nor had they made these animals their prey.

Those natives living near Sydney and other principal settlements, he said, 'live in a State of perfect Peace, Friendliness, and Sociality With the Settlers, and even Shew a willingness to Assist them Occasionally in their Labours; and it seems only to require the fostering Hand of Time, gentle means, and Conciliatory Manners to bring these poor Un-enlightened People into an important Degree of Civilization'.

Kindness and encouragement, he thought, might induce those responsible for hostility against the settlers to forego revenge. 'I have determined to make an Experiment towards the Civilization of these Natives, Which is the Object I have in View by this Address, and trust it Will Meet Your Lordship's benevolent Patronage.'

As a first step, Macquarie planned to establish a school at Parramatta under the direction of a former missionary, William Shelley, to educate and bring up 'to Habits of Industry and Decency, the Youth of both Sexes, Commencing at the Outset with Six Boys and Six Girls'.

Though he was not mentioned by name, the next part of Macquarie's plan would eventually involve Bungaree:

> I have it Also in Contemplation to Allot a piece of Land in Port Jackson bordering on the Sea Shore for a few of the Adult Natives, Who have promised to Settle there and Cultivate the Ground. Such an Example, Cannot, I think, fail of Inviting and Encouraging other Natives to Settle on and Cultivate Lands, preferring the productive Effects of their own Labour and Industry to the Wild and precarious Pursuits of the Woods.[17]

The Native Conference

William Shelley, who had been a missionary on the Pacific island of Tonga, suggested that Aboriginal children should be taught reading, writing and religion. The boys would learn manual labour, agriculture and 'mechanical arts' and the girls, sewing, knitting and spinning. Shelley reported to Governor Macquarie on 20 August 1814 that the Aborigines were eager to hand over their children. It has been suggested since that their parents may have been swayed by the fact that each child would receive a weekly ration of meat, rice, cornflour, wheat, sugar, soap, salt and pepper. The boys were to be given shirts, jackets, 'trowsers' and caps and the girls shifts, gowns and bonnets. They would sleep in beds with blankets and have one pair of shoes each.[18]

To 'make a personal Communication' to the Aborigines about the Native Institution he was about to establish, Governor Macquarie called a public conference to be held at the Market Place in Parramatta at 11 a.m. on Wednesday 28 December 1814, 'that being the next Day after the full Moon'. The date chosen for this event, which later became an annual affair, was the anniversary of the governor's arrival in Sydney in 1809.[19] All District Constables and Peace Officers were directed to inform natives in or near their districts in sufficient time to assemble.

The governor did not stint on food and drink, providing a feast capable of taking the minds of those attending off corn fields. He ordered the Commissariat to supply: one fat bullock weighing 500 pounds, 200 pounds of bread, 20 pounds of sugar, 100 pounds of lemons and 10 gallons of rum. Dinner was to be ready at 12 noon with a tub and tin mugs provided for drinking the grog.[20] It is an historical tradition that Bungaree, as 'host' of the Sydney Aborigines, always attended and introduced the other chiefs to the governor. It is known he was at the Native Conferences in January 1826 and January 1829 and that he did not attend in January 1818 (see Chapter 11).

The *Sydney Gazette* reported the first conference at length in a style and sentiment owing much to Macquarie's Secretary, John Thomas Campbell:

> On Wednesday HIS EXCELLENCY the GOVERNOR went to Parramatta, for the purpose of seeing and conferring with the Natives, agreeably to the benevolent design intimated in the General Orders of the 10th instant. At one o'clock HIS EXCELLENCY, accompanied by the LIEUTENANT GOVERNOR, and a number of Officers, Civil and Military, went to the Market-place, where the interview had been appointed to be held, and conversed with them for an hour, pointing out in an affable and familiar way the advantages they would necessarily derive from a change of manners, and an application of moderate industry.

However, only 60 Aboriginal men, women and children attended, 'owing as it was conjectured, to some false impressions which the more distant tribes had given way to, relative to the design of the conversation, suspiciously imagining that they were to be forcibly deprived of their children, & themselves sent to labour'. Other Aborigines were in the neighbourhood, but were afraid to come forward.

'Three children were yielded up to the benevolent purposes of the Institution.' After the talking, the feasting began. The Aborigines were seated in a circle, and served with roast beef, and 'a cheering jug of ale', after which Governor and Mrs Macquarie returned to Sydney. During the afternoon, more Aborigines came in and were welcomed by Shelley who gave them the remaining food and liquor. Another child was added to the list of 'candidates for civilization'.

The house being prepared for the native children near the church at Parramatta, said the *Gazette*, would be enclosed by a paling fence, so that the parents 'becoming eye-witnesses of the benefits accruing to their children' would feel thankful to 'the beneficence that projected and accomplished it'. The report closed with a sympathetic editorial, most unusual for the times, which candidly admitted the plight of the Aborigines caused by British settlers taking and clearing their land:

> The plan that has been adopted must appear the best suited to the ends proposed. At a tender age it affords to the children asylum against the distressing wants they feel, more especially

in June, July and August [winter], when the weather is cold, the woods afford them little or no food, and they become prey to many loathsome diseases which poverty entails upon the human frame. The kangaroo has almost disappeared about the Settlements; the opossim [possum], long substituted as their chief dependence, has at length become as scarce; the roots of the earth are by nature too sparingly administered to constitute any thing like a dependence to them; and the tribes of each district dare not incroach upon any other. In the summer those of the coast subsist by fishing, but in the winter, only for the occasional aid they derive from us, their situation would be equally miserable.—And whence have these evils originated, but in the clearing of the immense forests which formerly abounded in the wild animals they lived upon? This admission certainly gives them a claim upon the considerations of the British Settler; and we cannot imagine for a moment, that any one who bears that character will withhold any means that may fall within his power of forwarding the benevolent views of the Native Institution.[21]

Only two months after the Native School officially began on 18 January 1815, with six boys and six girls, Macquarie reported to London that by an 'unaccountable caprice' six children had been taken away from the school by their parents.[22]

William Shelley died on 6 July 1815, but his widow managed the school until 1823, when it was transferred to Black Town.[23] It was abandoned by 1824. In 1819 an Aboriginal girl aged 14 from the Native School took first prize in the Anniversary School Competition which was contested by 20 Aboriginal and 100 European children.[24]

Although in the governor's mind it had been done for the best of motives, the separation of the Aboriginal children from their parents to 'civilize' them was later to become an official policy of Australian governments which led to much heartbreak and sorrow.

The Native Conference lapsed in 1815, but it was revived in the following year and held annually for many years. It was finally abolished by Governor Sir Richard Bourke in 1835.

Bungaree's Farm

In a benevolent but naive attempt to break the Aborigines of their nomadic habits, Macquarie decided to settle 'friendly' Aborigines on land which they could farm. This part of his 'Experiment in Civilization' was officially inaugurated at a ceremony on Tuesday 31 January 1815 (Macquarie's birthday) when Governor and Mrs Macquarie and a large party of ladies and gentlemen travelled by boat 6 miles down the harbour to the peninsula of Georges Head. The *Sydney Gazette* reported:

On this occasion, sixteen of the Natives, with their wives and families, were assembled, and HIS EXCELLENCY the GOVERNOR, in consideration of the general wish expressed by them, appointed Boongaree (who had been long known as one of the most friendly of this race, and well acquainted with our language), to be their Chief, at the same time presenting him with a badge distinguishing his quality as 'Chief of the Broken Bay Tribe'.

Each Aboriginal settler received a suit of slop clothing, agricultural implements and other useful articles. A boat, called the *Boongaree*, was given to them for fishing, which, the *Gazette* noted, 'always furnished the principal source of their subsistence'.[25]

At the end of March 1815 Macquarie advised Earl Bathurst that the 16 adult natives had been settled on the farm, 'where I have had comfortable Huts built for them, and they and their families appear to be perfectly Contented'. They had already made 'some

Fig. 13.

Port Jackson, New South Wales   Watercolour, 10.7 x 35.21 cm.
[Georges Head at left]   Rex Nan Kivell Collection, National Library of Australia,
Augustus Earle, c. 1825.   Canberra.

little progress' in cultivating the ground 'and by giving them some trifling assistance now
and then from Government in the way of Slops and Provisions, I doubt not they will
become industrious, and set a good Example to the other Native Tribes residing in the
Vicinity of Port Jackson'.[26]

Corporal Patrick Geary and his party received a payment of £10 for constructing 'Huts
and Gardens at Georges Head' from the Police Fund for the quarter ended 31 March
1815.[27]

When George Howe, editor of the *Sydney Gazette*, recorded these events in his chronology
for the year 1815 in the *New South Wales Pocket Almanack*, he said of Bungaree: 'This
native, now between 40 and 50 years of age, has ever been distinguished for the docility
of his manners; his kind and tractable disposition, his friendly demeanour; his general
utility . . . thus has the effort been made to reconcile the adults to the manners of an
orderly society, to which effort every possible encouragement was given'.[28]

According to Dr Joseph Arnold, however, the attempt to establish the farm at Georges
Head was already a failure by July 1815. Arnold wrote in his journal: 'I was told however
that it was a foolish business, that they will not work on their farm, that they leave
it to ruin, that old Bungaree threw away his medal and cloathing, and that no good was
done'.[29] Arnold had a score to settle with Macquarie, who had coldly received him and
refused to reimburse his return passage to England when he arrived as medical officer
on the convict transport *Northampton*. He remained in Sydney from 19 June to 13 July
1815 and had to pay his own fare home.

Bungaree may have discarded his clothes and the gorget presented by Governor Macquarie,
or even sold them, but if he did he recovered the breastplate and wore it proudly for
many years afterwards.

But Bungaree was ill. On the same day that Arnold (bound for Batavia on the *Indefatigable*)
passed Newcastle, Macquarie addressed a letter from Government House, Sydney, to Surgeon
D'arcy Wentworth:

Sir, I request you will be so good as to order to be received into the General Hospital for
Medical care the Bearer Boongaree Chief of the Broken Bay Tribe of Natives—He is to be
victualled at the expence of Government.[30]

It is not known what illness Bungaree had, or how long he spent in hospital. D'arcy Wentworth filled many responsible roles in the colony's administration. He was colonial surgeon, superintendent of police, treasurer of the police and orphan fund and a magistrate.

Arnold's conjecture was premature. Bungaree was again at Georges Head on Tuesday 5 November 1815. Early that morning, Governor and Mrs Elizabeth Macquarie and a party which included Rev. William Cowper, Mrs Cowper and Captain John Gill of the 73rd Regiment went to visit the 'Native Farm at George's Head' in the Government Barge. 'Mrs Macquarie made Boongary the chief a presentation of a Breeding Sow & 7 Pigs— and also a Pair of Muscovy Ducks—together with Suits of Clothes for his Wife and Daughter', Macquarie wrote in his Diary.[31] The expense of £8 10s. 0d. for the sow and pigs 'purchased by Government as a present to Bungaree Chief of the Broken Bay Natives' was charged to the Police Fund and recorded in Police Reports and Accounts on 31 December 1816, signed by D'arcy Wentworth.[32]

William Cowper (writing in 1838) said an overseer was appointed to assist the Aborigines on their farm. 'But the European, feeling little, if any, interest in the welfare of the Natives, did not protect the property thus appropriated to them, and in a short period the Huts and gardens, &c. were destroyed, and the Boat was lost; and this attempt failed'.[33]

Russian explorer Captain Bellingshausen who was in Sydney in 1820 said that convicts were employed to teach agriculture to the Aborigines. 'At first they worked with great zeal,' he said, 'but they soon began to find it irksome, sold off their implements and returned to their former way of life. Boongarie was given a garden, specially laid out for him by a European. He still owns it, and gains a little money for the peaches which grow so abundantly in it.'[34]

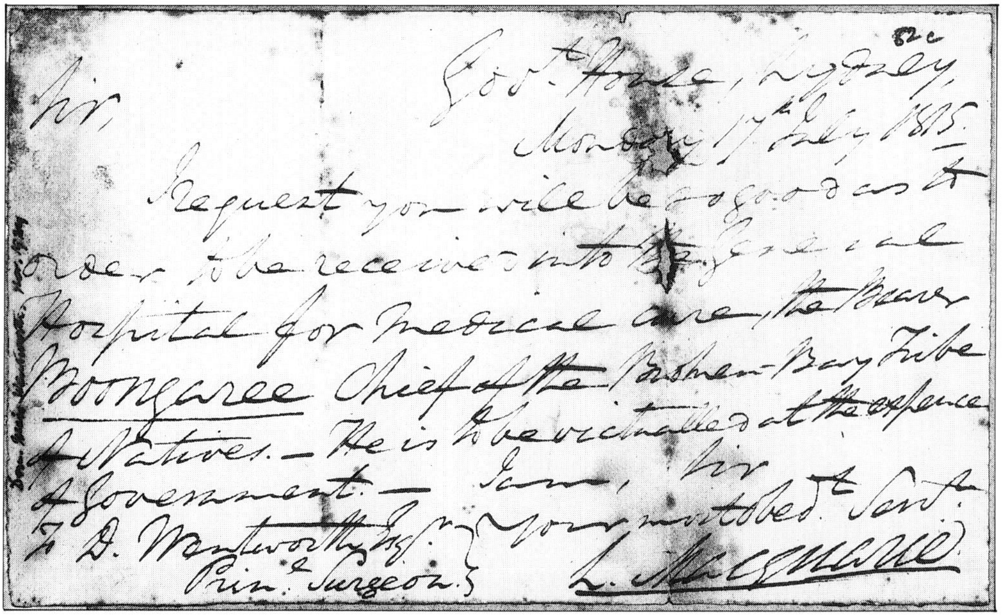

Fig. 14.

Lachlan Macqaurie.
Letter to Surgeon D'arcy Wentworth, asking that Bungaree
be admitted to the General Hospital, 17 July 1815.

Extract from *Memoranda and Related Papers*, Mitchell Library,
Sydney.

If Bungaree's boat had been lost, as Cowper said, it was recovered (or another boat was given to the Aborigines) because Bungaree in 1820 still possessed 'a dirty European boat'.[35] This was replaced in 1824 with another boat given to Bungaree (at Macquarie's suggestion) by Governor Sir Thomas Brisbane.

Bellingshausen had his own ideas on why the farm failed: 'the magic charms of drink and tobacco, the greatest of all temptations to these natives, are stronger than all the joys of a fixed, plentiful and quiet life and still attract them to the town of Sydney'.[36]

Gatherings and Gorgets

Lachlan Macquarie hoped to exert his authority over the natives of New South Wales without the force of arms by creating leaders among them who would be responsible for the behaviour of their people, a chain of command quite alien to Aboriginal culture. Selecting chiefs, presenting them with engraved metal breastplates or gorgets as a badge of office, establishing the Native School, and convening the Annual Native Conference were the crucial factors in Macquarie's 'experiment'.

The Native Conference was a masterstroke. The 'peaceful' Aborigines who attended were greeted in a friendly manner by the governor and his wife and feasted on ample liquor and beef. Afterwards they sang and danced together in a grand inter-tribal corroboree. In later years, the conference became a forum at which previously rebellious chiefs came in to make a formal surrender.

The germ of Macquarie's idea for the Native Conference may have been some stately reception or *durbar* he had attended while in India, or a folk memory from his Scots tribal origins. Biographer M. H. Ellis compared the gathering of the Aborigines to an incident in which the Scottish Highland chiefs were lured to the island of Iona for a feast and then forced to become Presbyterians and learn English.[37] More likely precedents were the great tribal congresses held in North America at which the British distributed gifts of cloth, hatchets, clothing, barleycorn and beans to the Indians.

Bungaree was the first Aborigine to be appointed a chief by Governor Macquarie and the first to be given a metal gorget bearing his name and title. It was inscribed: 'BOONGAREE—Chief of the Broken Bay Tribe—1815'. As far as we know this gorget no longer exists, but it was illustrated clearly in 1820 by the Russian artist Pavel Mikhailov (Fig. 26). Bungaree's breastplate was often mentioned by observers, who reported varying inscriptions such as the spurious 'King of Port Jackson' and 'King of the Blacks'. It is depicted in differing shapes in his other portraits. See, for example, Earle's first lithograph (Plate 3) in which the wording is reversed, Jules Lejeune's inscription 'Buggary—Roi des natifs' (Fig. 33) and Charles Rodius's portrait (Plate 19) in which the name is spelt as Bungaree and not Boongaree. It is possible that more than one gorget was given to Bungaree.

The gorgets issued in New South Wales were made of brass. They were usually shaped like a crescent moon and were suspended from a brass chain around the neck so that they hung on the chest. Strong and durable, they could be worn with or without European clothing. Holes were made in each of the top corners of the gorget plate to secure the neck chain.

Two similar gorgets presented to Bungaree's widow Gooseberry have survived in good condition. One is in the collection of relics in Mitchell Library, Sydney (Fig. 15)[38], along with her rum mug. The engraved inscription reads:

CORA GOOSEBERRY
FREEMAN BUNGAREE
QUEEN
OF SYDNEY & BOTANY

The other (Fig. 16) is the smallest gorget in the collection of the Australian Museum in College Street, Sydney. On each of the top corners is a drawing of a fish caught on a line leading to the chain holes. There is a stylised crown in the centre.[39] The inscription follows the curved shape of the gorget and reads:

GOOSEBERRY
Queen of Sydney to South Head

These gorgets were probably patterned on similar ornaments introduced by both the French and British in North America. As a young man, Lachlan Macquarie spent several years in the Americas. He arrived there in 1776 at the age of 15 at the start of the War of Independence. The next year he was promoted to ensign in Nova Scotia and became a lieutenant in January 1781, serving in New York and at Charlestown. In 1783 Macqaurie was in Jamaica.[40]

Fig. 15.

CORA GOOSEBERRY   Copper gorget, c. 1800, 11 cm x 8 cm.
FREEMAN BUNGAREE   [Small engraving of a fish at right above inscription]
QUEEN   Relics, Mitchell Library, Sydney.
OF SYDNEY & BOTANY

Fig. 16.

GOOSEBERRY   [Engraved with design of fish and fishing line, with stylised
Queen of Sydney to South Head   crown at centre.]
Brass gorget, 5 cm deep and 7.8 cm long. Australian Museum, Sydney.

The North American gorgets were crescent-shaped, but usually made of silver, with the likeness of King George III stamped on one side and the British coat of arms on the other. They were fastened below the neck with ribbons attached to loops at the top edges of the crescent. Such gorgets were bestowed on Indian warriors of the six Iroquois 'nations' who were Britain's allies against the French during the Seven Years War (1755–62). The French had their own Indian troops and 'medal chiefs'.

Some vain young chiefs decorated themselves with as many as 12 silver gorgets, each hanging below the other. The Indians were delighted by gaudy clothing like bright shirts, scarlet coats, silk handkerchiefs, shiny buttons and plumed hats. The Iroquois *satchems* (kings) favoured green silk waistcoats.[41]

The gorget had evolved between 1400 and 1600 from a small piece of armour between the helmet and breastplate which protected the throat. The English word is derived from the French *gorgete*, a diminutive of *gorge*, throat.[42] By the early eighteenth century this armour piece had become stylised as a crescent-shaped silver or brass plate worn at the neck in full dress uniforms by British officers.

Macquarie himself referred to the chest ornaments as gorgets. When describing the Native Conference held on Thursday 1 January 1818, he noted in his diary: 'I presented Gorgets to Cogie [Cogy] as Chief of the George's River Tribe, and to Norwong as Chief of the Botany Tribe and the Order of Merit to Tindall of the Cow Pastures and Pulpin of the Hawkesbury Tribe'.[43]

Macquarie's innovation, which started with Bungaree, began a long tradition of presenting gorgets to trustworthy Aborigines. George Howe, who usually reflected Macquarie's views, remarked that other deserving natives had received medals for good conduct 'and it is a pleasure to say that much good has been effected by it'.[44] While in Macquarie's view these awards may have had as much merit as any civil or military title or medal, by Victorian times their importance had been debased. They had become known as 'kingplates' and were handed out with flour and blankets to rural 'King Billys' (often the last survivors of their 'tribe') by petty officials, police, missionaries and squatters.[45]

War on the Frontiers

In 1816, after two further years of severe drought, the Gandangara, bent on vengeance and hungry for corn, came down again from their mountains. They attacked settlers in the outlying Cow-Pastures districts, burned their houses and sheds, speared their cattle and plundered their crops, forcing many to abandon their farms. They killed four of G. T. Palmer's men on the Nepean River and three of Mrs Macarthur's stock-keepers at Camden. A militia of 40 farmers armed with muskets, pistols, pitchforks and pikes clashed with the Aboriginal war party at Upper Camden and retreated under a shower of spears and stones.[46]

Bitterly disappointed by the failure of his efforts to pacify and civilise 'these Wild rude people' by peaceful methods, Governor Macquarie determined on a tough stand. He blamed the Aborigines rather than the settlers for the fresh outbreak of fighting and replaced conciliation with brutal reprisals. While persevering with his original experiment, Macquarie told Earl Bathurst in a dispatch to London dated 18 March 1816: 'It is my Intention, as soon as I shall have Ascertained What Tribes Committed the late Murders and Depredations, to send a Strong Detachment of Troops to drive them to a Distance from the Settlements of the White Men'.[47]

On 10 April 1816 Macquarie ordered three detachments of the 46th (South Devons) Regiment 'to proceed to those Districts most infested and Annoyed by them on the banks and Neighbourhoods of the rivers Nepean, Hawkesbury and Grose'. The troops were to take as many Aboriginal prisoners as possible. Those who resisted or fled were to be shot and their bodies hung 'on the highest trees and in the clearest parts of the forest'. The troops were commanded by Captain W. G. B. Schaw, who went north-west to the Grose and the Nepean, Lieutenant Charles Dawes, who marched to the Cow Pastures; and Captain James Wallis, who went to the Airds-Appin area with grenadiers. At the end of the operation, Schaw and Wallis were to meet at Woodhouse's Farm on the Appin Road.[48]

In his journal that day Macquarie wrote that he felt compelled, unwillingly, to chasten the tribes and to 'inflict terrible and exemplary punishments upon them'. It was a painful resolution, he said, but the Aborigines might construe any further lenience on the part of the government as fear and cowardice.[49]

As usual the Aborigines were elusive, disappearing into the bush as the military force approached. However, Lieutenant Dawe's troops, guided by an Aborigine from the Cow-Pastures named Tindall, killed an unknown number of Aborigines and captured a 14-year-old boy.

At dawn on 17 April, Wallis' men ambushed a band of Aborigines as they slept in their camp near William Broughton's farm at Appin. Roused by their dogs, the Aborigines attempted to escape, but 14 were killed and five were captured. The dead included several women and children, felled by bullets as they dashed from rock to rock or threw themselves in terror over the cliffs. Two men considered to be ringleaders of the raiders were among those killed, one of whom was the 'notorious chief' Carnanbigal.[50]

Macquarie followed up this military action by equally repressive measures against the 'Aborigines, or Black Natives of this Country', gazetted in his proclamation of 4 May 1816. From 4 June 1816 (the king's birthday):

> No Black Native or Body of Black Natives shall ever appear at or within one Mile of any Town, Village, or Farm, occupied by, or belonging to any British Subject, armed with any warlike or offensive Weapon or Weapons of any description, such as Spears, Clubs, or Waddies, on Pain of being deemed and considered in a State of Aggression and Hostility, and treated accordingly.

No more than six Aborigines, unarmed, could 'lurk or loiter' near any farm in the interior. Large assemblies for ritual battles between tribes at or near Sydney or other towns or in the bush were 'wholly abolished'. Aborigines judged to be peaceful would receive passports signed by the governor and would be protected from molestation. To those Aborigines 'inclined to become regular Settlers', Macquarie promised small land grants and six months' provisions, agricultural tools and wheat, maize and potatoes for seed. Each person would receive one suit of slop clothing and one 'Colonial Blanket' from the King's Stores.

The Governor called 'a general Friendly Meeting of all Natives residing in the Colony' to be held at the Market Place in Parramatta on 28 December 1816, at which he would acquaint them with the objects of the Native School and reward 'such of them as have given Proofs of Industry and an Inclination to be civilized'.[51]

Macquarie was lavish in his rewards to those Aborigines who had been helpful during the hostilities. On 7 May 1816 he gave Bidgee Bidgee, Harry, Bundell, Tindall Coelby and Creek Jemmy (Narragingy) 'each a complete suit of slops including Blanket, 4 Days Provisions, Half Pint of Spirits and Half Pound of Tobacco'.[52] On 25 May the governor gave Narragingy, Coelby and Tindall a further seven days provisions, half a pound of tobacco and blankets for each of their gins.[53]

A further proclamation, issued on 20 July 1816, outlawed 10 Aborigines, 'well known to be the principal and most violent instigators of the Late Murders'. They were named as Murrah, Myles, Wallah (alias Warren), Carbone Jack (alias Kurringy), Narrang Jack, Bunduck, Kongate, Woottan, Rachel and Yallaman. A reward of £10 was offered to anyone bringing in the outlawed Aborigines or proof of their having been killed or destroyed within three months.[54]

The outlying settlers were encouraged to form themselves into associations, or armed groups which were authorised to respond to any attacks by Aborigines. One such armed party went in quest of the mountain tribes in August 1816 after a shepherd tending sheep was found murdered on a remote part of the Mulgoa estate. The man's body was in 'a most mutilated and mangled state, having been perforated with spears in several parts, and otherwise barbarously used', said the *Sydney Gazette*. A twisted sense of poetic justice was evident in the methods used to slaughter the sheep:

The flock in charge of this unfortunate man consisted of upwards of 200 very fine sheep, most of which were thrown down an immense precipice by the savages, and the remainder, about fifty in number, were barbarously mangled and killed, many of the unoffending and defenceless creatures having had their eyes gorged with spears, which were afterwards driven into the head.[55]

Festivity and Good Humour

The assembly of the Native Tribes at Parramatta on Saturday 28 December 1816 was a 'novel and very interesting spectacle' attended by 179 'friendly' Aborigines, men, women and children in response to Governor Macquarie's invitation. Again the natives sat on the ground in a large circle, their 'chiefs' sitting on chairs in front of each tribe.

In the centre of the circle, long tables groaned under the weight of roast beef, potatoes and bread. 'A large cask of grog lent its exhilarating aid to promote the general festivity and good humour which so conspicuously shone through the sable visages of this delighted congress,' the *Sydney Gazette* reported on the following Saturday:

> The GOVERNOR, attended by all the members of the Native Institution, and by several of the Magistrates and Gentlemen in the neighbourhood, proceeded at half past ten to the Meeting, and having entered the circle passed round the whole of them, enquiring after, and making himself acquainted with the several tribes, their respective leaders, and residences. His EXCELLENCY then assembled the chiefs themselves, and confirmed them in the ranks of chieftains to which their own tribes exalted them, and conferred on them badges of distinction, whereon were engraved their names as chiefs, and those of their tribes.—He afterwards conferred badges of merit on some individuals, in acknowledgement of their steady and loyal conduct in the assistance they rendered the military party when lately sent out in pursuit of the refractory natives to the west and south of the Nepean.

When Mrs Macquarie arrived the 15 children from the Native Institution, led by their teacher, paraded around the circle, 'the children appearing very clean, well clothed and happy':

> The chiefs were then again called together to observe the examination of the children as to their progress in learning, and to civilized habits of life.— Several of the little ones read, and it was grateful to the bosom of sensibility to trace the degree of pleasure which the chiefs manifested on this occasion.—Some clapped the children on the head, and one in particular turning round towards the GOVERNOR, with extraordinary emotion, exclaimed 'GOVERNOR,— that will make a good settler—that's my Pickaninny!'—and some of their females were observed to shed tears of sympathetic affection at seeing the infant and helpless offspring of their deceased friends so happily sheltered and protected by British benevolence.[56]

It became the practice to give each Aborigine attending the annual congress a bright uniform consisting of 'frock' or loose jacket, a pair of red 'trowsers' and a leather cap for the men and a red jacket and petticoat for the women. Each pickaninny received a shirt; all received blankets.[57]

Governor Macquarie seems to have had a genuine warmth for those Aboriginal 'chiefs' like Bungaree, whom he perceived to be 'on side'. Roger Oldfield in the *South-Asian Register* mentions an incident which illustrates Macquarie's generosity and warmth towards them.

Some time after the 1814–16 clashes at the Cow-Pastures, 'Koogee' (Cogy) called unexpectedly to see Macquarie at Government House. His Excellency treated this as quite natural and introduced the unwashed chief and his gin to the British gentlemen present and invited him to take a glass of wine with them.[58]

By 4 April 1817 Macquarie felt confident enough to advise London that the measures he had taken, including disarming the Aborigines, had succeeded and 'all Hostility on both sides has long since Ceased; the black Natives living now peaceably and quietly in every part of the Colony, Unmolested by the White Inhabitants'. He cancelled the Proclamation of 20 July 1816 and pardoned all the outlawed natives. Outlawing some of the 'Most Violent and Atrocious Natives' he said, had made them 'Sensible of the Folly of their Conduct, and soon afterwards induced the Principal Chiefs to Come in at the Heads of their respective Tribes to sue for peace and to deliver up their Arms in all due Form'.[59]

The governor again rewarded his favourites at the annual meeting of the 'Native Chiefs and their Tribes at Parramatta', held on New Year's Day 1818. He wrote in his diary:

> Thursday 1 January 1818!!!
> The Native Chiefs with their respective Tribes assembled this day at the Market Place at Parramatta, agreeable to appointment, to the number of 130 Men, Women & Children . . . The whole of the Natives were plentifully and hospitably entertained with Roast Beef[,] Potatoes, Bread and Punch, and after having seen the 16 Native Children now at the Institution, mustered and marched round the Circle, the Native Meeting broke up and separated Peacably for their Several Homes.[60]

Bungaree was not present at the New Year's Day meeting at Parramatta in 1818, nor at his North Shore bush camp in Sydney. By that time he was far away at sea, somewhere in the Great Australian Bight, on another voyage of discovery.

7 Voyage of the Mermaid

Fourteen years after sailing on *Investigator* with Matthew Flinders, Bungaree volunteered to go to sea with naval explorer Phillip Parker King. King, aged 26, had chosen *Lady Nelson* for the survey, but while she was being repaired and refitted, the colonial cutter HMS *Mermaid* arrived in Port Jackson from India. He soon convinced Governor Macquarie that the cutter was better adapted to the proposed survey. *Mermaid* was a strong, snub-nosed vessel built in India of Bengal teak. Compared to *Investigator* she was tiny: only 55 feet long against 100 feet and 83 tons in weight against 334 tons. The cutter carried a crew of only 19 men compared to 88 on *Investigator*.[1]

King's task, in a survey jointly sponsored by the British Admiralty and the Colonial Office, was to chart the outline of the coast of western and northern Australia which Flinders had missed in 1803 when he was forced to cut and run for Timor in the leaky *Investigator*. King was instructed to search for any river mouths 'likely to lead to an interior navigation into this great continent'.[2]

Phillip Parker King, born on Norfolk Island in 1791, was the third and legitimate son of Philip Gidley King, third governor of New South Wales. A child named after such eminent seamen as Captain Arthur Phillip (his godfather) and Captain John Parker of HMS *Gorgon* was surely marked for a life at sea. Phillip King sailed to England in 1799, went to school there and attended the Naval Academy at Portsmouth. He joined the Royal Navy at the age of 16 on the *Diana* and served in the North Sea. He was promoted master's mate at the age of 19 and lieutenant at the age of 23 in 1814.

After receiving his commission for the Australian survey, Phillip King married Harriet Lethbridge in England and took his bride on a six and a half month 'honeymoon' voyage aboard the convict transport *Dick* which arrived at Port Jackson on 3 September 1817.[3]

Sir Joseph Banks, who had sent Allan Cunningham to New South Wales in 1816 to collect plants for Kew Gardens, arranged for the botanist to join King's expedition. Cunningham later became an inland explorer (he discovered the Darling Downs).[4] Like some Antipodean 'Johnny Appleseed', he would often stop to plant English peach tree stones in wild places. Cunningham, aged 27, wrote with appreciation of Bungaree's 'little attentions' during his botanical excursions ashore from *Mermaid*.

The cutter's two master's mates, Frederick Bedwell, a marine surveyor, and John Septimus Roe, aged 20, acted as naturalists and collected insects during the voyage.

Like his father, Phillip King was a protégé of Banks. A talented amateur artist, he was also keen on natural history. He drew the first known portrait of Bungaree (Fig. 24) and made many sketches of the little cutter, coastal scenery and incidents which occurred during his survey voyages of the Australian coastline. Some of these drawings were engraved

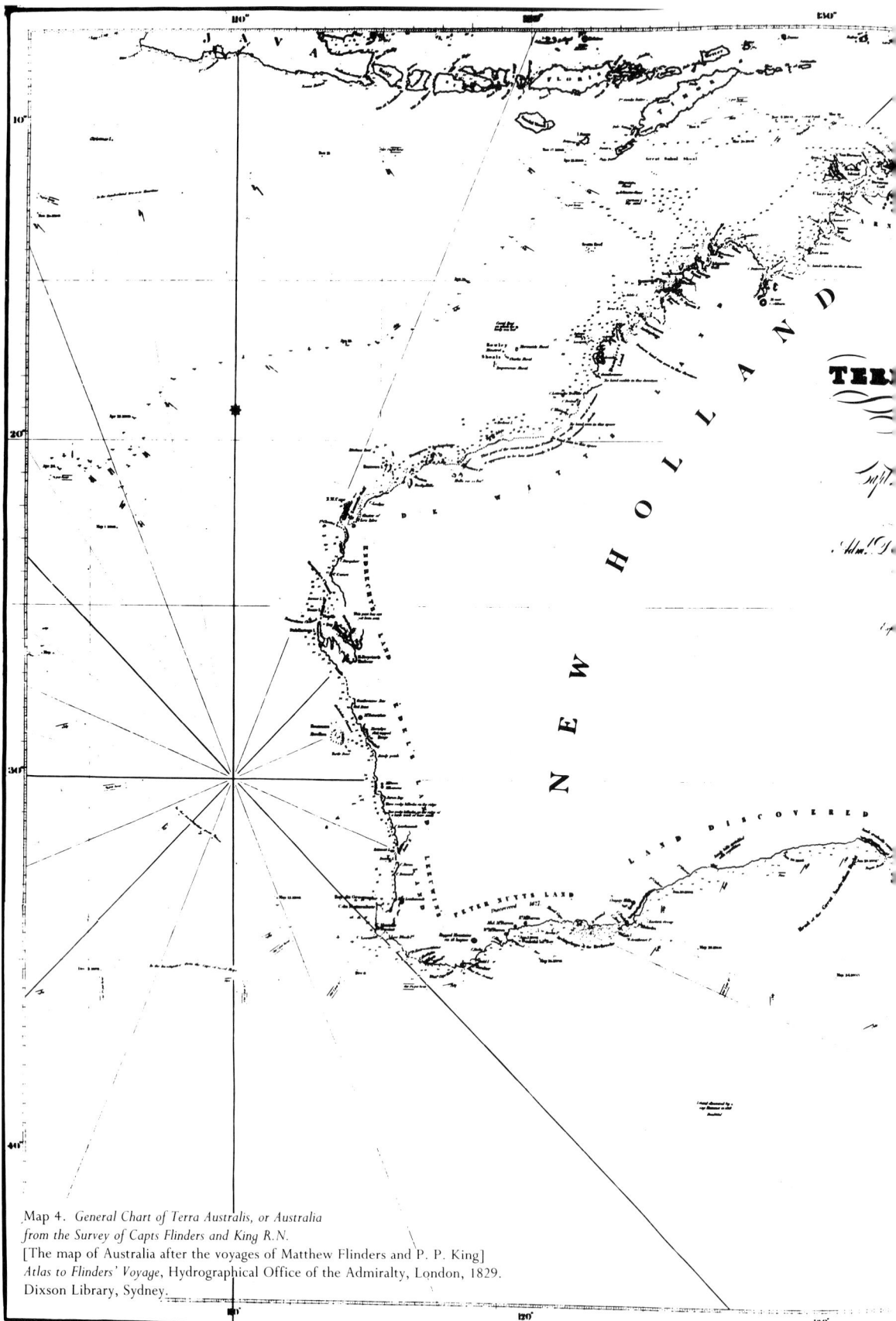

Map 4. *General Chart of Terra Australis, or Australia from the Survey of Capts Flinders and King R.N.*
[The map of Australia after the voyages of Matthew Flinders and P. P. King]
Atlas to Flinders' Voyage, Hydrographical Office of the Admiralty, London, 1829.
Dixson Library, Sydney.

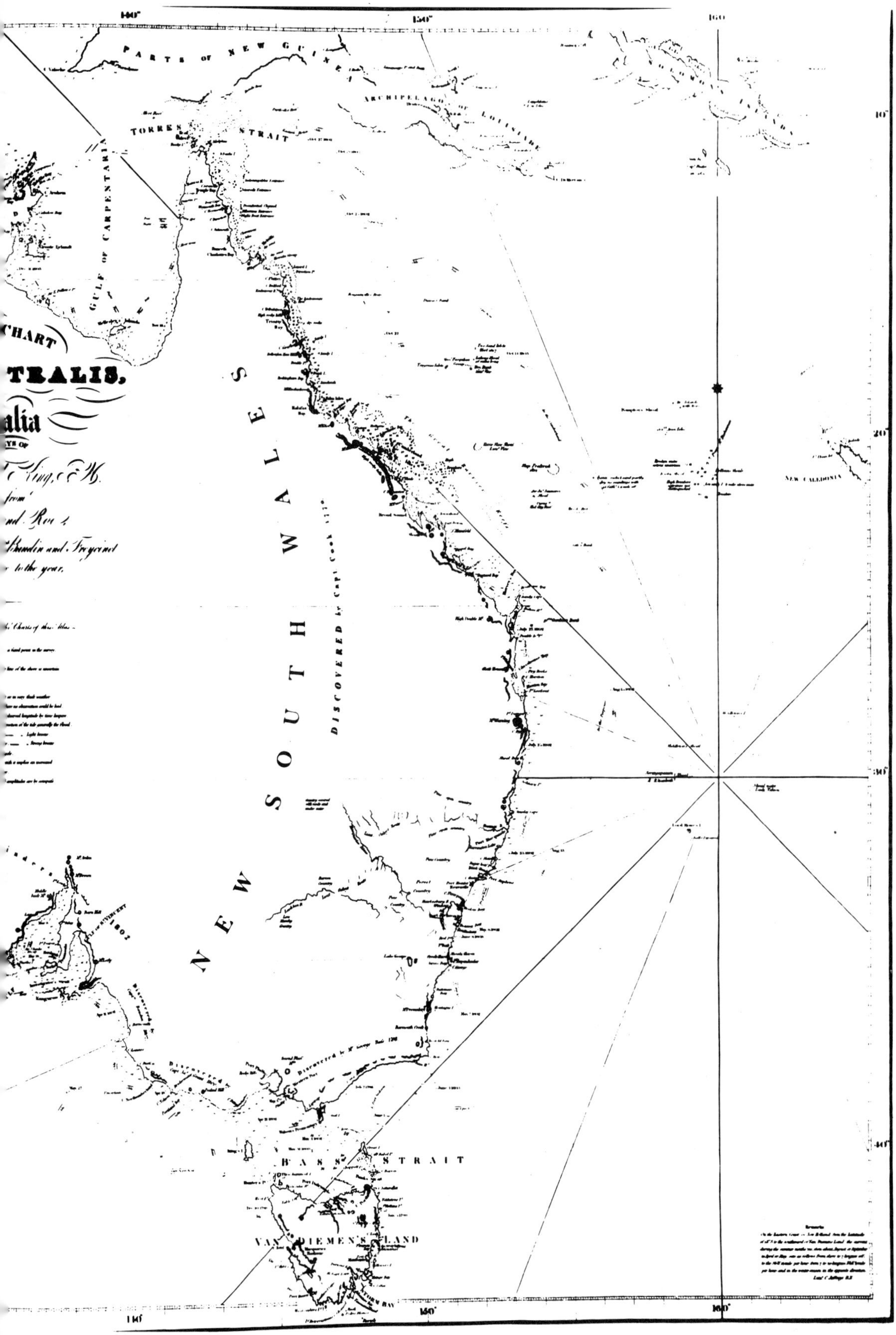

140°
150°
160°
10°
20°
30°
40°
PARTS OF NEW GUINEA
TORRES STRAIT
ARCHIPELAGO OF LOUISIADE
GULF OF CARPENTARIA
CHART
TRALIS,
alia
NEW SOUTH WALES
DISCOVERED by Capt. Cook 1770
NEW CALEDONIA
BASS STRAIT
VAN DIEMEN'S LAND

in his *Narrative of a Survey of the Intertropical and Western Coasts of Australia*, published in London in 1827. He wrote:

> I acquired the proferred services of Bongarree a Port Jackson native who had formerely accompanied Captain Flinders in the Investigator, and also, on a previous occasion in the Norfolk schooner. This man is well known in the colony as the chief of the Broken Bay tribe; he was about forty-five years of age, of a sharp, intelligent and unassuming disposition, and promised to be of much service to us in our intercourse with the natives.

Allan Cunningham made it clear that Bungaree had personally volunteered for the voyage.[5] Included in the crew, he said, was 'Bongaree, a chief of natives of a tribe of Broken Bay, who accompanied Captain Flinders in the Investigator, and who was taken on this voyage at his own particular request'.[6]

King, an admirer of Matthew Flinders, would have noted the many references to Bungaree

---

HM Cutter *Mermaid*

Colonial cutter, 83 tons, built in India of Bengal teak.
Purchased 1817.
Left Sydney on first survey 22 December 1817.
Returned to Port Jackson 29 July 1818.
Subsequent survey voyages 1818–24.
Sold at Sydney 1824. Wrecked 13 June 1829 on a reef east of Franklin Island, Torres Strait.

Dimensions: 55 feet long, beam 18 1/2 feet.
Arms: One 6-pounder muzzle-loader.
Boats: Whaleboat, jolly boat.
Crew: 12 seamen; 2 boys.
Deaths: None.
Commander: Lieutenant Phillip Parker King.
Masters mates: John Septimus Roe, Frederick Bedwell.
Botanist: Allan Cunningham.
Supernumary: Bungaree.

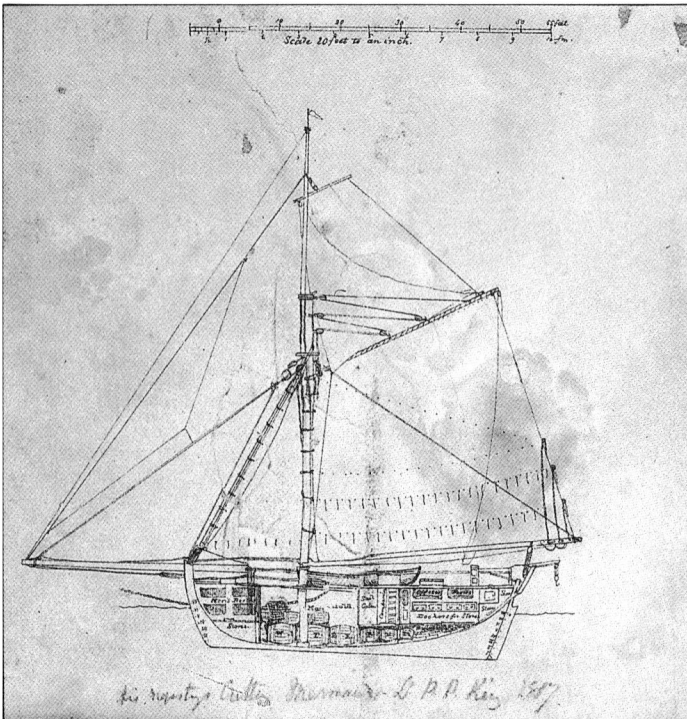

Fig. 17.

His Majesty's Cutter Mermaid
Phillip Parker King, 1817.
Etching.
Mitchell Library, Sydney.

in *Terra Australis*. Bungaree may also have been recommended by Governor Macquarie, who should have long since received Flinders' book and charts which he requested from London in June 1815.[7]

Mermaid, carrying provisions for nine months and water for 12 weeks, left Port Jackson on 22 December 1817. Four days later, after being battered by a gale on Christmas Day, the cutter put in for shelter and minor repairs at Twofold Bay, where Bungaree again took up his role as an intermediary between the Europeans and the Aborigines. They passed several Aborigines on Red Point as they entered the bay (Fig. 18). One defiant warrior stood at the edge of the rocks holding a spear and waving a club or throwing stick 'most furiously' over his head. Bungaree replied in his 'Port Jackson language', but neither man understood the other. Groups of natives around the bay seemed anxious to avoid contact.

The ship moored in Snug Cove in the northern part of the bay, where King went ashore with Roe and Cunningham. 'Boongaree also accompanied us,' wrote King, 'clothed in a new dress, which was provided for him, of which he was not a little proud, and for some time kept it very clean.'[8]

That evening, after hauling the fishing seine net on the beach without success, the ship's party was about to leave when they spotted 'three or four natives' peeping above the long grass about 70 or 80 yards up the hill, watching their movements. They walked towards the Aborigines, who suddenly 'scampered' up the hill to hide among thick trees.

> Boongaree called to them in vain; and it was not until they had reached some distance that they answered his call in loud shrill voices. After some time in parley, in which Boongaree was spokesman on our part, sometimes in his own language, and at others in broken English, which he always resorted to when his own failed in being understood, they withdrew altogether, and we neither heard nor saw any more of them.

When they passed Red Point as the cutter left the bay next morning (27 December), 20 or 30 Aborigines came to the cliff top 'shouting and hallooing and making violent gestures' while the women and children hid among the trees and bushes. At the same time, another group of Aborigines unconcernedly cooked fish near the beach where two canoes were hauled up on the rocks.[9]

Fig. 18.

Entrance to Twofold Bay
Phillip Parker King, 1817.
Watercolour.
Mitchell Library, Sydney.

Fig. 19.

Oyster Harbour King George Sound
Phillip Parker King, 1818.
Watercolour.
Mitchell Library, Sydney.

Mermaid rounded Cape Howe, where large fires were burning in the hills, and got into Bass Strait, almost running ashore in the dark at Cape Naturaliste in north-eastern Van Diemen's Land. They returned to Bass Strait, passed Seal Island and set sail westward along the Great Australian Bight.

At Oyster Harbour, an inlet of King George's Sound, where the cutter remained for 11 days during January 1818, Bungaree again proved his prowess as a spear-fisherman. 'Bungaree speared a great many fish with his fiz-gig; one that he struck with the boat hook on the shoals at the entrance of the Eastern River weighed twenty-two pounds and a half, and was three feet and a half long.'[10]

On Sunday 25 January King sent a boat to search for a river shown by Flinders and Baudin in their charts as running out of Oyster Harbour. Cunningham joined the party 'consisting of Mr King, Mr Bedwell, our friend Bongaree, the native, and four able hands'. The boat was soon stopped by sand flats and shallow water and the search for the river was abandoned. While the others lit a fire, Cunningham took the opportunity to plant a few peach stones.[11]

Mermaid rounded Cape Leeuwin at the extreme south-west tip of the continent, and headed north through the Indian Ocean, plagued with bad luck. On 10 February off North-West Cape a cable parted and she lost an anchor and three days later a fluke was broken off the second anchor. During the survey of Exmouth Gulf, Cunningham recorded (16 February): 'Bongaree, our native, had with great skill speared some fish, which afforded us a fresh meal'.[12]

Bungaree constantly went ashore in the ship's boats. On Friday 20 February he went with Rowe and King with four crew in the second whaleboat as they explored the sand and mangroves of a small island. On the following Wednesday he searched for shells on the beach with one of the officers.

King started the survey proper from Exmouth Gulf (18 February 1818), examining the curve of coastline to Depuch Island (5 March), Rowley Shoals (16 March) and the coast of Arnhem Land westward from Goulburn Island (26 March) to Van Diemen Gulf. He discovered Raffles Bay (16 April), which he named after the founder of Singapore Sir Thomas Stamford Raffles, and also Port Essington (24 April), site of a later unsuccessful settlement.

The first encounter with white men in their sailing ships must have been as startling and terrifying to the native Australian as aliens in spaceships would be to us today. Cunningham and King both record a clumsy incident which took place in the islands of the Dampier Archipelago on 25 February 1818, when Bedwell captured an Aborigine. The English sailors were not only surprised at the man's displeasure but were bemused when he cast away the presents they gave him.

The crew spotted three 'Indians' who from a distance looked as though they were wading over sandbanks towards Lewis Island. As they approached, they realised that the men were sitting on logs in the water, paddling along with their hands. The sight of the ship alarmed the Aborigines, who called out and cried even louder when the jolly boat was lowered and sent after them.

'On the boat's coming up with the nearest Indian, he left his log and, diving under the boat's bottom, swam astern; this he did whenever the boat approached him, and it was four or five minutes before he was caught, which was at last effected by seizing him by the hair, in the act of diving, and dragging him into the boat.' The man resisted strongly and two sailors were needed to hold him still. A group of about 40 Aborigines, mostly women and children, watched the kidnapping from a nearby island. Overcome with grief, the women cried out, rolled on the ground and covered themselves with sand.

> When our captive arrived alongside the vessel and saw Boongaree, he became somewhat pacified, and suffered himself to be lifted on board; he was then ornamented with beads and a red cap; and upon our applauding his appearance, a smile momentarily played on his countenance, but it was soon replaced by a vacant stare. He took little notice of any thing until he saw the fire, and this appeared to occupy his attention very much.[13]

Alan Cunningham described him as a 'fine figure of a man, of rather thin, spare shape'. He was 6 feet 2 inches tall, naked, had a strong bushy beard and was about 27 or 28 years of age. They gave him some biscuit, which he spat out, and sugared water, which he drank. He greedily ate sugar from a sailor's fingers and then licked the saucer dry. 'He took much notice of Bongaree, who had reluctantly at our persuasion stripped and exhibited a scarified body—a counterpart of his own,' Cunningham observed.[14]

Fig. 20.

Native of Dampier's Archipelago on his Log
Engraving after Phillip Parker King, 1818.

Title page: King, Phillip Parker, *Narrative of a Survey of the Intertropical and Western Coasts of Australia.* London, 1827.

Taken to the side of the boat from which he could see his own people on the island, the Aboriginal cried out 'coma negra', loudly and repeatedly. After an hour, during which he had been 'greatly caressed', to calm him, he was taken in the jolly boat to his log raft to which the sailors lashed a metal axe. A bag was hung around his neck containing biscuits and a little of whatever he appeared to like.

When he reached the shore, his companions treated him as if he had been contaminated by the aliens. He was ordered to stand apart from them until he had thrown away his new red cap, bag and axe. All this time they held their spears poised and pointed at him. The Aboriginal men stood 'huddled together in the greatest alarm' while the women hid in the bushes, peeping out to see what was going on. The native stood 'as motionless as a soldier' while he answered his friends' questions. He was soon allowed to approach them and they cautiously advanced, still with spears at the ready, and surrounded him:

> His body was then carefully examined; and upon the women and children being allowed to approach, they seated themselves in a ring and placed him in the middle, when he told his story, which occupied about half an hour. Upon its being finished, they all got up, and, after shouting, and hallooing to us, they went to the opposite side of the island, leaving our presents upon the beach, after having carefully examined them.[15]

The simple float used by the Aborigine was about 1 foot in diameter and 7 or 8 feet long, solid and cylindrical and tapering at the ends which were detached pieces joined by sticks.[16] He sat astride the partly submerged log in the manner depicted by Phillip King on the title page of Narrative of a Survey (Fig. 20).

Before sunset the jolly boat crew, with Cunningham, Roe and Bungaree aboard, rowed to the island. As the shore was too rocky for them to land, they gave a few presents to the Aborigines who waded up to their arms in the water to take them. 'The natives were much amused with Boongaree's appearance, and frequently addressed him, but his answering them in a strange language surprised them very much; on his taking off his shirt they shouted loudly, and were delighted.' They were disappointed when the boat turned back to the ship without landing.[17]

Two days later King, Bedwell and Cunningham went to the island in the whaleboat and landed on a sandy beach. The natives had left and the party found only their deserted temporary huts made of green boughs. 'It was with no small surprise we found near the huts the axe and other things we had given the native on board,' said Cunningham, 'the bag with provisions appeared not to have been even opened.'[18] Taking Bungaree with them, again 'divested of his clothes', the explorers parleyed with some 'friendly Indians' on a sandy beach on the opposite shore. 'Boongaree was of course the object of their greatest attention: the fashion in which his body was scarred was the subject of particular remarks; and when he pointed at the sea, to shew them whence he came, they set up a shout of admiration and surprise.'

This time the Aborigines shook hands with the British sailors as they departed.[19]

Cunningham takes up the story:

> We all landed, and found our commander with the natives, who . . . now amounted to about a dozen. We decorated their persons with beads, and the reflection of their frizzled visages in a glass [mirror] created much laughter among them. To the one who had advanced towards us first, we gave the cap and the axe and, having found a piece of wood on the beach, Bongaree was directed to show him how to use it. Some old rusty nails, files, sharpened chisels, were also presented to this person, who although he appeared the most intelligent among them received

all with a careless indifference and unconcern. It is evident they never saw iron before, and knew nothing of its valuable uses. The captured native was not among them, nor did we observe any so well proportioned as he was.[20]

Following this happy meeting with the Islanders, King gave the name Intercourse Islands to the seven islands between Lewis Island and the mainland.

Mermaid dropped anchor in South West Bay at South Goulburn Island on 26 March 1818. The next day, when the sailors went ashore for wood and water, Bungaree accompanied Cunningham, who was gathering botanical specimens. They followed some fresh footprints in the sand, but did not see any Aborigines. 'Bongaree, the native, was with me all the afternoon, and upon our return to the beach we found the jolly boat had gone back to the cutter, but returning at sunset it took us both off,' wrote Cunningham. The boat's crew found only a small amount of water, which was brackish.[21]

In his rambles on shore Bungaree discovered fresh water running into a natural basin from the foot of the cliffs on the beach. A well was dug and left to fill overnight.[22] However, the cutter's wooding party carelessly left their tools on shore when they returned that night. The Aborigines objected to this intrusion on their territory and, inevitably, a series of skirmishes followed. The next day, while the British party were at dinner, 'Boongaree, whose eyes were constantly directed to the shore, espied five natives among the grass, which was so high as nearly to conceal them, walking towards our wooding place'. The Aborigines had stolen one of four flags on the beach left to mark the base-line for a survey.

When they reached the cliff above the watering party, three of the Aborigines began to throw down timber from a wood pile the cutters had heaped up. The fourth man,

Fig. 21.

Allan Cunningham (1791–1839)
Phillip Parker King, 1817.
Pen and ink.
Mitchell Library, Sydney.

creeping on his hands and knees, carried off two more flags, but was detected as he was taking the fourth. Two muskets shots were fired at him and he fled into the bush with his companions who took the wooding tools with them.

Earlier, a canoe containing six or seven natives had been seen on the opposite shore under Point Ross. At Bedwell's suggestion, the explorers rowed around South West Bay and found the canoe pulled up on the beach with several Aborigines close by. One threatened them with a spear, but they all ran into the bush when the boat crew landed. The well-crafted canoe, which King assumed was Malay, was made of a teak log 17 feet long and 2 feet broad. It was launched and brought to the ship as a reprisal for the stolen flags and tools.

The South Goulburn Island Aborigines were determined to make their own reprisals. That afternoon, while King observed distances between the sun and moon, warriors armed with spears played a cat-and-mouse game, watching from the trees. In the evening they shadowed a group from the ship walking towards the north end of the bay. Before dark the explorers hoisted the canoe up to the cutter's stern and secured her other boats under it. However, later that night, 'when every thing was quiet', the Aborigines cut the whaleboat's moorings and 'swam away with her in tow'. Luckily, the boat was recovered 'before the tide had drifted her out of sight'.[23]

Early the following day (30 March) the cutter was moved in closer to the watering place Bungaree had found. When King saw a dozen Aborigines watching from the trees, he decided to take the opportunity of 'expressing our anger at their attempt to steal our boat, and of shewing them we were not Malays'. He ordered a shot to be fired over their heads by a six-pounder carronade (a short cannon). The report alarmed the Aborigines, but they quickly recovered from fright and kept their eyes on the white men.

The shore party had been filling up their wooden barrels for half an hour when the islanders suddenly appeared on the brink of the cliff overhanging the beach and threw down several large stones, which slightly wounded three men before the muskets could reply. After this surprise attack, the jolly boat was sent ashore and Bedwell was ordered to keep the whaleboat moored close to the beach with muskets at the ready. A warning shot was fired over their heads when they advanced towards the cliffs.[24]

Because of this hostility, King decided to leave South West Bay as soon as the water casks were filled and to obtain wood from the neighbouring North Goulburn Island. At Mullet Bay a shore party found an Aboriginal camp of conical-shaped huts nestled into the sand. These huts were 3 feet high and made of long sticks joined at the top to support a bark roof which was covered with sand. King thought the huts looked 'more like a sand-hillock than the abode of a human creature'.[25]

Allan Cunningham found a good spot of soil nearby in which he planted 'every sort of seed that we possessed'—peach, apricot, loquat, lemon, vegetable seeds, tobacco, roses, other European plants and coconuts. The bay was called Mullet Bay, wrote Cunningham, 'in consequence of the immense shoals of that fish which were seen near the shores, and of which Boongaree speared several with his fiz-gig'.[26]

Trepang were found in great numbers about the rocks on the beach as they had been at South Goulburn Island. Returning to South West Bay on 10 April, King was surprised to see the Malay trepang fleet steering through Macquarie Strait towards two of their prows anchored in a sandy bay on the south west side of Sim's Island. He then sailed west to Van Diemen Gulf and circumnavigated Melville and Bathurst Islands.

On 23 April at Knocker's Bay, west of Port Essington in Van Diemen Gulf, they were ambushed by Aborigines who leapt into the water armed with spears and clubs when the boat became entangled in thick mangrove roots in a swampy channel. The attackers fled to the other bank when muskets and small shot were fired over their heads and remained there, shouting and screaming threateningly. After the boat was freed, the Aborigines attacked again with a shower of spears and stones. Some spears struck the boat, but nobody was hurt. King punished this group of Aborigines by towing away their new bark canoe and its cargo of shellfish from a nearby beach.[27]

On 7 May King named two islands Barron and Field 'after my friend [Barron Field], then presiding as Judge of the Supreme Court of New South Wales'.

A shore party had another skirmish with the natives on 17 May, this time on Melville Island. After climbing Luxmore Head near St Asaph's Bay to take bearings, they were surprised by a group of natives armed with spears who 'obliged us very speedily to retreat to the boat'. In their haste to run downhill to safety, the mariners left behind a brass theodolite stand and Cunningham's insect net, which were instantly seized.

Muskets at the ready, the whites parleyed with the blacks and exchanged a silk handkerchief for a dead bird. When they made signs that they wanted fresh water, the Melville Islanders directed the boat around the headland and followed, skipping from rock to rock. Soon there were nearly 30 warriors gathered at the sandy beach on the north side of Luxmore Head. The Aborigines constantly demanded axes by imitating the action of chopping, so the Englishmen returned to the *Mermaid*.

That afternoon, while Bedwell's crew stood by in the whaleboat, King and some of his men in the jolly boat exchanged some metal chisels and files for a basket of fresh water and one of sago palm fruit. King threw a tomahawk to an old man and when he caught it, 'the whole tribe began to shout and laugh in the most extravagant way'. Phillip King's sketch (Fig. 22) captured this 'interview' with the Aborigines.

The Aborigines enjoyed the game of negotiating for the theodolite stand. At first they pretended they believed that what the sailors really wanted was an Aboriginal woman who was holding the instrument. When the boat rowed towards her, two nimble warriors sprang into the water, 'jumping at each step entirely out of the sea', which came up

Fig. 22.

Interview with the Natives at Luxmore Head [St Asaph's Bay],
Melville Island
Phillip Parker King, 1818.

Ink and wash, 15 x 23.2 cm.
Mitchell, Library, Sydney.

Fig. 23.

Coepang from Fort Concordia
Phillip Parker King, 1818.
Ink.
Mitchell Library, Sydney.

to their thighs. They tried to seize the remaining tomahawk, but King threatened one man with a club and pulled the boat further out. The Aborigines performed a defiant dance, laughing and shouting and leaping two or three times out of the water. Some kept their spears at the ready by floating them on the surface, while others carried them under the water between their toes. Although by this time he was 'thoroughly disgusted' with his opponents, King was impressed by their yellow-painted muscular bodies and long curly hair clotted with white paint. Finally, he gave up and the party returned on board without the theodolite stand.[28]

Phillip King mentioned Bungaree less frequently in his journal as the mapping voyage progressed. This may have been because he did not consider Bungaree much of an 'active seaman', as he wrote in 1821—or was it because Bungaree created such a stir whenever he went ashore and met other Aborigines? Allan Cunningham had no such doubts. After a day gathering botanical specimens in an area of sand and mangroves at Port Hurd on Bathurst Island on Tuesday 26 May, he wrote:

> During the whole of this day's excursion I was accompanied by our worthy native chief, Bongaree, of whose little attentions to me and others when on these excursions I have been perhaps too remiss in making mention, to the enhancement of the character of this enterprising Australian.[29]

Finding his water casks leaking and provisions running low on 31 May, King decided to put in at Timor for supplies. On 4 June 1818 *Mermaid* anchored at Coupang. From the Dutch Fort at Concordia Phillip King sketched the cutter riding at anchor in the bay, flanked by Malay trepang prows, with canoes drawn up on the beach and men fishing with nets nearby (Fig. 23). 'From the anchorage,' wrote King, 'Coepang provides a very picturesque and lively appearance. The houses, a few of which are built of stone, are roofed either with red tiles or thatch, and are shaded from the heat of the sun by thick groves of trees.'[30]

To illustrate the 'unquestionable intelligence' of the Australian 'savages' the French explorer Jules Dumont d'Urville many years later recalled 'a very droll flash of memory' told about Bungaree, who, he said, showed 'enthusiasm and despatch' while accompanying P. P. King to northern Australia:

On putting in to Timor, Boungari having gone ashore, made a call on a merchant to drink a glass of gin; he drank and offered a piastre in payment, knowing full well that he should be given small change in return for it. The shopkeeper, not having the exact change, took the piastre, saying that he would repay the balance another time. However, the ship having set sail, Boungari was forced to leave this credit. Nevertheless, he did not forget it, for the following year, the ship having put in again at the island, Boungari went off boldly towards the gin seller and asked him for spirits for the rest of his money.[31]

The story is probably anecdotal as there is no record of Bungaree going on a second voyage with P. P. King. Perhaps Bungaree had an even longer memory? He first called at Timor with Matthew Flinders on *Investigator* in 1803—15 years before his visit on *Mermaid*!

From Timor, *Mermaid* returned to chart the Monte Bello Islands and Barrow Island. Returning by the west coast, the survey ship anchored off Sydney Cove on 29 July 1818. She did not sail around the continent, so Bungaree obviously did not circumnavigate Australia a second time.[32]

Redrawing charts and refitting the *Mermaid* lasted until December 1818 when King visited Hobart Town and went to examine Macquarie Harbour on the west coast of Van Diemen's Land. He returned to Sydney on 14 February 1819 and left on 8 May to assist Surveyor-General John Oxley to map the mouth of the Hastings River at Port Macquarie, N. S. W., before resuming the charting of the north coast of Australia.[33]

The constant skirmishes with the Aborigines on King's first survey voyage, despite Bungaree's intervention, are a tribute to their bravery under fire and their determined resistance to the intrusion of strangers in their land.

A Victorian-era writer, M. Gaunt, author of 'Explorers by Sea' in Cassell's *Picturesque Australasia* (1889), claimed P. P. King's accounts of his voyages 'show that they were monotonous and devoid of incident, and, though his notes are most copious, they are of interest only to the seaman or naturalist'.[34] Judge for yourself!

Uranie at Neutral Bay

Phillip Parker King left a note to express his regret at not being able to meet French explorer Captain Louis Claude Desaules de Freycinet (1797–1842), commander of the 350-ton French corvette *Uranie*, which moored at Neutral Bay between 18 November and 25 December 1819.[35]

While in Sydney, de Freycinet and his wife Rose, who accompanied him during his long voyage through the Pacific, rented a house on Bunker's Hill at the Rocks (from which their silver and table linen were stolen on the first night) and became friends with their close neighbour Judge Barron Field. Governor Macquarie gave the French scientists permission to cross the Blue Mountains and provided them with horses and guides. They also had the use of a port building as an observatory.[36]

Governor Macquarie and his wife Elizabeth welcomed the de Freycinets to Parramatta, where Rose was impressed by the pupils at the Native School:

The boys cultivate the garden attached to the house they occupy. The girls are taught the tasks suitable to their sex . . . We saw the house where these little savages are kept: the advances they have already made are truly astonishing, and think how valuable a work! these children, thus taught, will carry to the homes of their families the germs of civilization, which cannot fail to produce good results: to appreciate this benefit it is only necessary to look at the present state, the miserable air, of the natives one sees in the streets of Sydney.[37]

Jacques Etienne Victoire Arago (1790–1855), a naval lieutenant and draughtsman with the French expedition, was entertained in Sydney by Judge Barron Field, Captain John Piper and Edward Woolstonecraft. His brother François Arago was a famous astronomer. Jacques Arago wrote a series of letters to a friend which were published in Paris in 1822 as *Promenade autour du monde* and translated into English as *Narrative of a Voyage Around the World* (1823).

Arago was appalled by the sight of 'savages' living in Sydney 'who wear no kind of clothing' and thought they should be compelled to cover 'at least certain parts' with kangaroo skin. At the home of a 'respectable merchant' he found the family and their guests, including 'elegant and accomplished young ladies' encouraging a group of Aborigines to fight each other, egging them on with offerings of bits of bread and a few glasses of wine and brandy. In the end: 'Two of them were stretched on the ground dangerously wounded, and a third received a mortal blow'. He witnessed a similar fight in the yard of an inn, and also described a ritual battle staged by Aborigines at the time of his visit, but does not say whether Bungaree took part in it.[38]

Fig. 24.

Boon-ga-ree Aboriginal of New St Wales 1819
who accompanied me on my first voyage to the N W
coast
Phillip Parker King, 1819.
Watercolour, 25 x 30 cm.
Album of Sketches and Engravings, 1802–29.
Mitchell Library, Sydney.

Uranie left Sydney on Christmas Day 1819 but ran onto a reef in the Falkland Islands in February 1820 and was wrecked.[39]

'All the Defects of His Race'

It was 'about Christmas that year' (1819), according to merchant and landholder Alexander Berry (1781–1873), that Bungaree was 'savagely beaten in a drunken broil [brawl]' with another Aborigine. He was brought to Berry's cottage on the north shore of Port Jackson suffering from a severe head wound and a fractured arm. Berry, a former ship's surgeon with the East India Company, treated the wound and gave instructions that Bungaree should be taken care of in his kitchen.

> There he remained for several days until he recovered from the bruise—the moment however he was able to move he escaped from the house as from a jail—and [*obs.* disencumbered?] the arm from the bandage—some weeks after he came back—on examining his arm I found that the ends of his fractured bones had healed without uniting—giving the appearance of a joint—and it remained for the rest of his life.

Recalling these events in 1838, Berry praised the character of 'old Bungarrie' who was, he said, the 'first Native in whom I took an interest':

> Bungarrie was a man decidedly of considerable natural talent—very faithful & trust worthy—but had all the defects of his Race—in consequence of which all the trouble & expence bestowed by the humane Macquarie to amiliorate his condition proved abortive, as in every other instance.[40]

Berry, a Scot, settled in New South Wales in 1819 and went into partnership with Edward Woolstonecraft. He died at Crow's Nest House (which gave the Sydney suburb its name) in 1873.

Fig. 25.

Alexander Berry (1781–1873).
Artist unknown.

Part 2: 1820–30
His Sable Majesty

8 The Russians at Kirribilli

Fresh from a perilous voyage deep into the icy Southern Ocean, His Russian Imperial Majesty's warship *Vostok* (East) of 900 tons, commanded by Captain Fabian (Thaddeus) Bellingshausen, anchored in Port Jackson before noon on 11 April 1820. The sloop and her companion *Mirnyy* (Peaceful) of 530 tons (which arrived on 19 April) had surveyed part of the South Georgia Islands then, skirting icebergs and hugging the ice-shelf, touched on latitude 67 degrees south and longitude 17 degrees, in sight of the Antarctic mainland.

Sent by Czar Alexander I, the Russian discovery ships left their Baltic Sea home port of Kronstadt near St Petersburg in July 1818 and passed Cape Horn on their way south in December 1819. Entering Port Jackson, the Russians found 12 merchant vessels at anchor, most from India or Canton, as well as the British convict transport *Coromandel* and the cutter *Mermaid*, being prepared to continue her survey of the northern coast of New Holland.[1]

Bungaree was the first to greet Captain Bellingshausen on his arrival in Sydney.

About midday a family of natives arrived on board, in a dirty European boat from the north shore. They spoke a little broken English, bowed very low to the Europeans, and made grimaces to express their delight. One of them wore the worn-out trousers of a British sailor, and on his forehead there was a plaited band, decorated with red clay and mud, on his neck he wore a copper plate, in the shape of a crescent-moon, with the inscription:

BOONGAREE
Chief of the
Broken—Bay—Tribe
1815

This plate was attached to a strong copper chain. From this inscription we knew who our guest was, and he added that he had accompanied Captain Flinders and Lieutenant King in their voyages off the coast of New Holland.

Boongaree presented his wife Matora to us. She was partially attired in a dress of English frieze [woollen blanket], and had adorned her head with kangaroo teeth. A daughter was almost half white, handsome in face and figure, which gave evidence of European blood; the son, like his father, was dark; all were naked.

Indicating his companions, Bungaree told Bellingshausen: 'These are my people'. Then, pointing to the north shore of the harbour: 'This is my land'.

The Russian captain ordered a glass of grog for each of his visitors and as much sugar and butter as they wanted. They begged him for tobacco, old clothes and ropes and 'whatever they happened to notice'. He gave Bungaree some Brazilian twist tobacco and told him that they would all receive clothes and ropes if they brought fish, live birds, a kangaroo and other animals. 'Oh yes, yes', was Bungaree's reply.

Боонгарее   Матора

Начальникъ Брокенъ-Байской Орды и его жена

Fig. 26.

Boongaree Matora   Lithograph by Ivan Pavlovich Fridrits, c.1826–29.
The Chief of the Broken Bay Tribe and his Wife   Atlas k puteshestviiu Kapitane Bellingsgauzena . . . St
Pavel Nikolayevich Mikhailov, 1820.   Petersburg, 1831.

'They left the ship half drunk, shouting horribly,' wrote Bellingshausen. 'Matora, who called herself "Queen", behaved with even greater vulgarity than the other guests.'[2]

Born a Baltic German on the island of Oesel (now Estonia) in 1778, Bellingshausen was baptised Fabian Gottlieb von Bellingshausen. He later altered his name to Faddei Fadeevich Bellingshausen to suit the Russian style. An explorer in the mould of Captain James Cook, whom he greatly admired, Bellingshausen took the opportunity while docked at Portsmouth to take a carriage to London to pay his respects to Sir Joseph Banks.

He kept a journal from which he wrote the official account of the scientific expedition: *Dvukratnyye izyskaniya v yuzhnom Ledovitom Okeane i plavaniye vokrug sveta, v prodolzhenii 1819, 20, i 21 goduv . . .* (Repeated investigations in the Southern Icy Ocean and a voyage around the world during 1819, 1820 and 1821 . . .), published in St Petersburg in 1831. This work was translated into English by Frank Debenham as *The Voyage of Captain Bellingshausen to the Antarctic Seas, 1819–1821* for the Hakluyt Society, Cambridge, in 1945.

Officers and midshipmen of the Czar's naval vessels were obliged to keep records which were handed in to officials at the end of the voyage. Canadian scholar and Professor of Russian Glynn Barratt, an authority on Russian naval history, has made a modern translation of parts of Bellingshausen's text as well as extracts of memoirs, journals and notes from other officers of the Antarctic expedition, including Ivan Mikhaylovich Simonov, Midshipman Pavel Mikhailovich Novosil'sky and Leading Seaman Yegor Kiselyov. These appeared in Barratt's work *The Russians at Port Jackson*, published by the Australian Institute of Aboriginal Studies in Canberra in 1981.

While in Sydney Captain Bellingshausen often encountered Bungaree and his people. His was the first of many descriptions of Bungaree's frequent visits to ships arriving in Port Jackson, and from it we learn that he was still wearing the brass breastplate given to him five years before by Governor Macquarie. Bellingshausen and his fellow officers were the first observers to comment on Bungaree's love of 'grog', frequent drunkenness and constant begging for tobacco.

The Russian crew put up their tents by the sandstone cliffs on the north side of Sydney Cove at Kirribilli Point, directly opposite Fort Macquarie (Bennelong Point). In one tent Simonov, the astronomer and physician, erected a telescope to make nightly observations of the stars in the southern skies. Sailors were kept busy cutting firewood and brush for brooms, filling water casks, repairing barrels and restoring the ships' rigging. A portable forge was brought ashore so the blacksmith could replace copper plates and nails damaged in collisions with ice floes.

Fig. 27.

View of the Town of Sydney in Port Jackson
Pavel Nikolayevich Mikhailov, 1820.
Lithograph by Ivan Pavlovich Fridrits, c.1826–29.

Atlas k puteshestviiu Kapitane Bellingsgauzena . . . St Petersburg, 1831.

On Sunday 16 April, when 'the day was beautiful', Bellingshausen allowed his crew, in two shifts, to go ashore 'in the woods near the tents'. It was better for them to wander around in the bush, he thought, than to be 'exposed to temptations, only damaging to their health, by visiting the town'.[3]

According to local tradition the rock baths at the south-east tip of Kirribilli Point were used by the seamen and the promontory was given the name Russian Point.[4] 'As the refit of the vessels neared completion, we sent the crew ashore to wash all the linen and clothes, and made them frequently have a bath,' Bellingshausen noted.[5] A wood-fired steam bath had been set up in a tent next to the observatory.

Freed by daylight from his astronomical instruments, Simonov strolled along the rocky shore with a few companions and found the surroundings delightful. 'At every step we encountered sublime *Banksia* of various sorts, quantities of beautiful flowers that we had never seen before, and birds likewise unusual to us.' They met a 'New Hollander' named Burra Burra who took them to see his shelter where his family was gathered around the remains of a fire. Back at the Russian tents, Burra Burra complained that a sketch of him by Mikhailov had not shown him 'in full attire'. Picking up a small stick, he thrust it through the slit in his nose so that it could be included in the portrait. After that, he asked the Russians for clothing.

A crowd of curious 'ugly native New Hollanders of both sexes' came to the tents, some of the men wearing 'ancient and threadbare clothing', shabby jackets and trousers of the sort worn by convicts. Having satisfied their curiosity, the women went off to fish, while the men sat making fishing implements which they smoothed down with pieces of bottle glass.[6]

Fig. 28.

Fabian Gottlieb von Bellingshausen (1778–1852)
Artist unknown.

Shortly afterwards, seven Aborigines approached. 'They were led by a man of about 55 wearing a shabby yellow jacket of the English convict's type and a torn pair of sailor's trousers. His proud step and bearing,' said Simonov, 'indicated an important personage.' This man was Bungaree, who wore the breastplate given to him by Macquarie. His black hair was curly and the band round his forehead was made of 'laces' decorated with red ochre.[7]

Vostok's Midshipman Pavel Novosil'sky, a graduate of the Naval Cadet Academy in St Petersburg, enjoyed early morning walks through 'the New Holland woods', often returning 'weary to the point of exhaustion' late in the evening. After visiting Simonov at his tent-observatory, Novosil'sky would set out with his pocket compass to walk many miles through the heart of the north shore bush, along a track strewn with boulders and crawling with snakes, examining the unfamiliar trees, plants, flowers and birds. He often met natives, armed with long 'pikes' (spears) made from the stems of the gummy plant, but he was not afraid of them 'since for a bottle of rum I enjoyed the friendship of Bongaree, the chief of these natives'. Novosil'sky found another hazard in the bush: 'His wife, an old woman smeared with fish-oil, was truly the personification of ugliness—but meeting one in the bush she always asked to be kissed'.[8]

Macquarie's Hospitality

'Captain Billinghausen waited on me soon after the Ship came to anchor, and afterwards saluted the British flag with 15 guns which was returned with an equal number from our Battery,' wrote Governor Lachlan Macquarie in his journal.[9]

Years before, in 1807, Macquarie had been arrested by Russian authorities as a suspected spy while returning overland from India to England via the Caspian Sea and detained near Baku (Azerbaijan). After his release, he was feted in Moscow and well received in St Petersburg and at the Kronstadt naval base, where he was shown over the forts and dockyards.[10]

Returning this hospitality, the governor gave the Russian explorers a warm welcome. He invited Bellingshausen and his chief officers to breakfast at Government House in Sydney on Wednesday 19 April and took them afterwards on an outing to the Macquarie Light at South Head.[11] He sent his carriage to Sydney to fetch Bellingshausen, Lazarev and Captain-Lieutenant Zavadovsky and bring them to Parramatta, where they and 10 others spent several days and were received by Macquarie in the garden at Government House.[12]

While at Parramatta the Russian officers visited Macquarie's school for 'the children of the native inhabitants'. At church that Sunday Bellingshausen was touched by the Aboriginal girls singing hymns: 'their little prayer books in their hands and with eyes uplifted to heaven . . . All the girls were modestly dressed in white . . . Their dark faces were the only signs of their origin.'[13]

Macquarie renewed his acquaintance with Mikhail Petrovich Lazarev, now in command of *Mirnyy*. It was Lazarev, who had served for four years (1804–8) with the British Royal Navy, who brought the welcome news of Marshall von Blücher's arrival in Paris to Port Jackson when in command of the *Suvorov* in August 1814.

On his return to the ship on 1 May, Bellingshausen found that preparations for sailing were proceeding well:

Every day we went ashore to the place where we had set up our little observatory and dockyard on the foreland. Boongaree and his family were encamped in the wood not far from this spot. We often visited them on our walks. Although he called himself 'King' of this place, his title was 'Chief of Broken Bay'. His 'palace', however, did not correspond to this high title, since his dwelling consisted of a semicircular wall, built of fresh branches 4 to 5 feet in height. This wall was always thrown up on the side from which the cold wind or bad weather comes. The roof of Boongaree's dwelling was the blue sky above him. Both men and women were naked except those who had a frieze blanket wrapped around them.[14]

This is the first instance in which Bungaree is reported to have described himself as 'king'.

'Those in a position to do so buy tobacco,' said Bellingshausen. There was always a fire of dry sticks at the Aboriginal camps, on which they cooked fish without removing the entrails. 'They also eat mussels and crayfish, animals of all sorts and birds, snakes and other reptiles found in the woods.' The native women collected the blossoms in large bark baskets and sucked the honey from them, or they soaked the blooms in a water trough and drank the sweet liquid 'which is probably nutritious'. Many species of *Banksia* trees were in flower.[15]

As the Russian expedition's camp was at the tip of Kirribilli Point, Bungaree's camp, further in the bush, must have been close to the present Admiralty House, the Sydney residence of the Australian governor-general.

Bellingshausen recorded that Governor Macquarie had given Bungaree a 'house and garden' (at Broken Bay, he thought), had made him a chief and had given him a boat. Other natives had been given boats for fishing in return for a part of their daily catch. They went fishing each day in their boats and, having given up the portion due, exchanged the rest for drink or tobacco. 'On their return from town to their camps on the northern shore, they had to pass near our ships, and every evening they came back drunk, shouting savagely and uttering threats: and often their quarrels with one another ended in a fight.'

He described the traditional method of fishing from rocks with 'fish-gigs'. To make canoes, the Port Jackson Aborigines cut strips of stringybark 11 or 12 feet long and 3½ feet wide from trees. This strip they bent up at the sides, thrust apart with stretchers, then tied with rope also made from stringybark. 'They move about in the bay in these poorly constructed canoes in which they always carry a fire.'

One morning Bungaree came on board *Vostok* to exchange some fish for a bottle of rum. 'In answer to my question "Who has broken your head?" he replied indifferently, "My people when they were drunk". From which,' Bellingshausen comments, 'his power over his so-called tribe may be estimated.'[16]

Simonov recounted a similar visit by Bungaree bringing fish:

'Where is your captain?', he proudly asked a sailor. He was escorted to the captain's cabin. 'This is a gift for you', said Boongaree to Captain Bellingshausen in his broken English dialect, and gave him the fish. 'Thank you Boongaree, thank you', said Bellingshausen, and gave orders for the cook to take the fish from him. 'One pound', then said Boongaree. 'For what? For a gift?' 'Yes, sir'. The captain reached into his pocket for a small silver coin worth about 30 kopeks, and handed it over. Scraping his feet, Boongaree expressed his liveliest gratitude and went off home as joyfully as if he had indeed received £1.[17]

A Little Night Music

Out of curiosity, Bellingshausen went to see how his 'friends disposed of themselves for the night and how they slept'. Bungaree's family were awakened by their dog barking. The chief got up to greet them, but the others remained where they had been lying. Some small fires were smouldering between the mixed group of men and women as they quietly slept.[18]

On another evening Simonov, attracted by 'wild sounds', went into the bush and stumbled on a kind of corroboree. Naked men and women were dancing 'to the measured beat of music' while others sat gazing at fires. They ate fish and mussels, cooked on the spot in burning twigs. Some of the dancers flaunted their 'strange conical coiffures' and their faces and bodies were covered with patches of red ochre. 'Their music consisted of the sound of two small sticks, which the single musician beat time with, and of his loud voice as he sang a dissonant song. The dancers, stood before him in a single line. They jumped at each blow of the sticks, and hummed: prrs, prrs, prrs.'

The next time Simonov went to his neighbours' camp by night he witnessed

> not a dance but a fight with burning logs—the result of a heavy drinking bout. I had no fear in visiting for I knew that the natives feared and respected the Europeans and that Boongaree, chief of the Broken Bay Tribe, had received private gifts from us—and hoped to get more. None the less, each time it was with shudders and a heavy heart that I gazed on the abasement to which Man may fall when lacking both science and faith.[19]

The Aborigines of New Holland, said Bellingshausen, were of 'middle size and very thin, legs and arms especially bony'. Their heads were large compared with the rest of the body, their skin was lighter than a negro, the hair curly, the nose broad and mostly 'hooked like a parrot's', the mouth large and the lips thick. Part of the body was painted in parallel lines and smeared with a red colour while white stripes were painted on the face and body.[20]

Mikhailov's portraits

Boongaree, Matora. The Chief of the Broken Bay Tribe and his Wife (Fig. 26), which appeared in Bellingshausen's published account in 1831, is a composite engraving of separate portraits of Bungaree and his wife Matora made by the Russian expedition's artist Pavel Nikolayevich Mikhailov (1786–1840).

It is the only picture of Bungaree in which he does not appear in European clothing, although at the time he was seen by Bellingshausen in a pair of worn-out sailor's trousers and by the astronomer Simonov in similar trousers and a shabby yellow convict's jacket. His wavy hair—'curled in rings, à la Titus' said Simonov—protruded from a headband around his forehead, described by Bellingshausen as a 'plaited band, decorated with clay and mud'. In this study, Bungaree is clean-shaven and has a stick (perhaps a bird bone) thrust through his nose. He has a rather serious, sullen expression.

Bungaree's bare chest reveals the raised pattern of scars on his skin. Dr Frederick McCarthy describes these cicatrices as 'a vertical set of three parallel straight bars on his shoulders and upper chest and two sets of five, one above the other on his right breast, those on the breast being slightly diagonal'.[21] The scarification, nose bone and headband are usually signs of initiation. Bungaree's wife, Matora, wears a similar headband and also has a pattern of body scars. These portraits appear as serious and accurate reporting and differ very little from the separate sketches Mikhaylov made 'on the spot' in Sydney in 1820.[22]

The engraving of the brass breastplate or gorget worn on a chain around Bungaree's neck is as clear as a photograph. The inscription, in English, confirms the wording given by Bellingshausen and by the *Sydney Gazette* in February 1815.[23]

Mikhailov, the son of an actor, graduated from the St Petersburg Academy of Art and was made an Academician in 1815 for his portrait of Count Tolstoi. During the voyage of *Vostok*, Mikhailov completed a portfolio of sketches of birds, plants, views and portraits of native peoples from which he later painted aquarelles (very transparent watercolours tinted with white lead). Many of Mikhailov's original pencil and sanguine (red or flesh-coloured crayon) sketches on brown paper are now in the Russian State Museum, St Petersburg (formerly Leningrad), while an album of aquarelles is in the State Historical Museum in Red Square, Moscow. Several of the aquarelles were lithographed by Ivan Pavlovich Fridrits (1803–60) for the Atlas of Bellingshausen's book published in 1831.

They include *View of the Town of Sydney in Port Jackson* (Fig. 27) which shows an Aboriginal family in the bush at Kirribilli, the Russian ships among others at anchor in Sydney Cove and Fort Macquarie and Sydney Town in the background. Prominent in the foreground is the 'gummy plant' or grass tree, from which the Aborigines obtained spear shafts and a resinous gum. Mikhailov's original pen, ink and watercolour study is reproduced in *First Views of Australia, 1788–1825* by Tim McCormick (Sydney, 1987).[24]

NOUVELLE - HOLLANDE.

COUR–ROU–BARI–GAL.

Fig. 29.

NOUVELLE-HOLLANDE.
COUR-ROU-BARI-GAL
Nicolas-Martin Petit, 1801.
Engraving, 35.5 x 24 cm by B. Roger.
Plate 21: Historique Atlas de MM. Lesueur et Petit. *Voyage de découvertes aux terres Australes.* Seconde édition. Paris, 1824.

Bungaree's Family

The engraving *Natives of New Holland* (Fig. 30), based on Mikhailov's aquarelle, is a revealing look at Bungaree's family group gathered in the sapling and brush shelter of their camp in the bush at Kirribilli. The figures are posed and rather stiff, but the faces of the Aboriginal men and women are animated and full of character. Items of ethnographic interest in the picture include hunting weapons, net bags, a bark container and the ornamental hair binding mentioned by Simonov, worn by the two men at left.

On the face of it, here is a scene showing how the Aboriginal fringe-dwellers lived on the shores of Sydney Cove more than 170 years ago. However, all is not as it seems. There is an element of puzzle and intrigue, because at some stage the artist has chosen to alter reality.

This conclusion is based on a comparison of the published engraving with colour transparencies of the original study for the 'family' group (titled 'Gagolbi')[25] and with Mikhailov's original individual sketches of these people, now in St Petersburg. These illustrations cannot be reproduced here due to copyright restrictions.

Among Mikhailov's portrait sketches is a watercolour of an Aboriginal man with his hair bound into a coil by a band of cloth or bark, titled *Native of New Holland Couz-*

Fig. 30.

Natives of New Holland
Pavel Nikolayevich Mikhailov, 1820.
Lithograph by Ivan Pavlovich Fridrits, c.1826–29.

Atlas k puteshestviiu Kapitane Bellingsgauzena . . . St
Petersburg, 1831.

chou-bari-cal and inscribed '*iz atl perona*' (Atlas of Péron)[26]. It was copied from an engraving titled *Nouvelle-Hollande—Cour-rou-bari-gal* (Fig. 29), published in Paris in 1824, as Mikhailov acknowledged, as Plate 21 in the 'Historique Atlas de MM. Lesueur et Petit', which accompanied Francois Péron's *Voyage de découvertes aux terres Australes*. The original pastel, charcoal, ink and pencil study was made in Port Jackson in 1801 by Nicolas Martin Petit (1777–1804), an artist with Baudin's French expedition.[27] It is now in the Muséum d' Histoire Naturelles, Le Havre.

To copy such a portrait from a book during a long sea voyage was not unusual. However, it was less usual to 'borrow' a portrait and 'import' it into another work as Mikhailov has done here. Looking at the Aborigine at far left with the moustache, headband and conical coiffure, apart from some changes such as his curlier hair and the clay pipe in his hand, we see the very Cour-rou-bari-gal of Nicolas Petit, no older in 1820 than he was 19 years before!

The long-limbed, extremely muscular Aborigine seated at the front of the group also wears a headband and similar hair wrapping. His rather languid pose is no doubt derived from a classical source. Because there is no evident original study of this man and because he has a nosepeg it is tempting to identify him as Burra Burra, whom Mikhailov sketched at full length, adding the detail of a nosepeg. There is a full-length pencil sketch of an Aborigine titled *Bara Bara vilam miny* among Mikhailov's St Petersburg sketches, but a colour copy could not be obtained for study as it is drawn on the reverse of another illustration.[28]

Even a casual glance at a copy of Mikhailov's pencil-and-chalk study ('Gagolbi') for the engraving of *Natives of New Holland* is sufficient to conclude that these two figures are out of character with the rest of the group. A close study reveals that they are more densely and artistically 'finished' than the others, which are only sketched in roughly. These figures were probably added by the artist, either for interest or to balance the composition. In Fridrits' published engraving, based on Mikhailov's later aquarelle (now in Moscow), all the figures appear in a more uniform style.

Again comparing the study and final engraving of *Natives of New Holland* with the individual portraits of the Aborigines, we are able to name most of the remaining people seated around the fire in 1820. The man at right, shown with a wispy beard, is Bourinoan; the young girl leaning on a net bag next to him is Gulanba Duby; the curly headed youth with a headband is Toúbi; and the woman with a blanket around her legs resembles Gouroungan (sketched by Mikhailov with Matora). The young, light-skinned girl (fourth from left), wearing a cloth neckband, is certainly Ga-ouen-ren, the daughter of one of Bungaree's wives and a European man. This 'young girl of pretty appearance' was easy to distinguish, said Bellingshausen—'Bungaree himself admitted to me that she did not resemble him'. The young woman at left, wrapped loosely in a blanket, with two large cicatrices above her breasts, was also sketched by Mikhailov, but he did not name her.[29]

Other Aborigines Mikhailov sketched but did not include in the completed family group include Movat and Salmanda (two young men), Tsoin or Boin (a young man), Volendens (a woman), a seated young female and a small family group of a man, woman and child also titled 'Gagolbi'.

There are several interesting ethnographic differences between the study and the completed engraving. In the original Bourinoan does not have a beard or wear a belt; the single fish on the ground near the weapons (there are two fish in the engraving) is sketchy and has not been tied with twine; the man at the front left (Burra Burra?) also does not wear a belt and the bark container behind him is absent (it may be based on other French drawings).

'At my wish,' Bellingshausen wrote, 'Boongaree procured for me a set of native weapons, a shield, a spear and a fork for catching fish. All these articles were sketched.'[30] A pronged fishing spear with bone points, a pointed spear, a 'sword club' and a woomerah with a tapering adze-shaped end (but no shield) appear in the engraving. In the original study, the weapon beside Bourinoan looks more like a curved boomerang than a club.

A pronged fishing spear or fiz-gig, a wooden spear and a small wooden shield appear in Glynn Barratt's *The Russians at Port Jackson* in photographs of artefacts brought from Port Jackson by Russian expeditions before 1828 and now held in the N. N. Miklukho-Maklay Institute in St Petersburg. The fishing spear in this unique collection is probably the only one from early Sydney now in existence, says Professor Barratt.[31] Some of these weapons may have been obtained for Captain Bellingshausen by Bungaree.

'Yesterday resumed their voyage of discovery, the Russian ships Wostock and Mornoy,' the *Sydney Gazette* noted in its Ship's News column on 20 May 1820.[32] Leaving Port Jackson, the ships cruised through the Pacific Ocean for four months, visiting Hawaii, Tahiti, Fiji, New Zealand and Tasmania. They returned to Sydney on 21 September to 'refresh' and load supplies before resuming their Antarctic explorations.

Bellingshausen's attitude to Bungaree seemed warmer than during his earlier stay in Sydney:

> When I visited Port Jackson for the second time, our old friend Boongaree and the members of his tribe came to pay us a visit at once. Boongaree complained that throughout the winter he had suffered from a bad cough. On my asking: 'How did you try to cure it?' he replied: 'Only with grog; and I drank a great deal'.[33]

In the concluding chapter of his book, headed *A Short Notice on the Colony of New South Wales*, Bellingshausen has much to say about the life and habits of the Aborigines dwelling on the fringes of white society around Sydney in 1820.

Fishing remained the most important means of survival for the coastal Aborigines, as it had been before the arrival of the white settlers. Aboriginal men treated their wives like slaves, said Bellingshausen. Near Sydney, 'the poor women have to sit all day in the canoes and catch fish, while their men folk lounge about or sleep. If the catch is poor they are not infrequently beaten.' Women also gathered wood, lit fires and collected blossoms from the *Banksias*.

Bellingshausen painted a picture of the general decline of the Aborigines from their former self-reliant life. Tobacco and alcohol had become indispensable to them. They frequently went on alcoholic binges and fought among themselves. Though they still fished and hunted and used their traditional weapons, they depended more on the white colonists, with whom they bartered fish and asked for handouts. Some worked in English homes. Despite their 'exceeding laziness' they willingly became 'hewers of wood and drawers of water' in return for tobacco and spirits. Although it was officially illegal, tavern owners hired the natives to wash out brandy casks. The first wash, called 'bull', which had a strong flavour of brandy, was given to the Aborigines as payment for their work. In many houses they were employed at such tasks as cleaning glasses at which, with their long, slender fingers, they were more skillful than Europeans. The black workers wore no clothes, 'but one soon gets accustomed to this', said Bellingshausen.

'All living in the neighbourhood of towns, more especially near Sydney, are able to speak a little English—such expressions as "Give me money" or "Will you not give me a guinea?" (about 6 silver roubles) or a "dump" (about 40 kopecks).'

Since their arrival in 1788 the Europeans had tried to make the natives understand 'both the usefulness and decency of clothing, all to no purpose'. Many received complete outfits, but bartered them for rum or tobacco. 'But as they were then warned that they would not receive any help or work unless they came clothed, they always appear in the towns in some sort of rags, which they take off as soon as they get home again. During the cold weather the women wear a woollen blanket over the shoulders. This forms their entire dress.' Three of the women sitting in the shelter in Mikhailov's *Natives of New Holland* have blankets wrapped around them, obviously more for warmth than for modesty.

In Bellingshausen's opinion the Aborigines were still attached to their land and resented its loss. They recalled their former independence very well. Some expressed claims to certain places, asserting they belonged to their ancestors and they were 'not indifferent' to being expelled from their favourite localities. 'Despite all the compensation offered to them, a spark of vengeance still smoulders in their hearts.'

Returning to Bungaree, Bellingshausen noted his generosity, gentleness and kindness of heart:

> Boongaree himself is worth a more detailed account. He is about 55 years of age; he has always been noted for his kindness of heart, gentleness and other excellent qualities and has been of great service to the Colony . . . He has often endangered his life in his efforts to keep the peace within his tribe. A few years ago an escaped convict fell into the hands of another tribe. They robbed him, took his axe away from him, and were about to kill him. Boongaree appeared on the scene, took the man under his protection, secured his freedom, and then for three days carried him on his back to Port Jackson, taking him across rivers and feeding him on roots. He asked for no reward, save the fugitive's pardon. The Government of the colony gave Boongaree a long boat as a present. He is a generous man, generally beloved for similar kind actions.[34]

Simonov told the same story. To illustrate the 'influence exerted on him by a constant intercourse with Europeans', Simonov related a further anecdote about Bungaree and his boat. As Sydney was a port town, he wrote, it was customary to give the polite title of captain to every skipper commanding a merchantman or sailing craft, no matter how small:

> As a result, captain is a pretty common title in Sydney town. Well: Boongaree had noted this fact and on one occasion brought a fellow New Hollander to Captain Bellingshausen, recommending him to him as Captain Bellau. This he did because Bellau had his own, insignificant boat. Highly amusing it was to see these two ugly natives, both in dirty rags, shuffling now on one foot, now on the other and bowing deeply; amusing, too, to see one proudly introducing the other as Captain Bellau! Both were served with a glass of rum. And the ceremonial introductions ended forthwith—for the rum had been their sole object.[35]

Leading seaman Yegor Kiselyov of *Vostok* pithily summed up his visit to 'the town and port of Zekson':

The residents of the town are English, but there are quantities of natives on the islands; they live like beasts in the woods, have no houses, feed themselves from the woods on cones and fish. There's a king, too: he has a sign on his chest, given by the English king. And our captain gave him a hussar's greatcoat and a bronze medal, and his wife a white blanket and a pair of woman's earrings.[36]

Vostok and *Mirnyy* sailed out of Port Jackson on 12 November 1820.[37] The ships completed the circumnavigation of the Antarctic continent and returned to Russia by July 1821. With their departure, Bungaree was forced to fall back for some time on his usual suppliers of food, grog, tobacco and clothing.

9 The Native Settlers

One week after their first visit to Port Jackson (18 April 1820), Captain Bellingshausen and some other Russian officers went to visit 'Mr King, Lieutenant in the British Navy' aboard *Mermaid*:

> He is in command of a small warship tender and is here for the purpose of exploring the northern coasts of New Holland and Van Diemen's Land, of which he has already surveyed half. The Government of New Holland may be proud that so important a task has been entrusted to one who has been born and bred in these new colonies.

Bellingshausen was impressed by the young man who later became the first Australian-born admiral. 'He combines a wide knowledge with charming manners and forethought for others,' he remarked.[1]

Phillip Parker King made three more survey voyages in the *Mermaid* between 1818 and 1822 but did not take Bungaree with him. As King prepared for the final voyage in the *Bathurst* to complete the survey, Bungaree offered to join him, but withdrew at the very last moment on the day of sailing, 26 May 1821. King wrote in *Narrative of a Survey*:

> Boongaree, the native who had formerly accompanied us, volunteered his services whilst the vessel was preparing for the voyage, which I gladly accepted; but when the day of departure drew nigh, he kept aloof; and the morning that we sailed, his place was filled by another volunteer, Bundell, who proved not only to be a more active seaman, but was of much greater service to us, than his countryman Boongaree had been.[2]

Bundell (also Bundle or Bondel) was about 40 years of age when he signed on the *Bathurst*. He was an orphan whose father had been killed in battle and whose mother had been bitten in two by a shark. As a young boy he attached himself to Marine Captain William Hill and went with him to Norfolk Island on the *Supply* in March 1791.[3] He returned to Port Jackson the following September on the *Salamander* convict transport, having gained 'a smattering' of English.[4] Bundell was named among other seafaring Aborigines who had 'made themselves useful on board colonial vessels employed in the fishing and sealing trade' by David Dickinson Mann in *The Present Picture of New South Wales* (1811).[5] Bundell may have been a more active seaman than Bungaree, but he was shamed during the voyage when an Aborigine nimbly climbed to the topmast of *Bathurst*. Bundell, wrote Phillip King on 26 December 1821, had 'never taken courage to mount so high'.[6]

Barron Field arrived in the colony of New South Wales in 1816 as the second judge of the Supreme Court, replacing Jeffrey Bent. A barrister and former dramatic critic of *The Times*, Field liked to write verses, but after publication of his *First Fruits of Australia Poetry* (1819) his poems were reckoned to be a 'barren field' indeed. His home from

1816 to 1824 was a two-floor mansion on the hill above Robert Campbell's Wharf House, overlooking Sydney Cove, from which the judge was in a good position to observe the comings and goings of the town's inhabitants.[7]

In a speech to the members of the Philosophical Society of Australia in Sydney on 2 January 1822, Mr Justice Field handed down his judgment *On the Aborigines of New Holland and Van Diemen's Land*, of whom he was among the first to call Australians:

> They have quick conceptions, and ready powers of imitation; but they have no reflection, judgment or foresight. They have no wants but such as are immediate; and they have therefore never become either builders, or cultivators, or mechanics, or mariners . . . they are the only savages in the world who cannot feel or 'know they are naked'.[8]

The Europeans, he said, had lived among them for 30 years, but despite the most persevering attempts to induce them to settle, 'they cannot be fixed, nor is it possible by any kindness or cherishing to attach them'. They had adapted none of the European arts of life, except 'exchanging their stone hatchets and shell-fish hooks for our iron ones'.

Judge Field's speech to the Philosophical Society was included in his *Geographical Memoirs of Australia*, published in 1825 after his return to London. In the Appendix, 'Journey of an excursion across the Blue Mountains of New South Wales', he commented further on the native Australians in quite a perceptive way. Perhaps Field had Bungaree in mind with this description?

> They will not serve, and they are too indolent and poor in spirit to become masters . . . They bear themselves erect, and address you with confidence, always with good humour, and often with grace. They are not common beggars, although they accept of our carnal things in return for the fish and oysters, which are almost all we have left them for their support. They are

Fig. 31.

Elizabeth Bay, Sydney.
With the bark Huts for the Natives
Attrib. Edward Mason, c. 1850s (signed 'E.M. del')
Pen and ink sketch cut out and pasted in an album.

(Presumed to be after an original of c. 1822).
Views of Sydney and Surrounding District. Mitchell Library, Sydney.

the Will Wimbles of the Colony; the carriers of news and fish; the gossips of the town; the loungers on the quay. They know everybody; and understand the nature of everybody's business, although they have none of their own—but this . . . They have bowing acquaintance with everybody, and scatter their How-d'ye-do's with an air of friendliness and equality, and with a perfect English accent, undebased by the Massa's and Missies, and me-nos of West Indian slavery.[9]

Elizabeth Town

The ever-patient Governor Macquarie was not prepared to easily abandon his 'Experiment in Civilization'. Despite the failure of Bungaree's group to settle down at Georges Head, he still believed he could make farmers or mechanics from the Aborigines.

On his sixth birthday, Tuesday 28 March 1820, Macquarie's cherished son Lachlan, dressed for the first time in a Scottish Highlander tartan suit and bonnet, set out in the Government Barge with 'a number of his juvenile friends' for an excursion on Sydney Harbour. They were accompanied by a cutter and 'three Boats full of the Natives'. Governor Macquarie wrote that day in his journal:

> The Fleet rowed slowly from Port Lachlan, where we all embarked, round Garden Island, and from thence to the beautiful little Bay on the south side of the Harbour, next to Wooloomoloo Bay, and which on this occasion, I christened 'Elizabeth Bay' in honour of Mrs Macquarie [who was ill], it having no distinguishing name before—and intending to establish some native settlers there.

After this water excursion the party returned to Government House where young Lachlan entertained 19 boys and girls at a 'sumptuous Breakfast' and dinner. He also welcomed 'Sixty Male and Female Natives' at a separate breakfast and dinner, "highly to their satisfaction'.[10]

One year and nine months later, on the first day of 1822 (the twelfth anniversary of his administration), the Governor, Mrs Macquarie and young Lachlan, 'paid a visit this Morning, before Breakfast, to Elizabeth Town, the Native Village in Elizabeth Bay'. They were accompanied by Macquarie's successor, Sir Thomas Brisbane, who had arrived in Sydney on 21 November 1821.[11]

Neat rows of huts in the European style, set on rising ground around a curving beach, had been built from sheets of bark over a sapling frame, each with its small cultivated garden. There was a larger hut next to an orchard, a haystack and long buildings on a forested ridge leading to the headland. These details are shown in a pen-and-ink sketch by Edward Mason. As Mason did not come to Australia until 1853, it is presumed that he copied an earlier illustration. Mason's drawing, *Elizabeth Bay, Sydney With the bark Huts for the Natives* (Fig. 31) was also engraved by the Government Printer. Both versions survive in an album of *Views of Sydney and Surrounding District* which once belonged to Sir Henry Parkes and is now in the Mitchell Library, Sydney.

The last day of January 1822 was another anniversary for Macquarie, this time his sixtieth birthday. He celebrated the occasion in his own way. 'My dear Mrs M. gave a Breakfast to a few select Friends at Elizabeth Town, the Native Village where we have established the Sydney Tribe . . . We also treated 42 Natives to Breakfast and Tobacco.'[12]

In 1828 Edward Smith Hall, former editor of the *Monitor*, in a letter to Sir George Murray, said that the land at Elizabeth Bay had been owned by an Irishman called O'Donnell, 'some eighty years of age, I believe an old pensioned soldier, remarkable for his venerable appearance and great stature'. It was 'very much frequented and delighted in by the Sydney Blacks, to a family of whom it belonged'. O'Donnell shared the land with the Aborigines and after his death it was resumed by the Government:

> Governor Macquarie built huts for the blacks at the cove or bay in question . . . being earnestly desirous of trying what could be done in the way of civilizing the adult natives, who still resorted thither . . . Besides building huts for them, the General ordered the natives a fishing boat with fishing tackle, and as I have heard, salt and casks to salt their fish withal, and so established the cove as a native village. To the row of huts, he gave the name of Elizabeth Town in honour of his spouse Mrs Macquarie.

Soon after he took office, Governor Sir Thomas Brisbane decided to build a lunatic asylum at Elizabeth Bay, 'as the natives had gradually disappeared from there'. But after Brisbane left, 'the claims of the Aborigines or the Lunatics of the Colony were forgotten' and the land was given by the next governor, Sir Ralph Darling, to Colonial Secretary Alexander McLeay.[13]

Though Macquarie clearly states that it was established for members of the Sydney Tribe, there is some confusion over whether or not Bungaree was involved in Elizabeth Town. Some contemporary observers and, consequently, later historians, have placed Bungaree there, despite the fact that he and his people were at that time being resettled at their old stamping ground further up the harbour at Georges Head.

Roger Oldfield, writing about Elizabeth Town in 1828, said the farm was sited on 'a plot of good ground rising gently from a sandy beach, and sheltered from the south wind by a declivity of rocks'. He continued:

> In this pretty nook, Macquarie invited Bungaree to become a settler. He caused several rude huts to be erected, and covered them with sheets of bark; he laid the ground out in gardens, and assigned the chief a servant victualled from the store, to assist in the cultivation. But the scheme proved abortive. The materials of the huts, in a short time, were used for fuel: the sheets of bark, were taken to Sydney to be exchanged for bread and drink; the gardner's sinecure was abolished, and nothing remains of what was called Elizabeth Town, but the local denomination. The place is now granted to Mr M'Leay [McLeay], who has converted it into an excellent garden, with a prospect of erecting a Grecian villa contiguous. As Bungaree showed no great penchant for settling, Macquarie presented him with a boat, which was infinitely more congenial to him and his 'vagrant train'.[14]

Oldfield probably confused Elizabeth Town with Bungaree's venture at Georges Head either in 1815 or 1822. Scots-born 'Merchant' Robert Campbell, writing to Mr Justice Burton in 1838, recalled that land was cleared and huts built 'on the Richmond Road' (Blacktown) and 'about the same time' huts were constructed at Elizabeth Bay. 'Mrs Macquarie zealously endeavoured to prevail upon the Port Jackson Tribe to settle there, furnishing their Chief Bonjaree with boats to enable them to obtain fish, for which they could always find a market in Sydney.'[15] Elizabeth Macquarie was frequently credited with starting the establishment named in her honour.

Alexander McLeay (1767–1848), colonial secretary of New South Wales, 1826–37, was an enthusiastic naturalist. His beautiful landscaped garden at Elizabeth Bay spread over 56 acres. In 1832 McLeay employed architect John Verge to design a Palladian-style villa, Elizabeth Bay House, which was completed in 1835 and stands today, superbly restored.

Plate 12. *Lachlan Macquarie (1761–1824)*
Unknown artist, undated (c. 1800–20s).
Miniature, watercolour on ivory, oval, 16.2 x 14 cm.
Mitchell Library, Sydney.

Plate 13. *Elizabeth Henrietta Macquarie*
Unknown artist, undated (c. 1800–20s).
Miniature, watercolour on ivory, oval, 10.2 x 7.9 cm.
Mitchell Library, Sydney.

Plate 14. *Phillip Parker King*
Unknown artist, undated.
Oil, 59 x 49 cm (inside mount).
(Plate on frame inscribed, 'Admiral Phillip Parker King')
Mitchell Library, Sydney.

Plate 15. *The Annual Meeting of the Native Tribes at Parramatta,*
New South Wales—the Governor meeting them
Augustus Earle, 1826.
Watercolour, 17.1 x 26 cm.
Rex Nan Kivell Collection, National Library of Australia,
Canberra.

Plate 16. King Bungaree 1829   King Bungaree 1829
                 Sydney   Sydney
              [Half-right profile]   [Left-face profile]
Attrib. Ambrose Wilson, 1829 (Charles Rodius?).
Pencil, cut out and pasted on paper, 20.5 x 26.9 cm.
Fol. 20. *Australian Aborigines* [bound volume], Mitchell
Library, Sydney.

Plate 17. *Bungaree*
King of Port Jackson Tribe Sydney
John Carmichael (attributed), c. 1833.
Pencil, ink and watercolour, 13. 5 x 9.5 cm.

[Caption at side] *By John Carmichael of Sydney an Engraver,*
About 1833. et seq (He was deaf and dumb).]
Collection of Denis Joachim, Melbourne.

Plate 18. *BUNGAREE.*
Chief of the Broken Bay Tribe
N. S. Wales
Charles Rodius, 1830.
Hand-coloured lithograph, 20.7 x 17.5 cm.
[Caption] *Drawn upon stone by C. Rodius.*
Rex Nan Kivell Collection, National Library of Australia,
Canberra.

Plate 19. *KING BUNGAREE.*
CHIEF OF THE BROKEN-BAY TRIBE. N.S. WALES DIED
1832 [sic].
Charles Rodius, 1834.
Hand-coloured lithograph, 22 x 15 cm.
[Caption] *Drawn from Life, 1831, and on Stone, 1834 by Chaˢ.*
Rodius.
Printed by J. G. Austin, 15 Phillip St. Sydney .
Rex Nan Kivell Collection, National Library of Australia,
Canberra.

Plate 20. *BUNGAREE, a Native Chief of New South Wales*
Augustus Earle, 1830.
Hand-coloured lithograph, 31 x 20 cm.
[Caption] *London, Published August 10th 1830 by J. Cross 18*
Holborn . . .
Plate 1, Part 2, Earl, Augustus, *Views in New South Wales*
and Van Diemens Land.
London, J. Cross, 1830.
Rex Nan Kivell Collection, National Library of Australia,
Canberra.

Plate 12.

Plate 13.

Plate 14.

Plate 15.

King Bungaree 1829.
Sydney

King Bungaree 1829.
Sydney

Plate 16.

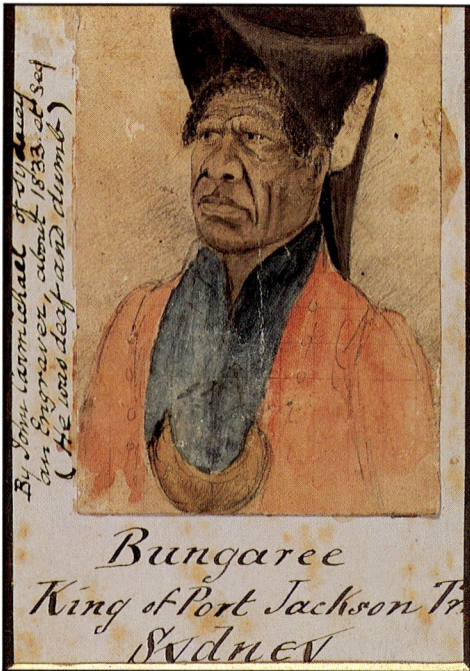

By John Carmichael of Sydney
for Bungaree, about 1833. at sea
(He was deaf and dumb)

Bungaree
King of Port Jackson Tr
Sydney

Plate 17.

Bungaree
Chief of the Broken Bay Tribe
N.S. Wales

Plate 18.

KING BUNGAREE

CHIEF OF THE BROKEN-BAY TRIBE N.S.WALES.

DIED 1832.

Drawn from Life 1831. and on Stone 1834. by Chaˢ Rodius .

Printed by I.G.Austin. 15. Phillip Sᵗ Sydney .

Plate 19.

Plate 20.

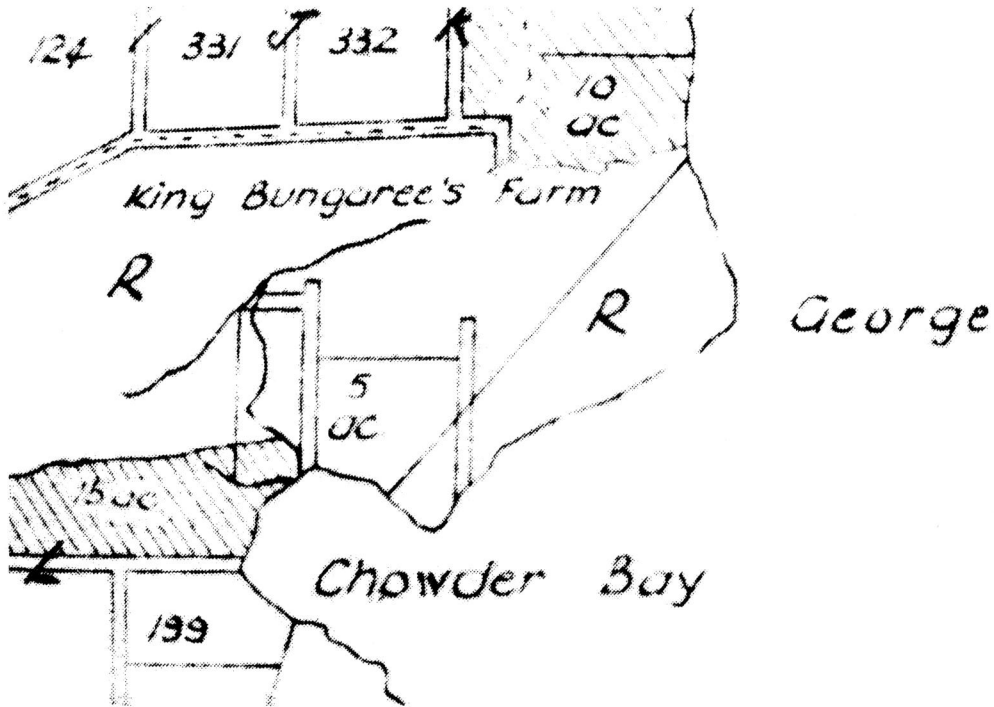

Map 5. *King Bungaree's Farm* [Georges Head, Sydney]
Detail: Map of Mosman dated 30 October 1841.
Carroll Collection, Mosman Library, Sydney.

Back at Georges Head

Eleven days after his birthday breakfast at Elizabeth Town, on the day before his departure for England (11 February 1822), Lachlan Macquarie went to visit his old friend Bungaree for the last time. It was the final official act of his 12 years of public service in New South Wales.

> Sir Thomas Brisbane came down to Sydney . . . and having taken early Breakfast with us at Government House, he was so good as to accompany Mrs M., Lachlan and myself, immediately afterwards on a Water Excursion in the Government Barge to 'George's Head' for the purpose of witnessing our Settling *Boongaree* and his Tribe of the *'Pitt Water'* Tribe of Black Natives on their former Farm for the second time at that pretty place, Barney Williams [overseer of government boats] having put the Farm in very neat order for them, built good Huts for their residence, and made a most excellent and romantic road from the Landing Place to the Village.— Mrs. M had ordered a plentiful Feast, with grog, for Boongaree & his Tribe consisting of 15 men and Women, and I gave him an old Suit of General's Uniforms to dress him out as Chief.— We strongly recommended Boongaree & his Tribe to the kind protection and good offices of Sir Thomas Brisbane, which he had promised to extend to them.—He has, also, at my request, promised to give Boongarie for himself and his Tribe a Fishing Boat with a Nett. Having staid at George's head for about an Hour, we took leave of our sable friends, and returned to Sydney.[16]

The *Surry*, with Macquarie's family on board, finally left Sydney Harbour after sheltering from wind and weather for several days. Did the 'Old Viceroy' glance towards the cliffs on the far shore as she sailed through the Heads, or spy the figure of his 'sable friend' in his fishing boat bidding him farewell, just as he had been welcomed by an Aborigine that day in January 1810? Cynics would say that Bungaree was already in Sydney exchanging the uniforms so lately given to him by his great benefactor for a bottle of rum.

The settlement at Georges Head, like that at Elizabeth Town, was to fade away in time, leaving a place on the map of Mosman in 1842 (Map 5) marked as 'Bungaree's Farm'. This covered the present Suakim Drive and George's Heights Oval south of Middle Head Road, not far from Rawson Park. Grotesque stories were told about the Aboriginal settlers, who were regarded as being 'backward'. Could it be that the Europeans who attempted to make them 'sit down' and become farmers were at fault? Dr George Bennett, in *Wanderings in New South Wales* (1834), tells a droll anecdote about the 'celebrated' King Bungaree, 'who recently ended his mortal career':

> It is related, that in the time of the government of General Macquarie there was an attempt made, by distributing seeds among them, to induce the natives to cultivate the ground: among the packets of seed sent for distribution were some which contained fish-hooks; these together with the seeds, were given by the governor to the sable monarch, King Bungaree. Some time after the Governor asked him how the seeds had come up and he replied—'Oh berry well, berry well', exclaimed Bungaree, 'all make come up berry well, except dem fish-hooks, them no come up yet'.[17]

A story current in the Sydney suburb of Mosman at the time of writing is that when Bungaree and his people at Georges Head were each given a bag of seed, some planted the seed, some stored it away and some ate it the next day.[18]

Addressing the Royal Society of Literature in London in 1882, J. Henniker Heaton, who interested himself in the customs of the Aborigines, thought little of the chances of Bungaree's people at Georges Head becoming farmers:

> The soil of the locality was so barren that if they had been ever so well disposed to settled habits and agricultural industry they could have produced nothing: but had the soil been ever so fertile, it is hardly probable that the result would have been different. Settled habits and steady industry are things too foreign to the nature of wandering savages to be acquired at once, or even in a single generation.[19]

Bungaree, via Peter Cunningham, deserves to have the last word in all these arguments:

> I have often seen [the Aborigines] prefer the open air to the shelter of a hut even in a cold night . . . King Boongarre appearing to think very lightly of the governor's judgment in providing such a hamlet, by the contemptuous shrug he gave in replying to a question 'how he liked the houses?' 'Murry boodgeree (very good), massa, '*pose he rain.*'[20]

Bungaree's Club

Trading in Aboriginal implements with the crews of ships visiting Port Jackson seems to have been one of Bungaree's sideline activities. In 1820 he supplied Captain Bellingshausen with a set of weapons, but four years later he failed to fulfil a commission given by Jules Dumont d'Urville to obtain a returning boomerang.

A fighting club now in the Pitt Rivers Museum at the University of Oxford is said to have been used by Bungaree in 'the war between the Tribes Liverpool and those of Five-Dock in about 1823'.[21] There is no record of any ritual battles or hostilities at that time between the Sydney tribes mentioned, but it is known that 'about 100 less natives than usual' (normally about 300) attended the annual Native Conference at Parramatta on 29 December 1823.[22] In contrast, about 400 Aborigines were at Parramatta the following year.[23] A similar fall-off in attendance was evident in 1826 when the Liverpool and Illawarra Aborigines were involved in a 'war' with the Cow Pastures tribe.[24]

The club is supposed to have been given by Bungaree to 'Mr Smith an assigned servant to Mr Kenyon of Smithfield'. The club was donated to the Pitt Rivers Museum in 1900 by R. F. Wilkins as part of the Norman Hardy Collection.[25]

Very little is known about Norman Hardy, but he appears to have obtained much of his collection from Harry Stockdale, an artist, explorer and pioneer ethnologist who made many drawings of Aboriginal weapons, utensils and decorations. These are included with Stockdale's manuscript essays on Aboriginal weapons, ceremonies, mysteries and folk stories now in the Mitchell Library, Sydney. His article 'On The origin and Antiquity of the Boomerang' appeared in *Town and Country Journal*, Sydney, on 12 June 1897.

During and after his travels in north-west Western Australia in 1844–46, Stockdale collected thousands of Aboriginal implements. While living in Sydney at the turn of the century, he sold scores of weapons in small lots to the Australian Museum in Sydney. These replaced the Museum's collection of early Aboriginal artifacts destroyed in the fire which swept through the Garden Palace exhibition building in 1882.

Bungaree's club resembles many fighting clubs and waddies of a later date collected by Stockdale in northern Australia. Documents in the acquisition files at the Australian Museum show that Stockdale acquired a few weapons from the Sydney area, including 'a very old shield', from Windsor, north-west of Sydney.[26]

10 French Connections

Jules Sébastien-César Dumont d'Urville was a big, robust and heavily built man according to his shipmate René-Primevère Lesson. 'Everything in physique as in habits and costume,' said Lesson, 'recalled in d'Urville a man of primitive times. He joined to the excessive soberness of a Spaniard the disdain of a beggar for his appearance.' While at sea, d'Urville rarely put on a uniform and was 'more untidy than most sailors'. He wore an unbuttoned baggy drill jacket with no cravat and worn trousers without stockings. Like Matthew Flinders, d'Urville had a straw hat, but it was a poor one 'with the daylight showing through it'.[1]

Two years after Governor Macquarie's departure, the French corvette *Coquille*, on a voyage of discovery to South America and the South Seas, came into Port Jackson on Sunday 17 January 1824. She saluted HM *Tees*, 'which courtesy was promptly returned'.[2] *Coquille*, launched in 1811, was a refitted transport vessel of 380 tons with a crew of 65 men. Her commander was hydrographer Louis-Isidore Duperry who had sailed with Louis de Freycinet as an ensign on *Uranie*.

The two young naval officers with the flowery names were gifted scientist-mariners who would soon cross Bungaree's path while in Sydney. D'Urville, aged 34, and second in charge of the expedition, was its ethnologist, botanist and entomologist, while Lesson, aged 30, combined the posts of assistant surgeon, pharmacist, zoologist and natural-history painter.

Without Jules d'Urville the world would be a much duller place. Walking one day on the island of Milos while charting the Greek islands on the *Chevrette*, he and his friend Lieutenant Armand Matterer came across a marble statue of Aphrodite, unearthed near the village of Klimi. D'Urville at once recognised the merits of the masterpiece destined to be known as the Venus de Milo (2nd C BCE). When found the arms of the statue were intact, but the hands were missing. D'Urville urged the French envoy in Istanbul to acquire the statue, but the arms were broken off in a clash between Greek brigands and the French sailors who were removing it. That is why the coldly beautiful Venus stands today without arms in the Louvre in Paris.[3]

Jules Sébastien-César Dumont d'Urville (1790–1842) was born in Normandy, where his father was the *sieur* or squire of Urville. He joined the French navy at the age of 17 as a cadet midshipman on *Aquilon*. He studied botany and in 1815 married Adèle-Dorothée Pépin, daughter of a watchmaker. Following his discovery of the Venus de Milo, Dumont d'Urville was made a Chevalier of St Louis in 1820 and awarded the Légion d'honneur in 1821. He continued his botanical studies at the Museum of Natural History at Le Havre.[4]

Coquille left her home port of Toulon on 11 August 1822 and remained one month at the Falkland Islands where d'Urville began an algae collection which at the end of

Fig. 32.

DUMONT D'URVILLE
Contre-Amiral (Rear Admiral)
Artist Unknown.
Engraving. Frontispiece: Hulot, E. Baron. *Le Contre-Amiral*
Dumont d'Urville.
Paris, Société de Géographie, 1872.

the voyage made up 106 species. He also brought back lichen and ferns and 3,000 species of plants of which some 400 were new.

The corvette rounded Cape Horn and called in at Chile and Peru before crossing the Pacific to visit Tahiti, Tonga and the Solomon Islands. At Waigeo in Papua, Lesson first saw the enchanting red and gold bird of paradise, but could not bring himself to shoot one. While in Sydney he was able to buy a male king bird of paradise with plumage of 'a bright red vermillion which shone like spun glass'.[5]

Coquille anchored at Port Jackson 'in the midst of a forest of masts' as Lesson put it. New South Wales was in the grip of a severe drought, but during nearly eight weeks in port the French sailors and scientists were warmly received by the soldier-scientist Governor Sir Thomas Brisbane. Lesson studied birds and fish and made a trip across the Blue Mountains where he found a red-throated pademelon (kangaroo) unknown to the English naturalists. Lesson accompanied d'Urville to the tomb of La Pérouse's chaplain Father Receveur at Botany Bay. Allan Cunningham gave d'Urville many of his duplicate botanical specimens which could not be obtained because of the drought.[6]

In 1820, Bellingshausen and the Russian explorers looked at Bungaree and the Sydney Aborigines through the eyes of interested observers, ready to praise or condemn on the merits of observation or anecdote. In contrast a tone of arrogance and derision runs through the accounts by the French. This same group of people are described by Lesson as 'puny creatures . . . close to the vilest animals'[7] and 'great black monkeys indulging in ridiculous contortions'.[8] Bungaree he called 'the wretched chief'.[9] This shift in attitude may have been influenced by Peter Cunningham's colourful descriptions of the Aborigines in *Two Years in New South Wales* (1827), which was translated into German in 1828 and French in 1836. Both Lesson and d'Urville drew on Cunningham's text and quoted from it.

Six years passed before even the first tome (there were 14 volumes with five Atlases) of Dumont d'Urville's epic *Voyage de la corvette L'Astrolabe . . .* was printed. It mainly concerned the task given to d'Urville by the French King Charles X during 1826–29 to survey areas of the South Seas and to try to find what had happened to Comte Jean-François La Pérouse's ships, last seen at Botany Bay in 1788. However, d'Urville mentions Bungaree several times in his description of an Aboriginal ritual 'trial by ordeal' which he had seen on 29 February 1824 during his first visit to Sydney. This has been translated by Helen Rosenman in *Two Voyages to the South Seas*, published by Melbourne University Press in 1987.

On the evening of 28 February 1824, d'Urville, accompanied by Major Edward Marley (barrack master of the Sydney Regiment) and John Uniacke, a New South Wales government official, went to visit Bungaree's camp 'on the peninsula on the north side of Sydney Harbour'. Bungaree told d'Urville that several tribes were meeting the next day near Sydney to 'punish' some Aborigines. 'I promised him some brandy, that he was mad about', d'Urville wrote later, 'and he undertook to let me know the next morning at the ship on his way to the battlefield.'

Early next day, 'two boats carrying Bungari's tribe and his allies' passed the corvette. The explorers followed them ashore and were touring the streets of Sydney when Bungaree, his wife and a friend came to tell them it was time to leave. On the way out of town, wrote d'Urville, they saw Bungaree 'at the head of all the warriors of his tribe moving out, leaping and prancing through the bush in all directions. It was a very strange and picturesque sight, rather resembling those flocks of little imps we sometimes see in our operas.'

The battle, which took place in a cleared space somewhere near today's Surry Hills (between the Brickfields and the road to Botany Bay), broke up before noon. D'Urville was fascinated by the returning boomerang which the warriors made 'curl and whine all around them', though he thought it was best suited to frightening someone than causing actual harm:

M. Uniacke pointed out to me a native who was said to be very skilled at boomerang throwing. I knew nothing of this implement, and on my asking him, the savage hurled it four or five times. Thrown horizontally at first, this projectile, which looks like a wooden sabre bent in the middle on two different planes, quickly rises, turning from right to left to an extraordinary height and well away ahead of the person throwing it. I estimate at almost 45 degrees the angle under which it slowly rises and at 150 feet at least, the distance it reaches. After describing pirouettes and undulations for this tremendous distance, it turns back on its tracks with the same movement and comes back to fall near the thrower; so that anyone beside him at first does not know what to do to avoid the boomerang; but he soon works out the direction of its trajectory and then it becomes easy to get out of its way. The savage in question never failed to bring it back right to his feet, and to do that you need a lot of practice.

D'Urville does not say whether or not he saw Bungaree throwing the boomerang at this combat. He was surprised not to find the use of 'this singular projectile' mentioned in the works of Collins or 'Barrington'. 'Might it not be a new invention on the part of the savages, or, more likely, a weapon peculiar to some tribes outside Port Jackson of which the authors had no knowledge?' However, most of the English colonists to whom he spoke said it certainly belonged to the Aborigines.

'Bungaree had promised me one of these strange instruments; when I left he failed to keep his word on this matter as on several others,' d'Urville added caustically.

Fig. 34.

René-Primavère Lesson (1794–1849)
Artist unknown, 1838.
Engraving.
Frontispiece: *Voyage autour du Monde* . . . Paris, P. Pourrat
Frères, 1838.

The three 'chiefs', Bungaree, Bidgi-Bidgi (of Kissing Point) and Cogai (Cogy or Gogy of the Cow Pastures), invited the Frenchmen to a 'marri' (big) corroboree that night, but 'this day and the ones following we had foul weather and these savages, bored with waiting around and not keen to dance in bad weather, disbanded, and made their way back to their homes, leaving as usual Bungari's and the Sydney tribe the sole inhabitants of these parts'.[10]

Dumont d'Urville embellished his account of these events in *Voyage Pittoresque Autour Du Monde*, published in 1830 (see Appendix II). The combat was also described by Lesson.

René-Primevère Lesson (1794–1849) was born and died in Rochefort. He joined the French Navy in 1811 as an assistant surgeon but became a pharmacist in 1816 while in charge of the botanical gardens at Rochefort. He was for many years professor of botany at the naval school in Rochefort and was finally Pharmacein-en-chef of the French Marine. Following the voyage of *Coquille*, Lesson wrote *Voyage médical autour du monde* (A medical voyage of the world), published in 1829, and then a two-volume memoir of the *Coquille* expedition (1838). His physical examination confirmed Bungaree's severe head wound and incorrectly healed fracture of the arm which Alexander Berry had treated at Crow's Nest in 1819:

> . . . there are found among them quite a few old men, who all bear more or less extensive scars as a result of battles during their lives. Bongarri, for example, the wretched chief of the Sydney Cove tribe, showed us his skull, quite shattered by numerous blows of a club which would have felled a strong animal. One of his arms also had been broken by a blow from the same weapon; and the two ends of the fractured humerus, constantly rubbing against each other, did not knit together properly, resulting in a false joint. Despite this, Bongarri used his arm with dexterity, whether to row a dinghy or to handle his weapons.[11]

In *Voyage autour du monde*, Lesson showed scant esteem for Bungaree and did not mince words in his description of him.

> The corvette La Coquille had scarcely dropped anchor in Sydney Cove when Bongarri and his band, composed of almost half a dozen individuals, came to levy a tribute on our curiosity . . . This chief has had the reputation of a fine warrior, he is also esteemed by neighbouring tribes and his honourable scars prove that blows from spears and war clubs have never made him retreat; but it is hard to find the hero in the arrant drunk and stubborn beggar who comes each day during our stay in port to harass us for brandy or tobacco. Miming, bowing and scraping and pulling faces, his grotesque get-up made him look more ridiculous for an old dragoon's helmet covered his skull and on his torso floated a greatcoat with frogging, which the last Russian expedition had left him.

Lesson saved his most scathing insults for Bungaree's two wives, whom he called 'the most striking, the ugliest, the most disgusting creatures that I had ever seen. These ladies, wrapped in a dirty woollen blanket instead of a cambric gown, had their hair covered in nits and lice: the whole seasoned with a smell capable of asphyxiating the most obstructed nose in creation'.

Several times Bungaree and his companions came to visit the French ship in what Lesson called 'grand ceremonial dress'. Their bare bodies, especially their chests, were smeared

Fig. 35.

Indigenos de nouvelle hollande   Pen and ink, 19 x 24.5 cm.
[Natives of New Holland]   Service Central Hydrographique de la Marine, Paris.
Jules Lejeune, 1824.

with a dusting of red ochre, their noses and cheeks were painted with red vermilion and white stripes extended from the centre of their foreheads. Their hair was bound by small bands of bark. Lesson was present on the evening of 28 February 1824 at 'one of the great festivals or *corobari*' (corroborees), but gave no details of it. Bungaree came to the ship by canoe to ask the French explorers to attend:

> Preoccupied and anxious, Bongarri, this famous chief of the Australian tribes, had swallowed in one gulp the glass of rum with which I never failed to regale his black majesty when he visited the corvette. Bongarri sprang into his bark canoe, filled with spears and war clubs. The formidable *boumarang* [boomerang] rested near a half-burned log which, like the fire of Vesta, these negroes never allow to go out; the words *Coroboree, coroboree*, were forced with effort from his drawn mouth; while speaking Bongarri could only by gesture invite me to come to the rendezvous at the east of the bay.[12]

The Old Viceroy

Lachlan Macquarie, who had served 12 years as the King's representative in New South Wales, lived only two more years after his return to Britain. Like Matthew Flinders, he died in a lodging house in London. The date was 1 July 1824. He was buried on the Isle of Mull.[13] Late in 1824, news of Macquarie's death reached Sydney, where the 'Old Viceroy' was greatly mourned.

Young Lachlan, the apple of his father's eye, who had entertained the Sydney Aborigines to breakfast on his sixth birthday, was to die tragically at the age of 32 after a fall downstairs while drunk.[14]

Bungaree's Boat

While Lesson told of Bungaree's canoe, d'Urville mentioned 'two boats' carrying Bungaree's family and friends.

Indigenous de nouvelle hollande (Natives of New Holland), a pen-and-ink sketch by the expedition's artist Jules Lejeune (Fig. 35), gives us a glimpse of Bungaree' group in their fishing boat. Bungaree stands at the bow, wearing his plumed cocked hat and the long Russian greatcoat with frogging described by Lesson. His left arm is extended, waving or pointing, and he holds a rope in the other hand. Apart from Bungaree, there are six men, two women and a baby on board. Two standing men with headbands are naked, as are the women, who do not wear even woollen blankets. Two men holding spears and two men rowing seem to wear only old uniforms coats (one has a military hat), without trousers, but the child is carried in a blanket. At the stern, a fire for cooking fish is attended by a woman wearing only a headband.

Walking by the Parramatta River with his brother George (Commissary at Parramatta) 'one beautiful evening' in 1824, the Rev. John Dunmore Lang met 'Bungary chief of the Sydney tribe of the black natives . . . pulling down the river, in a boat which he had received as a present from the Governor with his two jins or wives'. They stopped to talk and 'the good natured chief immediately desired his two jins to rest their oars'. Bungaree was wearing his cocked hat and an old military uniform.[15] The boat drawn by

Fig. 36.

Rev. John Dunmore Lang (1799–1878)
Charles Rodius, 1850.
Crayon, 34.3 x 26.7 cm.
Mitchell Library, Sydney.

Lejeune and described by Lang must be the one given to Bungaree by Governor Brisbane
at Macquarie's request.

The Lost Sailor

On 29 June 1825 the frigate *Thétis* and the corvette *Espérance* sailed into Port Jackson
and dropped anchor in Neutral Bay. This large French scientific expedition with a contingent
of 580 men was commanded by Hyacinthe Yves Philippe Potentien, Baron de Bougainville
(1782–1846), eldest son of the famous circumnavigator Antoine de Bougainville.

At the age of 18 Hyacinthe de Bougainville had spent three months in Sydney as a
midshipman on *Géographe* in Captain Nicholas Baudin's expedition.[16] Now as commander,
he kept his sailors well away from the vices of Sydney Town, while traveling widely
himself. He met the Corsican-born superintendent of police, Captain Francis Nicholas
Rossi, saw Samuel Marsden at Parramatta and invited Marsden's Maori religious students
on board *Thétis*. Accompanied by Captain John Piper and the expedition's artist Vicomte
Edmond Bigot de la Touanne, de Bougainville went to Botany Bay and later arranged
for a stone Doric column to be erected as a memorial to La Pérouse.[17]

In *Journal de la navigation autour du globe . . .* published in Paris in 1827, Hyacinthe de Bougainville recorded his impressions of Bungaree during his visit to Port Jackson. It was no novelty, he wrote, to see 'those unfortunate natives' condemned to drag out their existence by begging around Sydney:

> They often visited us and few days passed without the celebrated Boongarie, chief of the Broken Bay tribe and travelling companion (as the cabin boy is to the admiral) of Captains Flinders and King, coming aboard with his family, to drink our health with a few glasses of French brandy which he loved so much.

It was well known, he added, that most of the 'savages' living near European settlements indulged their fondness for strong drink. 'The natives of Australia are no more exempt than others from this fatal craving and Boongarie shares it, at the very least as much as his compatriots.'

The French sailors admired the skill with which Bungaree manoeuvred his boat (which had one sail bearing in large letters the words 'King Bungaree'), in spite of his intoxication:

> A black coat, three-quarters worn, an old uniform hat adorned with ribbons and sometimes decorations made of gold cardboard, comprised the town costume of S.M. [His Majesty], who used to withdraw in the evening into the bush on the North Shore of the harbour. There men, women and children, shedding all types of garments, lay down higgledy-piggledy on the ground, after lighting fires to protect them from the damp and the insects.

The scene at Bungaree's camp was no different than it had been five years before when described by Bellingshausen and Simonov.

Early one morning Baron de Bougainville sent a party of sailors in a ship's boat to the North Head of Sydney Harbour to gather palm leaves for making hats. While the men were at work, strong winds blew up suddenly from the south and a heavy swell struck the boat head-on. The two sailors guarding the boat could not prevent it running ashore, where it was staved in at Collins Beach, a small bay just inside North Head.

Midshipman du Bouzet led some of the men back to the ship along the harbour foreshores and cliffs, leaving others, well-armed and commanded by a coxswain, to guard the boat. As they returned, a sailor named Daniel wandered off into the bush and was lost. He did not answer gunshots fired to recall him. When du Bouzet arrived at dusk to report the shipwreck, de Bougainville immediately sent out search parties with lanterns along the coast and the fringes of the bush. They questioned without result groups of Aborigines on the north shore whose campfires should have guided the lost sailor. 'Next day, after further searches had proved useless, the longboat brought back the wrecked boat, but Daniel did not appear, so I decided to resort to Boongarie, who refused to accompany us unless he was given a bottle of brandy.'

Daniel was brought to the ship by two Englishmen who had given him shelter overnight. He had been back on board for 48 hours before Bungaree came to see de Bougainville, claiming he had broken his arm in an accident while searching for the lost sailor and was in great pain. This upset the baron, who did not know what compensation to offer. He was dumbfounded when the surgeon major, whom he had called in immediately, told him that Bungaree's arm had been broken three years ago. This 'master cheat' (*maître fourbe*), de Bougainville wrote, had not rested his arm and it had formed what the doctor called a 'false articulation' caused by the continual rubbing of the severed ends.[18]

As we know, Bungaree's arm had been broken in 1819, almost six years before.[19] Angered by Bungaree's attempt to deceive him, the French commander rebuked himself for not having previously noticed this physical disability. In a later reference to 'Boungari, then chief of a Port-Jackson tribe', de Bougainville claimed he had 'by no means thought to employ the latter as an agent on whose skill one would rely'.[20]

The two French ships sailed for Chile on 21 September 1825.

Entrée de la baie de Sidney. (Page 320.)

Fig. 37.

Entrée de la baie de Sidney   Engraving by Léon Benett.
[Entrance to Sydney Harbour]   Verne, Jules, *Histoire des Grands Voyageurs*. Paris, 1887.

11 'A King of Shreds and Patches'

Although the Australian Aborigines had no traditional hereditary leaders, Bungaree became known, to blacks and whites alike, by the spurious title of 'King' Bungaree. The genesis of this elevation to the monarchy lay in his appointment by Governor Macquarie in 1815 as 'Chief of the Broken Bay Tribe'. Macquarie presented Bungaree with the brass gorget 'distinguishing his quality' and later gave him a suit of old general's uniforms 'to dress him out as chief'.[1]

Bungaree's own claim to be 'king' of Port Jackson was first recorded by Captain Bellingshausen in 1820.[2] By 1825 he was generally styled 'King Bungaree' by curious new arrivals in New South Wales. The Sydney newspapers of the day described him, with varying degrees of irony or ridicule, as 'His Sable Majesty', 'King of the Blacks' and 'Chief of the Sydney Tribe'. Although Bungaree put on the mantle of 'royalty' with his gaudy uniforms, in the words of Geoffrey Dutton, 'he had only to look down at his bare feet to know where he stood'.[3]

Henry Thomas Ebsworth arrived in Sydney on the *York* in 1825 to take up a position as accountant for the Australian Agricultural Company at Port Stephens, N. S. W. Ebsworth kept a journal, written in neat copperplate lettering, of the six-month voyage from Cowes on the Isle of Wight, during which he saw that the AA Co's livestock on board was well cared for—only 17 sheep were lost from a flock of 730:

> Nov. 13. Sunday—Arrived in Sydney . . .
> On entering the harbour Ships receive a visit from one of the Natives in a Boat, who styles himself 'King Bungaree' accompanied by two Wives and a few friends; this he has done for many years: this royal party live principally upon what they can get given them from Ships.

Ebsworth thought the Sydney Aborigines were 'without exception the ugliest race of people ever beheld. The blacks at Rio are handsome to them.' They were lazy and could not be persuaded to work. Natives who refused to wear clothes, he said, were forbidden to enter the town.[4] In an undated letter written in 1826, Ebsworth further noted that on his shipboard visits, Bungaree 'forgets the quality of Royalty by bowing obsequiously to all on board'. He always concluded his speech by begging permission 'to have the honour of drinking the Captain's health'.[5]

In March 1826 the *Sydney Gazette* reported that 'His sable majesty, Bungaree' had been ordered by Captain Rossi to report to the Police Office. There Bungaree was told to warn his people and the chiefs of other tribes that 'rioting, drunkenness, and disturbing the quiet of the streets at night' would be punished by a sentence of hard labour or the treadmill. The treadmill, set up in 1823 next to the Carter's Barracks (site of the present Central Railway), was a place of punishment where 18 convicts marched ceaselessly up the endless revolving steps of a large wheel which drove a corn mill. 'Bungaree bowed politely, promised to use every exertion to put the orders of their worships into effect, and retired.'[6]

Naval officer Richard Sadleir (1794–1889) first saw Bungaree when he arrived in Port Jackson the following month (11 April) as a young naval lieutenant. More than half a century later he recalled the meeting in his book *The Aborigines of Australia* (1883):

> My acquaintance with His Majesty was very short. As was his usual habit, he visited the ship 'Thames' in which I arrived in the Colony. His sable majesty, in his native barge, a bark canoe, presented himself to make the usual inquiries as to the name of the captain, and to inspect the steward's pantry, receiving tribute of various articles of food and raiment; and although he was adorned with a cocked hat and a brass plate, I could not help contrasting, to his disadvantage, His Majesty's Appearance with that of the North-American chieftains with whom I had been in the habit of mixing; however, years of drunkenness and some starvation no doubt had their effect in emaciating his frame—the blessings which civilization has bestowed upon the unfortunate aboriginal population.[7]

Bungaree with his family and followers continued to camp in the bush on the North Shore, which the Aborigines retained, said the Rev. John McGarvie, 'as a place of retreat to which they retire almost every night'. The Presbyterian minister, naturalist and art critic first saw Bungaree as the *Greenock* came into port on 21 May 1826:

> Having come to anchor we saw a boat coming alongside with Bungarie chief of the Broken Bay Natives. He had 2 or 3 Gins with him who remained in the boat. He got a glass of brandy, and retired after making most profitable revenewes. He is a Drunken bare legged & barefoot Savage having a brass plate on his breast intimating that he is chief of the tribe.[8]

McGarvie and Sadleir agreed that Bungaree continued to wear the gorget given to him by Governor Macquarie, although de Bougainville does not mention it. Sadleir and de Bougainville commented on his cocked hat and McGarvie on his bare feet, but neither they nor Ebsworth mentioned Bungaree's colourful uniform jackets. This was left to Peter Miller Cunningham (1789–1864), who made several voyages to Australia as a navy surgeon on convict ships. He lived in New South Wales for two years while establishing a farm on the Upper Hunter River, travelled extensively, and 'came in contact with the aborigines in a variety of ways'. Cunningham's racy description of Bungaree and numerous anecdotes about him in his book *Two Years in New South Wales*, published in London (1827) and reprinted in the *Sydney Gazette* (11 January 1828), coloured many later accounts.

> King Bongarree, too, with a boat-load of his dingy retainers, may possibly honour you with a visit, bedizened [dressed vulgarly] in his varnished cocked hat of 'formal cut,' his gold-laced blue coat (flanked on the shoulders by a pair of massy epaulettes), buttoned closely up, to evade the extravagance of including a shirt in the catalogue of his wardrobe; and his bare and broad platter feet, of dull cinder hue, spreading out like a pair of sprawling toads, upon the deck before you. First he makes one solemn measured stride from the gangway; then turning round to the quarter-deck, lifts up his beaver with his right hand a full foot from his head, (with all the grace and ease of a court exquisite) and carrying it slowly and solemnly forwards to a full arm's-length, lowers it in a gentle and most dignified manner down to the very deck, following up this motion by an inflection of the body almost equally profound. Advancing slowly in this way, his hat gracefully poised in his hand, and his phiz [face] wreathed with many a fantastic smile, he bids massa welcome to his country. On finding he has fairly grinned himself

into your good graces, he formally prepares to take leave, endeavouring at the same time to take likewise what you are probably less willing to part withal— namely, a portion of your cash. Let it not be supposed, however, that his Majesty condescends to thieve: he only solicits the loan of a dump, on pretence of treating his sick gin to a cup of tea, but in reality with a view of treating himself to a porringer of 'Cooper's best,' to which his Majesty is most royally devoted.[9]

The Martinet

In December 1825 there was a change of guard at Government House, Sydney, with the replacement of the *laissez-faire* Brigadier-General Sir Thomas Brisbane by Sir Ralph Darling (1775–1858), the very model of a methodical lieutenant-general. At the age of 18 Darling had joined his father's old regiment, the 45th Foot, as an ensign. He was a captain by 1796 and lieutenant-colonel by 1801, serving in the West Indies. He was adjutant-general of the Horse Guards at Whitehall in London, an influential post, from 1806 to 1818. Darling married Eliza Dumaresq, daughter of an army officer killed during the Napoleonic Wars. He had command of the British Garrison at Port Louis, Mauritius, for five years (1819–23) and was effectively governor of the island for 18 months.

Aged 50, the seventh governor of New South Wales was something of a martinet, stiff-necked and a stickler for the rules. He enraged the fiery John Macarthur by refusing to make a distinction between emancipists (ex-convicts) or the land-owning 'exclusives'. Darling's appointment of three of his wife's brothers to public office (including his private secretary Henry Dumaresq), brought accusations of nepotism against him.[10]

Darling had orders from London to 'promote Religion and Education among the Native Inhabitants'. He was also to protect their persons and 'the free enjoyment of their possessions',[11] a task that was 'somewhat difficult', as C. D. Rowley observed in *The Destruction of Aboriginal Society* (1970), 'while at the same time establishing the settlers on their land'.[12] The governor encouraged ministers and missionaries in their attempts to 'civilise' the Aborigines and asked Anglican Archdeacon Thomas Hobbes Scott (1783–1860) for proposals on how they might be converted and educated.[13] Scott dispatched Richard Sadleir, who had experience of the North American Indians while serving on the Great Lakes in Canada, on a tour to investigate the condition of the Aborigines and their relation with the settlers in the Argyle district, south-west of Bathurst.

Darling paid an allowance to the Rev. Lancelot Threlkeld, Congregational minister in charge of a 10,000-acre mission and native reserve at Lake Macquarie (today's Toronto) which had been granted to the London Missionary Society by Governor Brisbane. He praised Threlkeld's initiative in compiling a vocabulary of the Awaba Aboriginal language.

Darling reported on his task to Earl Bathurst without much optimism, referring to the 'disgusting excess' of indulgence in spirits by those Aborigines who lived near Sydney and other towns and settlements. Though many of the natives who frequented Sydney spoke English 'remarkably well', it seemed impossible for them to abandon their 'vagrant habits', which he described as 'Those of Mankind in a Savage State'.[14]

Princes and Princesses

Darling continued to sponsor the annual Native Conference at Parramatta inaugurated by Macquarie, but because of wet weather he sent Lieutenant Governor Colonel Dumaresq, accompanied by the Rev. William Cowper and the Rev. Samuel Marsden, to represent him at the gathering of 214 Aborigines held in January 1826. 'Rain descended in torrents,' said the *Sydney Gazette* in a somewhat tongue-in-cheek report:

> Sixteen gallons of rum were converted into tolerably good grog, which many of the whites there thought was quite in season. The eatables were served up in the usual aboriginal style— we mean on such occasions; there were no tables elegantly equipped, but there was the table which Nature had spread for her sons, and the plots of grass were here and there interspersed with a small rivulet of water, or a lump of mud . . . It was quite amusing to see the temporary indifference to all distinction amongst this motley groupe—there were subjects, constables, chiefs, wives, daughters, mistresses, and even kings, all mingled up higgledy-piggledy; and as familiar one with the other as if they were all downright Republicans.[15]

In its report on 'the corroborie or annual festival' the rival *Australian* said that despite the downpour of rain, those attending, 'including the native princes and princesses', gave three loud cheers when the feast was set before them. 'The chiefs, who were present on the occasion, consisted of Bungaree, Blang, Dual, Cogle, Boodeny, Niaggan, and Jobinge. They were seated at the head of their respective tribes, who were arranged in semi-circular form.'[16]

Governor Darling, Colonel Dumaresq and Alexander McLeay attended a smaller gathering of the tribes on 28 December 1826 at the Market Place in Parramatta. This time only about 100 Aboriginal men, women and children were present owing to hostility between the Cow Pasture tribes and those of the Liverpool and Illawarra districts which was said to be going on with 'much spirit'.

However, some of the warriors had agreed upon an armistice and the abundance of food and drink, the *Sydney Gazette* suggested, seemed to temper the passion for war:

> It was supposed there would be some warm work, in the spearing way, as soon as the parties had plentifully regaled themselves, which they took good care to do, amply lining themselves with all sorts of the best substances, as well inside as outside. Considering their belligerent disposition, the sable gentry soon forgot the campaign in which they were engaged, and grew as cheerfull and lively, and as civilised, as abundant eating and drinking could possibly make their more cultivated fellows . . . HIS EXCELLENCY . . . was evidently much gratified with the business of the day, and none were more highly delighted than the guests themselves, who, at a late hour in the afternoon, retired to their native fastnesses, in order to prepare for the din of arms.[17]

This small 1826 gathering was visually recorded in Augustus Earle's watercolour, *The Annual Meeting of the Native Tribes at Parramatta, New South Wales, the Governor meeting them* (Plate 15). Earle was in New Zealand at the time of the 1827 Native Conference and left Sydney in October 1828 before that year's meeting.

The governor and his party, wearing uniforms and cocked hats (two with plumes), are being greeted by an Aborigine—probably Bungaree—who has on a cocked hat, red jacket and brown trousers. Other Europeans, including some women in bonnets, watch the spectacle from behind a fence and a garlanded gateway. Naked Aboriginal men, women and children sit in a semicircle on the ground while their 'chiefs' and 'constables' sit on stools. One man, seen at left talking to a European, sports a tall yellow top hat, while two others at right wear cocked hats. Food is being taken from boxes and rum from a barrel at left, rear.

Government House, Parramatta, crowns the hill in the background while the Church of St John with its twin spires is at right.

In true military style, Governor Darling sent troops to subdue Aborigines who rebelled against settlers in the Hunter River area in 1826 and again in the districts of Argyle and St Vincent in 1830, which resulted in many Aboriginal deaths.

The Gallant Commodore

On 17 October 1826 Sir James Brisbane, the 'gallant Commodore of His Majesty's squadron', a second cousin of the former Governor Sir Thomas Brisbane, sailed into Port Jackson on HMS *Warspite*, flagship of Britain's China and East India station.[18] With 500 crew and 74 guns she was the largest battleship ever seen in an Australian port.

Warspite left Trincomalee, Ceylon (now Sri Lanka) on 26 August to cruise the Pacific islands *en route* to the South American station. Sir James, who had contracted chronic dysentery at Rangoon in 1824 while serving in the Burma Wars, became ill and decided to call at Sydney. Passengers on board included the commodore's wife Lady Brisbane and his two daughters, while his son, a young lieutenant, was a crew member. *Warspite* was accompanied by the frigate HMS *Success* and the brig-sloop HMS *Fly*.

Governor Darling welcomed Sir James and 'Master Brisbane' to an 'elegant déjéune' at Government House on Saturday 21 October and paid an official visit to *Warspite* that afternoon. 'A large *partie* of Naval heroes, from the Warspite, Volage, and Fly, and a few other gentlemen' had dined with the governor the previous evening.[19]

While *Warspite* was moored in Neutral Bay her crew one night saw bushfires raging on the North Shore. At daybreak the sailors rescued a number of settlers who were sheltering in the water and ferried them across to Sydney Cove in the ship's boats.[20]

A military dinner was given to Sir James Brisbane on 27 October. However, his illness continued. At the end of October, Sir John Jamison sent a carriage to take the commodore to Regentville, his mansion on the Nepean River at Penrith, 'that he may recover that health that has been seriously affected'.[21]

On Wednesday 6 December the *Sydney Gazette* stated that Commodore Brisbane's health was 'not so hopeless as report makes it',[22] but on 19 December 1826 he 'expired at his residence in Macquarie-place'.[23] Governor Darling gave the commodore a lavish State funeral.

Astrolabe, on Discovery

On 2 December 1826, according to the *Sydney Gazette*, 'arrived the French corvette Astrolabe, 82 men, and 12 guns, captain D'Urville, from Toulon . . . on discovery'.[24]

Jules Dumont d'Urville, now a frigate captain aged 35, was in command of a new French scientific expedition sent to the Pacific by King Charles X. He was given his former ship *Coquille* but changed her name to the *Astrolabe* to commemorate one of La Pérouse's missing vessels.

Astrolabe sailed from Toulon on 25 April 1825 with 13 officers who included the two surgeon-naturalists Jean-René Constant Quoy and his assistant Joseph-Paul Gaimard, a zoologist. Pierre Adolph Lesson, younger brother of the *Coquille* naturalist, was the expedition's pharmacist and botanist, while artist Louis Auguste de Sainson was its official artist.

Governor Darling received the French explorers warily. The corvette had anchored at King George Sound and surveyed Oyster Harbour and it was rumoured that the French government intended to establish a penal colony there. To counter any possible territorial claims, Darling hurriedly sent a detachment of the 39th Regiment and convicts in the *Amity* to King George Sound, where they landed on Christmas Day 1826. Its commander, Major Edmund Lockyer, proclaimed the western half of Australia as a British possession. Dumont d'Urville also called at Western Port, where the crew met some sealers, and at Jervis Bay, south of Sydney.

Jules Dumont d'Urville was impressed with the changes that had taken place in Sydney since his visit in *Coquille*. 'Straight away we noted with some admiration how much the town had grown and improved in just three years,' he wrote.[25]

He collected plants in the Blue Mountains and went to Parramatta where he saw the Rev. Samuel Marsden who gave him information about New Zealand, his next port of call. Charles Fraser, superintendent of the Botanical Gardens, gave the French botanists a batch of newly discovered plants.

Bungaree in George Street

Louis de Sainson (1801–1887) painted the Governor's Stables (today's Conservatorium of Music) and the Macquarie Light at South Head, both designed by architect Francis Greenway. He included the figure of Bungaree in the foreground of a street scene in *Vue de George's*

Fig. 38.

View from the Sydney Hotel   Earle, Augustus. *Views in Australia.* Sydney: Earle's
Augustus Earle, 1826.   Lithography, 1826.
Lithograph.

Street à Sydney (Nouvelles Galles du Sud) (View of George Street, Sydney, New South Wales), lithographed by Alexis Nöel for the Atlas accompanying Dumont d'Urville's *Voyage de la Corvette l'Astrolabe*, published in Paris in 1833 (Plate 5). Bungaree wears his cocked hat, brass gorget and a long military coat with trousers and—uniquely—shoes. He carries a swagger stick or waddie in his right hand.

De Sainson copied the street scene from *View from the Sydney Hotel* (Fig. 38), an earlier lithograph by Augustus Earle which was on sale at the artist's gallery at No. 10 George Street, Sydney.

The identical view in both prints shows George Street, looking north from Charlotte Place (now Grosvenor Street). At left is the Main Guard with sentries on the verandah, at right the home of shipbuilder James Underwood and in the background is the arched door and white walls of Sydney gaol (site of today's Regent Hotel) at the corner of Essex Street. While leaving the buildings intact, de Sainson replaced the human figures, substituting Bungaree for Earle's Aborigine holding a spear. Bungaree's figure may be modelled on that in *Indigenous de nouvelle hollande* (Fig. 35) by Jules Lejeune in which Bungaree wears the same long coat. It is notable that Bungaree wears his cocked hat across his head (with the peaks at the sides) only in these two works.

Louis de Sainson's original aquarelle, titled *Vue prise dans George Street à Sydney, Xbre 1826* (View of George Street, Sydney, December 1826) is now in the collection of the Société de Géographie in Paris.

Astrolabe left Port Jackson for New Zealand on 19 December 1826, the same day that Commodore Brisbane died.

In 1827, according to Roger Oldfield in *The South-Asian Register*, the Parramatta feast was attended by 160 Aborigines, 'being most probably as many as there are, on this side the mountains, between Broken Bay and the Five Islands (Illawarra)'.[26]

The Bennelong of his Age

Bungaree and his band were unwitting players in a satirical article published in the guise of a letter to the *Sydney Gazette* on 24 March 1827 under the heading 'A Ride to the Wharf'. The author, who signed himself with the pseudonym 'XYZ', recounted an unfinished 'journey' from the Lumber Yard in Hunter Street to the Wharf at Sydney Cove. His attention was first attracted by Billy Blue, 'twirling a stick which he held betwixt his fingers and thumbs'. Blue, a black Jamaican boatman who rowed passengers over the harbour to the North Shore, was another well-known Sydney character. 'Here, however I came within sight of the snuff merchant's,' XYZ continued:

> I could descry Bungaree moving about in his uniform with a pipe in his cheek and a waddie stuck under his left arm. His gins and the rest of his tribe were ranged in front of the tobacconist's shop, and they seemed as if they had just purchased a supply of the deleterious weed, for volumes of smoke were steaming from their dingy lips.

The writer was so much amused by the scene that he put up at an inn and decided to continue his journey the next morning.[27] This tongue-in-cheek piece should be seen as a 'squib' fired in the constant war of words between the *Sydney Gazette* and its rivals, *the Monitor* and *The Australian*. Beginning on 13 March a rather florid account of a journey across the Blue Mountains, titled 'A Ride to Bathurst 1827', appeared in parts in *The Australian*. Its author XYZ has been identified by historian M. H. Ellis as Captain William John Dumaresq, brother of Henry Dumaresq and brother-in-law of Governor Ralph Darling.[28]

Bungaree appeared in a new role in November 1827, as an interpreter in a Supreme Criminal Court trial in which 'Tommy, alias Jackey Jackey, an aboriginal native, was indicted for the wilful murder of Geoffrey Cornell, a stockman in the employ of Mr George Kable, of Reedy Swamp, near Bathurst, on the 20th of June last'. Evidence was given that the stockman's body was found in his burnt-out hut. His skull was fractured and his brain was protruding from injuries probably made by a tomahawk. The jury returned a verdict of guilty.

Said the *Gazette*: 'The Rev. Mr Threlkeld, and Boongaree, the native chief, who attended on the part of the Crown, as interpreters, were unable to draw any thing from the prisoner beyond a denial of having taken any part in the transaction'.[29] Tommy and four white men were executed a few days before the 1828 Native Conference at Parramatta. His last words from the scaffold were reported to be: 'Bayal [no] more walk about'.[30]

A new journal, the *South-Asian Register*, styled after the British *Gentleman's Magazine*, was added to the Sydney scene in 1827. Its editor, Dr Roger Oldfield, a magistrate and former missionary, wrote at length about the 'Sydney tribes', their dress and behaviour in the second number (January 1828) as part of a series of essays titled 'New Holland'.

Echoing Arago's remarks of 1819, Oldfield wrote that, until recently, the Sydney Aborigines had been allowed to walk the streets without any clothing ('the troublesome disguises which we wear'), but in 'the Metropolis' they were now required 'to observe a certain degree of decorum'. This had become a general rule with the Aboriginal women, who were issued with blankets from the Commissariat store. These they wore around their necks 'mantle-wise, but from being worn night and day without washing, they add no grace to the person':

> In the same group we sometimes see a man with only a pair of trowsers, another with a shirt, another a jacket without any sub-tegument [under-garment]; or a female wearing a full-bodied gown with flounces; another wearing only a skirt with a frilled cap stuck on her hair obliquely; another has perhaps a red or yellow jacket over a skirt; every one in short wearing what the humour of individuals has bestowed, no matter how motley and fantastic.

Oldfield compared Bungaree's situation with that of Bennelong:

> Bungaree, the chief, often receives cast-off clothes from naval and military officers; but they are generally too valuable to be long retained, when his exchequer is empty. Every one that visits Sydney, knows Bungaree, who is the Bennilong of the present time, though a more hybrid species of savage, and therefore less interesting. He has not the attention shown him which was paid to Bennilong . . .
>
> Bungaree accosts any gentleman he meets, quite in a familiar manner; but if the intercourse extends beyond a passing compliment, he always avails himself of it to make a serious request— for the loan of one dump, (1s. 3d). His tribe are also fond of borrowing silver, but in lieu of that, they will accept of 'coppers', if they amount to the value of a loaf, which to them is the lowest standard of computation. The familiarity of their address is often taken to be impudence.[31]

Oldfield attempted to bring some literary wit to Sydney in the *South-Asian Register*. Reviewing a book titled *Sketch of the Mosquito Shore, including the Territory of Poyais*, written by Thomas Strangeways, he suggested: 'Had he [Strangeways] been in service in this "radiant realm,'' he might have become Colonel of Bungaree's 1st regiment of Life Guards'. The magazine ceased publication in 1828.[32]

At this time Bungaree in his fishing boat with his two wives at the oars and 'about six attendants' were allowed to row around Port Jackson unmolested. 'In this they frequently make excursions,' Oldfield wrote, 'and row into the open sea; employing themselves in catching fish, which they cook over a fire that is carried in the boat, and as they often catch more than they want, the surplus is brought to town for barter. A sailor's life would suit these blacks more than any other, except a gentlemen's.'[33]

Peter Cunningham said that the Sydney tribes lived chiefly by fishing, 'being supplied with hooks and lines by individuals in the town, to whom they bring all the fish they catch. They received payment from the hawkers in the form of old clothes, bread and rum.' Kingfish, mullet, mackerel, rock cod, whiting, schnapper, morwong (sea bream) and flathead were all in good supply.[34]

Plenty of small game and traditional food plants remained in the bush around the Aboriginal camps on the North Shore of Sydney Harbour, most of which was not closely settled until well into the 1850s. Oldfield noted that the Aborigines continued to return there

Fig. 39.

SYDNEY.
From the Parramatta Road
Drawn and engraved by John Carmichael, 1829.
[Caption]
'The last engraving is a view of Sydney from the south at the toll gate on the Parramatta Road, where are represented a few of the homeless inhabitants of the forest accompanied by their Chief—Bungaree.'
Plate 6: Select Views of Sydney New South Wales. Drawn and Engraved by John Carmichael, Sydney 1829 (Price four dollars). Mitchell Library, Sydney.

each day, just as they had eight years earlier. 'Neither Bungaree or his tribe sleep in Sydney, but at sunset retire into the bush, carrying a lighted stick with which they kindle a fire; choosing a place where the trees are thickest, or one of the hollow rocks with which the caves of Port Jackson abound.'[35]

About 200 Aborigines from the Sydney area attended the Native Conference held at Parramatta on 2 January 1828. As usual, the governor's black guests enjoyed beef, plum pudding, grog and tobacco and a cartload of slop clothing was divided amongst them. This time, however, wrote Dr Oldfield, 'Bungaree was not there, but remained with several others in Sydney'.[36]

In its issue of 4 January *The Australian* newspaper elaborated on his absence:

> But few strangers visited the place of festivity. Bungaree was not there, nor his tribe: that venerable chief having made away [sold] his fishing boat (it is suspected to purchase some extract stronger than that derivable from the suction of sugar-bag) a day or so before, had no suitable conveyance, and not feeling disposed to undertake the journey by land to Parramatta on foot, enjoyed his *otiom cum dignitate* [dignified leisure], the better part of Wednesday and Wednesday night, reclining by his fire upon the grassy upland bordering on Bennelong's Point.[37]

Tribal Diplomacy

It is impossible to fully gauge the effect on other Aborigines of Macquarie's elevation of Bungaree to 'Chief' of Broken Bay or his acquired title of 'King' of the Sydney tribes. However, it seems to have earned Bungaree some degree of respect among his people. He took an active role in tribal affairs, even to meeting Aborigines from distant places when they visited Sydney. Robert Dawson, a magistrate and chief agent for the Australian Agriculture Company, came to Sydney by ship some time in 1828 with M'Quarie and Cooribah, two Aborigines from Port Stephens.

> . . . on our voyage . . . I pointed out to them the character of the drunken and celebrated King Bungaree, and cautioned them to beware of him and his black associates. The morning after we landed, I received a visit from his sable Majesty, who had on an old military cocked hat, and an old black suit of clothes. 'Your tarben tir,' was his salutation [many Aborigines had difficulty pronouncing the letter 's']; he then said he understood two of my men had arrived with me from Port Stephens—that he always wished to see all black people who come to Sydney—and that if I would allow them to go with him, he would show them Sydney, and desire his men to take good care of them. I immediately introduced my two attendants to the old king, and told them they might go with him if they wished it for a few hours.

Bungaree's diplomacy in this case may simply have veiled a ploy to obtain another 'loan'. After persuading the reluctant visitors to go with him, Bungaree addressed Dawson again:

> 'Lend me one dollar sir, if you please.' 'No, Mr Bungaree,' I said, 'I shall do no such thing. I see you want to make my men drunk, and if you do I shall not allow you to see any more of them, nor shall I take them with me to Sydney again.'
>
> Bungaree assured me he would not even ask them to drink, and as he had no money I could easily understand his intended forbearance. A short time after they had left me I saw the two Port Stephens blacks in the street staring in amazement at a person riding in a gig,—a spectacle they had never before witnessed. Bungaree however had left them, and they soon returned to the house.[38]

Dawson was dismissed from his position at the AA Co. and left New South Wales in September 1828.

Bungaree continued to exert great influence as a leader among his fellows. He seemed able to easily separate the two cultures from each other, living a traditional Aboriginal life in his bush camp while visiting the white man's town for rum or bread whenever it suited him.

The Rev. Lancelot Threlkeld, adept at unravelling the strands of the Awaba language, also attempted to follow the thread of Aboriginal spirituality. In a circular letter to members of the London Mission Society, dated 8 October 1828, Threlkeld marvelled at how speedily Aborigines from different parts of New South Wales communicated with one another using messengers, 'even where the dialects are supposed so much to differ as to prevent communication'. The messengers, he said, were always armed and painted red and were often adorned with down feathers in their hair.

When some whales became stranded on a beach at the Central Coast, some of the Awabagal made a day's journey to take part with others in the feasting. Here they met a black messenger from Sydney who had come to collect the Aborigines to punish a murderer. This was his story, as recorded by Threlkeld:

> A black woman, the messenger's own wife, was intoxicated, and close to the bathing house on the Government Domain, Sydney; a black named William Munnan, cut her mouth, from ear to ear, split her head with a tomahawk, and then, with other blacks, jumped upon her body, until they supposed she was dead; her husband took her, in the black's boat, to Broken Bay, where she expired, and buried her at Pitt Water. Boongaree, the chief of the Sydney Tribe, ordered him to collect all the Blacks he could, and come and punish the man. The dead woman's daughter, a little girl, urged revenge, and some of every tribe will, at some favourable opportunity, have blood for blood.[39]

One cool morning in July 1829, walkers in the Government Domain were confronted by the strange figure of a man 'in a state of perfect nudity, with the exception of his old cocked hat, graced with a red feather'. The 'poor fellow', who supported his trembling body with a large staff, was none other than the 'veteran native, chief, Boongaree'. Reporting this apparition, the *Sydney Gazette* said he appeared to be 'in the last stage of human infirmity'.

'Boongaree is identified with Sydney,' the writer commented, 'and something ought to be done to make his few remaining days easier.'[40]

The King is Dead

Age, alcohol and malnutrition had done their work. In 1830, Bungaree suffered a serious illness which lingered for several months. Something *was* done to help him. Colonial Secretary Alexander McLeay arranged for Bungaree to be admitted to the General Hospital (central block of Macquarie's Rum Hospital), where he received medical attention and remained for several weeks. Impatient to be released, Bungaree was allowed to return to his people and was put on the full government ration.[41]

A short time before his death Governor Darling ordered that Bungaree be taken to the house of the Irish Catholic priest John Joseph Therry (near today's St Mary's Cathedral), where he was 'treated kindly'. Therry, who had been authorised as a priest by Macquarie, often gave food to the local Aborigines, who still held their dances and funerals nearby

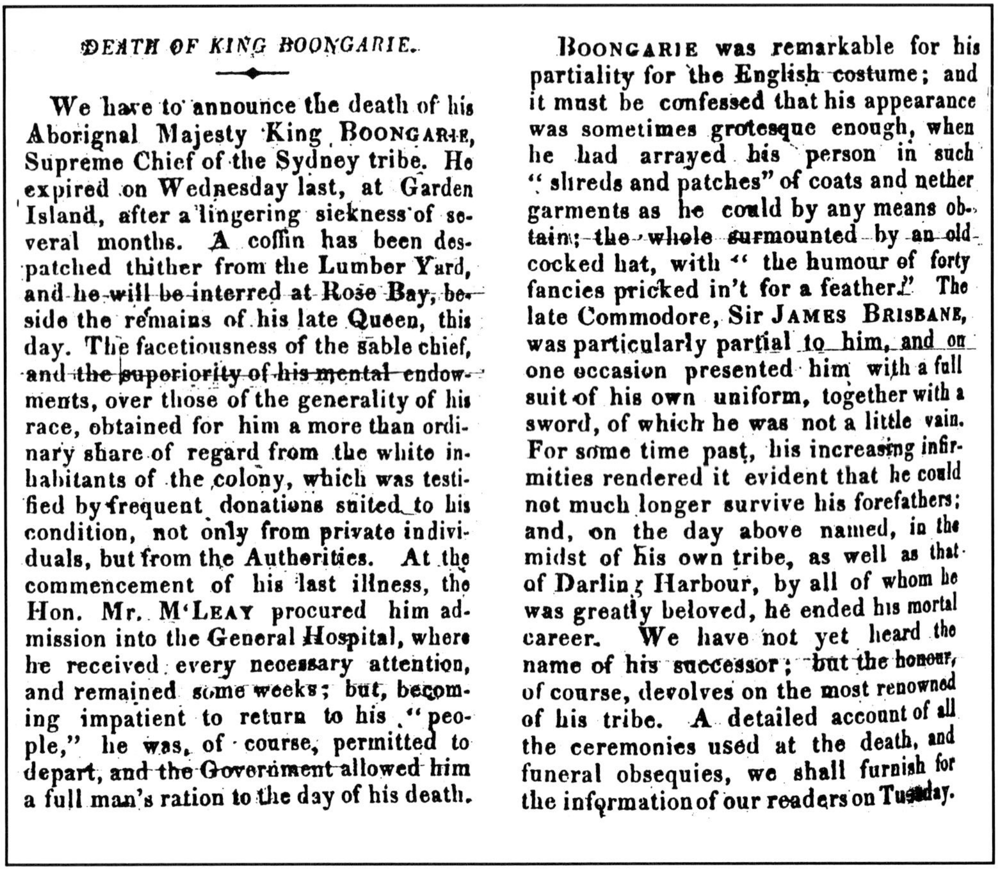

DEATH OF KING BOONGARIE.

We have to announce the death of his Aborignal Majesty King BOONGARIE, Supreme Chief of the Sydney tribe. He expired on Wednesday last, at Garden Island, after a lingering sickness of several months. A coffin has been despatched thither from the Lumber Yard, and he will be interred at Rose Bay, beside the remains of his late Queen, this day. The facetiousness of the sable chief, and the superiority of his mental endowments, over those of the generality of his race, obtained for him a more than ordinary share of regard from the white inhabitants of the colony, which was testified by frequent donations suited to his condition, not only from private individuals, but from the Autherities. At the commencement of his last illness, the Hon. Mr. M'LEAY procured him admission into the General Hospital, where he received every necessary attention, and remained some weeks; but, becoming impatient to return to his "people," he was, of course, permitted to depart, and the Government allowed him a full man's ration to the day of his death.

BOONGARIE was remarkable for his partiality for the English costume; and it must be confessed that his appearance was sometimes grotesque enough, when he had arrayed his person in such "shreds and patches" of coats and nether garments as he could by any means obtain; the whole surmounted by an old cocked hat, with "the humour of forty fancies pricked in't for a feather." The late Commodore, Sir JAMES BRISBANE, was particularly partial to him, and on one occasion presented him with a full suit of his own uniform, together with a sword, of which he was not a little vain. For some time past, his increasing infirmities rendered it evident that he could not much longer survive his forefathers; and, on the day above named, in the midst of his own tribe, as well as that of Darling Harbour, by all of whom he was greatly beloved, he ended his mortal career. We have not yet heard the name of his successor; but the honour, of course, devolves on the most renowned of his tribe. A detailed account of all the ceremonies used at the death, and funeral obsequies, we shall furnish for the information of our readers on Tuesday.

Fig. 40.

DEATH OF KING BOONGARIE
Obituary from the *Sydney Gazette*, Saturday 27 November 1830.

at Woolloomooloo. One day, while Father Therry was out, Bungaree's friends carried him off to the neighbourhood of Elizabeth Bay.[42]

Bungaree died at Garden Island on Wednesday 24 November 1830, 'in the midst of his own tribe and that of Darling Harbour, by all of whom he was greatly beloved'. He was buried at Rose Bay the following Friday, 'beside his dead Queen' in a wooden coffin. The *Sydney Gazette* published a lengthy obituary (Fig. 40) which took up most of the second column on page 3, its main news page (not a full page, as sometimes stated)[43]. By this time the *Gazette* had a new editor and manager, the Rev. Ralph Mansfield, who filled the position when Robert Howe, son of the paper's founder George Howe, drowned off Fort Macquarie (Bennelong Point) in 1829 at the age of 34. A detailed account of Bungaree's funeral was promised for the newspaper's following issue, but was never printed. William Charles Wentworth's *The Australian* recorded Bungaree's passing more briefly:

BOONGARIE, the venerable Aboriginal Chief of the Broken Bay and Sydney tribe of black natives breathed his last one day last week, and was solemnly interred on Friday, in a grave dug at Rose Bay beside his deceased gin. His naturally strong constitution gave way under a predilection for hard drinking which he indulged when practicable to excess, and which has so thinned and enervated such of the tribe as frequent Sydney. Some spears were thrown on the occasion of their chief's demise.[44]

Bungaree's Family

Bungaree left a family which included his widow Queen Gooseberry, a younger wife (whose name may have been Rose) and her baby son named John Bungaree and a stepdaughter known as 'Miss Diana Bungaree'. There were two other sons, 'Young Bungaree' and 'Long Dick', and probably other sons and widows.

Through the 1820s, Bungaree was usually accompanied by two of his wives. His obituary says he was buried beside one of his dead wives at Rose Bay. This may have been Matora.[45]

Queen Gooseberry

Bungaree's widow, Cora Gooseberry, commonly known as Queen Gooseberry, was a Sydney identity for 20 years after his death. Wrapped in a blanket, her head covered by a scarf and with a clay pipe in her mouth, Gooseberry was often seen with her family and other Aborigines camped on the footpath outside the Cricketer's Arms, a hotel at the corner of Pitt and Market Streets, Sydney, kept by Edward Borton (or Berton)[46]. When explorer John Frederick Mann (1819–1907) first saw her in the mid 1840s, he noted 'she had little on beyond an old straw bonnet',[47] but in *goosberry one Eyed Poll, Wife of King Bonjarry*

Fig. 41.

goosberry one Eyed Poll
Wife
of King Bongarry
Charles Rodius , April 1844.
Pencil, 20.3 x 14.3 cm.
Mitchell Library, Sydney (transferred from Art Gallery of New South Wales, 1921).

(Fig. 41), a portrait by Charles Rodius (1844), she is wearing a modest 'Mother Hubbard' dress with a wide collar.

Gooseberry, who could spin a yarn as convincingly as Bungaree, told artist and writer George French Angas that Bungaree had been the ruler of the Sydney Aborigines when the First Fleet arrived in Port Jackson in 1788. 'His queen has survived her glories,' Angas wrote, 'and she now totters about, very aged and decrepit, known as "Old Gooseberry;" but her memory is still good.' In July 1845 Gooseberry, in exchange for flour and tobacco, conducted Angas and Inspector W. A. Miles of the Water Police on a tour of Aboriginal rock carvings at North Head and told them 'all that she knew and all that she had heard her father say' about these places sacred to the *koradgees*, men potent in casting spells.[48]

Edward Borton had a soft spot for Gooseberry and allowed her to sleep at night in the kitchen of his new hotel, the Sydney Arms, in Castlereagh Street. She went there on the night of Thursday 29 July 1852 and was found dead the next morning.[49] Borton paid for her burial and a gravestone in the Presbyterian section of the Devonshire Street Cemetery (the 'Sandhills' Cemetery on the site of Central Railway). The gravestone is now in the Pioneers Cemetery at Botany, but its inscription is indecipherable. Happily, before the carved words faded, they were recorded by Mrs A. G. Foster in her *Epitaph Book* (1901): 'Stone erected by MRS STEWART and MR E. BERTON, Junior, in memory of Gooseberry QUEEN of the Sydney Tribe of Aborigines who died 30th July 1852 aged 75 years'.[50]

Miss Diana

The comments by both the *The Australian* newspaper and Dr Oldfield in his *South-Asian Register* that 'Bungaree was not there' (at the 1828 Native Conference), carries with it the inference that it was unusual for Bungaree not to attend the gathering of the tribes.

Fig. 42.

Gooseberry's rum mug
Bronze, c. 1800—8.5 cm in diameter; 5.3 cm high.
Relics, Mitchell Library, Sydney.

His attendance at the feast held at Parramatta on 19 January 1829 was noted by the *Sydney Gazette*:

> The venerable *Boongaree*, with his gin, and daughters, one of whom by the bye, *Miss Diana*, is distinguished by a less sable hue than her parents, was present in the midst of the interesting and delighted group. The HON. Mr McLeay paid particular attention to *Miss Boongaree*, who would not venture to look up, until her angry Sire gave a *sensible* token of his displeasure, accompanied with expressions which could not have been grateful to the young lady's ear.[51]

'Miss Diana' was the pretty light-skinned girl named Ga-ouen-ren, the daughter of one of Bungaree's wives by a European, who was first mentioned by Captain Bellingshausen in 1820. She appears as one of the group around a camp fire in Pavel Mikhailov's illustration *Natives of New Holland* (Fig. 30). Bellingshausen described her as 'almost half white, handsome in face and figure'.[52] Bungaree's good nature could stretch to a joke against himself, as Peter Cunningham related:

> It was our good-humoured facetious Boongarre of whom the story is told about the mulato child which his gin brought forth. If you ask Boongarre about it even now, he will shrug his shoulders, laugh heartily and exclaim, 'Oh, yes! *My gin eatit too much white bread!* ' accompanied by that sort of knowing humorous look which shows he both understands and relishes the import of the joke.[53]

The French explorers Jules Dumont d'Urville and René-Primevère Lesson also appreciated this anecdote and repeated it in their books for the benefit of French readers. To quote Lesson: 'Bongarri, a truly practical philosopher, replied to the jeers of those who questioned him about this curious phenomenon: *My wife is greedy for white bread and has eaten a lot of it; it's not so astonishing that her child is white*'. Referring to Peter Cunningham's book, published 10 years earlier, Lesson added: 'M. Cunningham has also recorded this ingenious answer. I attribute it to Bongarri by the intermediary of the Irish Major Marlay of the Buffs, who reported it to me as I quote it.'[54]

Young Bungaree

Bungaree's heir inherited his father's taste for liquor, ritual spear fights and drunken brawls. At a night 'corroborra' at Woolloomooloo in 1831, said the *Sydney Herald*, 'Young Bungaree did the honours of the ceremonies. Before the party broke up, his sable majesty had become done up with *bull*; and in consequence of some pranks played by him he was floored by a waddie, on which a regular melee ensued.'[55]

In 1843 John Hood said that Bungaree's son was 'by this time the last of the royal line', which, through his 'debauchery and debased habits' he had 'tossed away for ever'.[56] J. C. Waterman, writing in the *Journal of the Royal Historical Society* in 1923, recalled: 'Bungaree's party in 1846 comprised eight men, women and children, including Jacky Jacky, Ricketty Dick and Gooseberry, Bungaree's widow. They gave exhibitions of boomerang throwing in Hyde Park and roamed about Sydney by day and camped near Centipede Rock in the Domain.'[57]

There is pictorial evidence that Young Bungaree also obtained his father's European clothes and perhaps his brass gorget. The Aborigine wearing a tailcoat and raising his cocked hat to a trooper in John Carmichael's engraving *BARRACK from George Street* (Fig. 45), published in *Picture of Sydney* (1839), appears to be a young man. So is the Aborigine wearing a cocked hat, breastplate and torn uniform jacket grappling with a rum cask in William Fernyhough's lithograph *Natives of New South Wales Drinking 'Bull'*, from which a further print was copied by William Nicholas in 1840.

Long Dick

Long Dick may have been Young Bungaree's younger brother. We know about him only through John F. Mann, who described him as 'an influential native of the Cammeray tribe a son of Bungaree and Queen Gooseberry'. Mann met Long Dick at Brisbane Water (Broken Bay) in 1842 and later recorded a list of Aboriginal names obtained from him.[58]

John Bungaree

Born in 1829, John Bungaree was a tragic figure destined, like his father, to be set apart from his own people. The boy was adopted on Bungaree's death in December 1830 by Stephen Coxen, a farmer at 'Dartbrook' on the Hunter River, north of Sydney.[59]

John was sent to school at the Normal Institution at Hyde Park, Sydney, where he boarded with 90 other boys. He was a clever student who excelled at arithmetic, could draw maps from memory and won prizes for writing and geography at the age of 12.[60]

When Stephen Coxen died in 1844, his brother Charles assumed responsibility for the boy, who went to live with his family at Daradine Station on the Darling Downs near Toowoomba (now Queensland). John Bungaree worked as a servant and stock rider and joined the Native Police at Callandoon on the Macintyre River,[61] eventually reaching the rank of sergeant. There is no mention of him ever drinking to excess, but he does not seem to have had a happy life. As proof of this we have the words of Lieutenant George Fulford, repeated by William Ridley before the Select Committee of the Native Mounted Police held in Brisbane in 1861:

> Bungaree, who after taking prizes at Sydney College, speaking good Latin, and behaving as a gentleman in elegant society, returned to the bush, and then entered the black police, once said in a melancholy tone to Lieutenant Fulford (who repeated the remark to me at Surat on the Condamine) 'I wish I had never been taken out of the bush, and educated as I have been, for *I cannot be a white man*, and they will never look on me as one of themselves; and *I cannot be a blackfellow*, I am disgusted with their way of living'.[62]

12 An Actor in the Streets

Viola:
This fellow is wise enough to play the fool,
And, to do that well, craves a kind of wit:
He must observe their mood on whom he jests.
The quality of the persons, and the time . . .
This is a practice,
As full of labour as a wise man's art . . .

—William Shakespeare, *Twelfth Night*, Act III, Scene i

Begging or Borrowing?

Selling or bartering fish, as we have seen, was one of the methods used by Bungaree to support himself, his wives and children and other remnants of his Broken Bay 'tribe'. For many years he enjoyed the patronage of Governor and Mrs Macquarie. He sometimes found a buyer for Aboriginal weapons on the ships visiting Port Jackson.

After an initial revulsion, those Aborigines living close to the settlements of New South Wales developed a taste for European food and stimulants such as alcohol, tobacco, tea and sugar. To gain a share of these imported luxuries they at first attempted to draw white explorers and settlers into a relationship of mutual obligation, for example by bringing them into their kinship system by exchanging names, taking white names, or offering their women for sexual and domestic services. They were startled and mystified at the violent response of their white 'brothers' when they 'helped themselves' to the crops of corn or potatoes grown on their land.

By 1826 the Aborigines living around Sydney had become dependent on the white settlers, so much 'that without what they beg, earn or steal, they could not well exist', declared Peter Cunningham. They were fringe-dwellers of European society, pitiful drunkards, decimated by disease, malnutrition, inter-tribal fights and drunken brawls. 'As beggars, the whole world will not produce their match,' wrote Peter Cunningham.[1] 'They do not attempt to coax you, but rely on incessant importunity; following you side by side, from street to street, as constant as your shadow, pealing in your ears the never-ceasing sound of "Massa, gim me a dum [dump]!, massa, gim me a dum!" '[2]

Many Aborigines were forced to work at menial tasks for their white masters and mistresses. Black women became prostitutes, 'the husbands disposing of the favours of their wives to the convicts for a slice of bread or a pipe of tobacco'. Cunningham claimed that the half-caste children of these unions were 'generally sacrificed' as was the second born of twins. 'On Boongaree being once remonstrated with for allowing a woman to destroy a twin-child, he shrugged up his shoulders, and merely said, "*Bel boodgeree* (not good) *kill it pickininny*", but made no subsequent efforts to check the practice.'[3]

In the last 10 years of his life, when the whites had somewhat derisively dubbed him 'king' of the Sydney Aborigines, Bungaree made his living by his wits, chiefly through the role he had invented as a kind of 'actor in the streets'. This role was the sum of his good humour, his foppish manners, his flamboyant dress and, above all, his comic ability as a buffoon and mimic. In time he assumed the identity he played. Drunk or sober, this distinctive image set Bungaree apart from other Aborigines in Sydney.

Bungaree's attitude is interesting. Though he pestered visitors and demanded goods or money, he had convinced himself that he was a borrower rather than a beggar. He preferred to ask for a 'loan', which he obviously never intended to repay. Strangers to the colony, such as the French explorers, certainly considered this as begging, while regarding payment as the price for their curiosity. Although it was a 'burden on the foreigner', said Dumont d'Urville's fictitious Dr Harry: 'it has its interesting side and besides it is not very costly. Boungari is easily pleased with a little gin and brandy.'[4]

Like Shakespeare's clown in *Twelfth Night*, Bungaree was 'wise enough to play the fool'. This part he played with such talent, it seems, that he was usually able to obtain his desires. Other Aborigines, already awed by his cocked hat and governor's breastplate, must have envied the steady flow of rum, tobacco, bread and cast-off clothing Bungaree was able to obtain. Had he, they must have wondered, found some secret or magic to tap the white man's generosity?

Dr Oldfield captured Bungaree's routine in 'A Walk Through Sydney', an article in the *South-Asian Register* for December 1828:

> Who comes here? A troop of blacks walking to the military band to feed their ears with the music . . . Bungaree is at the head, with his military cocked hat on, tipping with invariable politeness to every gentleman—Good morning Sir, how are you? 'Quite well Bungaree, thank you.' 'Can you lend me one dump, Sir?'[5]

The Magic Charms of Drink

Although they resisted at first, the Aborigines around Port Jackson were soon corrupted by alcohol. In this they followed the example of a majority of the whites in the early days of the convict settlement when rum, brandy and other spirits had replaced ready money. Until the time of Governor Macquarie, the sale of spirits was a monopoly run by the notorious New South Wales Corps, which became known as the 'Rum Corps'. Rum was the colony's currency. A cartel of officers speculated in cargoes of liquor and there were times when soldiers and convict workers were more often paid in rum than in money or rations.

It was a simple step to entice the Aborigines to work in return for liquor. 'On the first occupation of a new country,' wrote Robert Dawson, 'civilized men have too frequently looked only at the easiest mode of procuring the present services of the poor natives, by the temptation of ardent spirits, which have never failed to degrade uncivilized beings into half-civilized brutes.'[5]

'These fellows . . . will do anything for rum,' wrote Dr Joseph Arnold while in Port Jackson early in 1810.[7] Judge Barron Field, writing in 1822, spoke of the frequent drunken quarrels among the Sydney blacks:

A rum, or even sugar-cask, filled with water furnishes these poor creatures with intoxicating liquor, and the invasions of civilisation are reproached with the introduction of a new vice, which operates as an inflamer of all their old ones. It is a melancholy sight to witness the drunken quarrels and fightings of the simple natives of Australia, in the streets of Sydney.[8]

Little had changed five years later, when the Rev. Laurence Halloran expressed disgust at the 'shocking scenes' of 'large parties of the Natives, armed, parading in a state of intoxication; and in repeated instances, fighting, and desperately wounding each other'.[9]

Macquarie had forbidden the sale or supply of liquor to the Aborigines. Bellingshausen saw how easily the Sydney tavern keepers flouted this law by making a bargain with the Aborigines to wash out their empty rum or brandy casks. In return they were allowed to drink the liquid from the first wash, which still had a strong taste of liquor and was called 'bull'.[10]

For all his wit, humour and stratagems, there is no denying that in the last years of his life, Bungaree was addicted to alcohol. From 1819 onwards he was frequently seen drunk. Whether it was begging or borrowing, or drinking the health of too many ships' captains, Bungaree's passion for brandy and rum inevitably took its toll on his health. In its obituary, *The Australian* newspaper in 1830 concluded that hard drinking, 'in which he indulged when practicable to excess', had undermined Bungaree's constitution and hastened his death.[11]

In 1820, after meeting the Russian navigator Captain Bellingshausen, Bungaree and his wife Matora had left the *Vostok* half drunk, 'shouting horribly'.[12] Each evening the Aborigines who had gone across the harbour to barter fish for liquor returned by boat to their camps on the North Shore, 'shouting savagely and uttering threats'. Often these quarrels ended in a fight. 'The magic charms of drink and tobacco,' said Bellingshausen, had quickly become indispensable to the Aborigines and attracted them to the town. Although lazy, 'they will willingly become hewers of wood and drawers of water for the sake of tobacco and spirits'.[13]

'Everyone knows with what eagerness most of the savages living near the European settlements indulge their fondness for strong drink! The natives of Australia are no more exempt than others from this fatal craving and Boongarie shares it, at the very least, as much as his compatriots.' So French explorer Baron Hyacinthe de Bouganville remembered Bungaree, whom he met in Sydney in 1825. Few days passed, said de Bougainville, without Bungaree coming aboard the frigate *Thétis*, 'to drink our health with a few glasses of old French brandy which he loved so much'.[14]

Jules Dumont d'Urville characterised Bungaree as a 'worthy brandy lover'.[15] The Rev. John McGarvie used no pious substitutes, but called Bungaree frankly, 'A Drunken bare legged & barefooted savage'.[16] The Russian midshipman Pavel Novosil'sky considered he had bought Bungaree's friendship for a bottle of rum.[17] Pastoralist Robert Dawson warned two Port Stephens natives he took to Sydney to beware of 'the drunken and celebrated King Bungaree' and his associates.[18]

We do not and cannot know why the Aborigines of early Sydney Town were so susceptible to alcohol and why it was so destructive to them. There were no unbiased observers to speak on their behalf, only outraged whites with notoriously racist attitudes and, all too often, double standards. We can speculate about some of the possible reasons. The Aborigines had been dispossessed, without recompense, of their lands and food supply. They had no knowledge of imperialism or any notion of the supposed superiority of an aristocratic class. In their own culture they were accustomed to sharing everything with members of their own band. Without firearms, they had no power to repel the invaders or to resist their influence. When they realised with horror that the Europeans had come to stay, they knew their old ways of life, culture and spiritual beliefs were doomed and they were weighed down with helplessness. They soon found that white man's food, such as flour, corn, beef and potatoes, was necessary for survival. They turned for solace to the new stimulants of tobacco, tea and alcohol. Today, we can only ask: 'Who provided the rum?'

No Aboriginal would have been in a better position, from his travels and friendship with Europeans, to know these bitter truths than Bungaree.

The pattern was usually the same. Wherever Europeans established colonies in the New World they corrupted the native people. In North America, to enlist their help to fight the enemy, both the British and the French gave the Indians coats, shirts and hats, 'but

Fig. 43.

NATIVES OF NEW SOUTH WALES.
As seen in the Streets of Sydney
Augustus Earle, c. 1825–8.

Plate 1, Part 4: Earle, Augustus. *Views in New South Wales*
and Van Diemens Land. London, 1830.

found that rum was the most popular of all gifts'. The French declared that the persistent use of rum actually sent the Indians crazy. Under its influence they fought each other, threw babies into fires and traded their clothes for more 'firewater'.[19] In Tahiti, Pomare, son of Tu (or Otoo), the Matavai chief who had known James Cook, conquered his enemies with the help of English missionaries and called himself King Pomare. In 1820 Pomare, whom Herman Melville called 'a sad debauchee and drunkard', begged Bellingshausen for bottles of rum and wine. He died of drink the following year.[20]

In 1830 Augustus Earle arrived back in London after an absence of 12 years. In August that year he published *Views in New South Wales and Van Diemen's Land*, an album of eight lithographs which included *BUNGAREE, a Native Chief of new South Wales* (Plate 20).

In this portrait, Bungaree stands in exactly the same pose and wears the same uniform he does in Earle's oil painting of 1826 (Plate 6), but by changing the background and some details, the artist has reinterpreted his subject. In place of the fort, ships and harbour, there are European houses behind Bungaree. An Aboriginal woman, smoking a pipe, sits beside him on a rock. Her hair is in untidy ringlets and she is wrapped in a blanket. She is thought to be Queen Gooseberry, Bungaree's widow, whose own rum mug (Fig. 42) is among the relics of the Mitchell Library, Sydney.

Bungaree's face, features, expression and unkempt hair are closer to Earle's lithograph (Plate 3) than the oil. He looks older, his face is thinner, lined and weathered. The effects of alcohol upon Bungaree are further symbolised by two grog bottles in a basket close to his bare feet. Comparing this London lithograph to the Sydney portraits, Richard Neville commented in 'The Many Faces of Bungaree' (1991): 'Earle understood his market: he knew that Sydney-siders would not want to buy such an unflattering vision of their town'.[21]

The warm shades applied by Earle to the hand-coloured version in the Nan Kivell Collection (Plate 20) tend to soften the starkness of the black-and-white impression. Bungaree's face, when painted, is more in the lineage of Earle's 1826 lithograph than the oil. As in the oil portrait, Bungaree wears a red jacket and a blue-green vest, but his tattered trousers are light blue.

There is another side of the story in Earle's lithograph, *Natives of New South Wales in the Streets of Sydney* (Fig. 43), a graphic statement of the degradation of the Aborigines of Australia, yesterday and today. While it pokes fun at the Aborigines and their craving for 'bull', there is a clear sub-textural message in the background, which shows the figures of 'respectable' Europeans entering the inn to drink liquor.

Augustus Earle was appointed artist on board HMS *Beagle*, and shared a cabin with Charles Darwin, but he resigned in Rio de Janiero in 1832 due to persistent fevers and was replaced by Conrad Martens. Earle died in London on 10 December 1838 of 'asthma and debility'.[22]

The Mimic

Mimicry was a natural talent of the Australian Aborigines, who cleverly copied the sounds made by birds and animals in their hunt for food. In their corroborees they told stories in song and dance, copying in a stylised ritual the action and movements of crocodiles, kangaroos, emus, crows, dogs and so on. They acted out myths and legends from the Dreamtime or everyday scenes of hunting, fishing or fighting.

Surgeon George Worgan, who had recorded the 'Mimicking and Frisking about' of the Aborigines Governor Arthur Phillip met on his first visit to Broken Bay, added some comments in a letter to his brother Dick from Sydney Cove in June 1788:

> They are wonderfully expert at the art of Mimickry, both in their Actions and in repeating many of our Phrases, they will say—'Good Bye' after us, very distinctly. The Sailors teach them to swear. They laugh when they see us laugh . . . In a Word, to sum up the Qualities, personal & Mental (those at least we have been able to discern) They appear to be an Active, Volatile, Unoffending, Happy, Merry, Funny, Laughing, Good-natured, Nasty, Dirty, Race of human creatures as ever lived in a state of Savageness.[23]

It was Bungaree's good nature and easy disposition which first won him the approval of Matthew Flinders. Others were impressed by his manners. The *Sydney Gazette* described him in 1804 as 'a native distinguished by his remarkable courtesy'.[24] Bellingshausen in 1820 praised Bungaree for his kindness of heart, gentleness and generosity.[25]

Bungaree's talent for mimicry seems at first to have been confined to aping the manners of the Europeans. It culminated in his elaborate display when welcoming ships to Sydney. The effect of this ritual was enhanced by the tattered jackets, trousers or uniforms which Bungaree wore. In 1822 Governor Macquarie had given Bungaree 'an old Suit of General's uniforms to dress him out as a Chief',[26] At various times he was seen wearing a drab brown suit, a Russian hussar's greatcoat, a canary-yellow jacket and other convict 'slop' clothing, a bright blue dress coat with gold frogs and loops and a full dress naval uniform (probably with a red jacket) given to him by Commodore Sir James Brisbane 'of which he was not a little vain'.[27] Bungaree's hats over the years had included a Russian dragoon's helmet, but his cocked hat, sometimes with and sometimes without either a red or black plume of feathers, was his everyday headgear.

After his death in November 1830, Bungaree's reputation as a Sydney 'character' expanded as time passed. To quote Dr Frederick D. McCarthy in the *Australian Dictionary of Biography* (1966): 'He affected the walk and mannerisms of every governor from Hunter to Brisbane and perfectly imitated every conspicuous personality in Sydney'.[28]

It is surprising, then, to find that of all the colourful stories written about him, Bungaree's fame as an outstanding mimic is supported by so few contemporary descriptions. One is merely a caption which accompanied Augustus Earle's London lithograph of 1830: 'These people (and particularly this man) are great mimics, and the graceful bow he makes to strangers he copied from one of the Governors, and those who recollect the original, say it is exact'.[29]

Another reference, by the Rev. John Dunmore Lang, in *An Historical and Statistical Account of New South Wales* (1834), recalled an incident which took place 10 years earlier. Lang and his brother George, then in charge of the Commissariat at Parramatta, were walking along the banks of the Parramatta River when they met Bungaree in his boat, being rowed down the river by his two wives:

> . . . my brother requested Bungary to show us how Governor Macquarie made a bow. Bungary happened to be dressed at the time in the old uniform of a military officer, and accordingly standing up in the stern of his boat and taking off his cocked hat with the requisite punctilio, he made a formal bow with all the dignity and grace of an officer of the old school. My brother requested him to show us how Governor Brisbane made a bow, to which Bungaree

very properly replied in broken English: "'*top, 'top; bail* me do it that yet; 'top nudda Gubbana come'* ['Stop, stop, I will not do that yet, until another Governor comes']. In short, Bungary could exhibit the peculiar manner of every Governor he had seen in the colony; but he held it a point of honour never to exhibit the reigning Governor.
* *Bail* is a particle of negation in the language of the Aborigines.[30]

Dickens as Myth-Maker?

The assertion that Bungaree was an 'amazing' mimic comes from a long article titled 'Bungaree, King of the Blacks', which first appeared in the London weekly journal *All the Year Round*, 'conducted' by Charles Dickens, in its fourth issue, dated 21 May 1859.[31] 'The action, the voice, the bearing, the attitudes of any man, he could personate with astonishing minuteness,' wrote the anonymous author:

> It mattered not whether it was the attorney-general stating a case to a jury, the chief justice sentencing a culprit to be hanged, a colonel drilling a regiment in the barrack-square, a jew bargaining for old clothes, a drunken sailor resisting the efforts of the police to quiet him— King Bungaree could, in a mere dumb show, act the scene in such a way as to give you a perfect idea of it.[32]

Scholars and historians over the years have relied on this 'biographical memoir' for many anecdotes about Bungaree. It is the only source of the reputed names of his many wives, but does not mention his widow Gooseberry. A cursory investigation is sufficient to conclude that this document does not provide a reliable historical basis. Although it would have added a great deal to our story, it has been deliberately excluded as a source of this biography. There are many sticking points. You will recall that there is ample documented proof that Bungaree died on 24 November 1830.

The veracity of the biographer falls down immediately after the extract above when he says that every new governor of New South Wales 'from Governor Macquarie down to Governor Gipps (during whose administration Bungaree died), supplied him with an old cocked-hat and full dress-coat'. Sir George Gipps did not assume the office of governor of New South Wales until 24 February 1838. Bungaree died eight years earlier during the governorship of Ralph Darling.

There follows a comparison of Bungaree's imitation of Governor Sir Richard Bourke's brisk walk with Lieutenant General Darling's military swagger, while later Bungaree's character during Bourke's administration is mentioned. Bourke arrived in Sydney in 1831.[33]

The author was either unaware of the date of Bungaree's death, or wished to ignore it, perhaps because this fact may have got in the way of a good story. Obviously, events mentioned after 1830 are deliberate inventions either by the writer or editor. A puzzle remains because, although there is a general tone of exaggeration throughout, most of the basic facts about Bungaree have the ring of truth.

'Bungaree, King of the Blacks' circulated widely throughout Britain, the United States and the British Empire, including Australia, in Dickens' temendously popular magazine, which began in April 1859 with the serialisation of *A Tale of Two Cities*. A shortened version was printed in Volume 4 of *The Australian Home Companion* (Sydney, 1859),[34] while an edited text of what he called a 'spirited sketch' was included by Richard Sadleir in *The Aborigines of Australia* (Sydney, 1883).[35]

It has proved impossible, at this distance, to discover the indentity of the writer or to establish whether or not he knew Bungaree. The narrator says he is an Australian who first met Bungaree when he was a boy of 12 and Bungaree was 'an old man, over sixty'. At the age of 16, he 'lost sight of Bungaree for a long time' when he was 'banished' to England, first to study with a tutor and then at Cambridge. A plausible Australian atmosphere is established by quoting customs such as calling 'cooey' (cooee) when lost and by the use of Sydney settings, including 'Bandye Bay' (Bondi). Seven years later the writer returns to Sydney and resumes his acquaintance with Bungaree. He left the Colony once more, he says, in 1843.

A possible candidate for authorship of the apocryphal biography of Bungaree is Peter Miller Cunningham, who had written amusingly about Bungaree in *Two Years in New South Wales* (1828). After the book was published he returned to Australia in 1828. Cunningham had intended to settle permanently on his farm Dalswinton at the Hunter River, but following droughts and other setbacks he left New South Wales in October 1830. He returned to the Royal Navy and served in South America 1830–34. In 1834–35 he made a final visit to Australia, staying at Darlington (now Singleton). He resumed his naval post on HMS *Asia*, serving in the Mediterranean 1836–41 and was at the blockade of Alexandria in 1840.[36]

While overshadowed by his famous elder brother, the poet Allan Cunninham (no relation to the distinguished botanist), Peter Cunningham had aspirations as a writer. He was the author of *On the Motions of the Earth* (1934), a scientific work, and *Hints for Australian Emigrants* (1841), a practical book. The *Australian Dictionary of Biography* says he was 'a prolific contributor to Periodicals'.[37] There are many similarities of style, notably the vivid, anecdotal, rather journalistic descriptions, between 'Bungaree, King of the Blacks' and *Two Years in New South Wales*.

Peter Cunningham left Australia in 1830, just two months before Bungaree's death, and may not have heard about this event during his visit in 1834–35.

Cunningham's nephew, an intelligent young man also called Peter (son of the poet Allan Cunningham), was a constant companion of Charles Dickens. He visited Dickens in company with the Honourable Mary Boyle (the novelist's 'darling Mary') at the Châteaux des Moulineaux in France in the summer of 1852.[38]

Serious consideration must also be given to the possibility that some sections of the biography were added by Charles Dickens himself.

Charles John Huffam Dickens had a kind of long-distance love affair with Australia, which he promoted as a true 'working man's paradise'. In *David Copperfield* and *Great Expectations* he dispatched his fictional characters to this southern Utopia. In real life, Dickens sent two of his sons to Australia when their careers did not live up to his expectations. Alfred d'Orsay Tennyson Dickens settled in Australia for a time and later went to live in America. His brother, Edward Bulwer Lytton Dickens, nicknamed 'Plorn', was packed off to Australia at the age of 16. He eventually bought a property at Moree and became a member of the New South Wales parliament.[39]

In *Household Words* and its successor *All the Year Round*, Dickens, ever the Victorian reformer, published a series of articles about Australia, often promoting emigration from Britain. After the death of Peel in 1850, Dickens wrote that he thought of 'flying to Australia, and taking to the bush'.[40] He also hobnobbed with the Rev. Sydney Smith, editor of the *Edinburgh Review* and a self-appointed expert on Australia and the British convict system.

Dickens, known to his staff as 'The Chief', stamped his character on both journals, imposing a strong editorial attitude and style on the works of his anonymous contributors. He made numerous alterations to manuscripts and proofs in a quick-drying blue ink. 'It is not inaccurate to refer to Dickens as author, or at the very least, part author of these works,' concluded Coral Lansbury in 'Charles Dickens and his Australia' in the *Journal of the Royal Australian Historical Society* (June 1966).[41]

The novelist, who set a high standard for his public readings and his family's regular amateur theatrics, used mimicry as a stimulant to 'get inside' his characters. His daughter Mamie watched him at work one day, pulling 'extraordinary facial contortions' in the mirror and afterwards talking rapidly to himself in a low voice while all the time writing furiously at his desk.[42] George Lear, a fellow clerk working for the solicitor Edward Blackmore at Gray's Inn, London, during 1827–28, was struck by Dickens' dramatic gifts. 'He could imitate, in a manner that I have never hear equalled, the low population on the streets of London in all their varieties, and the popular singers of that day, whether comic or patriotic,' wrote Lear, 'as to his acting, he could give us Shakespeare by the ten minutes, and imitate all the leading actors of the time.'[43] This passage makes an interesting comparison to the quote about Bungaree above.

What could be more Dickensian than the names given to Bungaree's wives in the *All the Year Round* biography: Onion, Boatman, Broomstick, Askabout and Pincher?[44] No mention of these names can be traced to any other available published or unpublished historical source.

Taking 'Bungaree, King of the Blacks' at face value, Dr John Joseph Healy in 'Dimension and Grandeur', an article published in *Hemisphere*, analysed the episode in which Bungaree was received on board HMS *Warspite* in a mocking way by Commodore Sir James Brisbane. Brisbane wears his full dress uniform and the ships's band plays 'God Save the King'. Bungaree, however, refuses to acknowledge the commodore as the 'real' (Governor Sir Thomas) Brisbane. Borrowing a telescope, Bungaree acts out his imitation of the former governor. By doing this, says Healy, Bungaree has turned 'the current of ridicule' firmly against the commodore. [45]

In his book *Literature and the Aborigine in Australia* (1988), Healy further examined what he called the 'Warspite incident':

> The tables had been turned. This was partly because what was a joke to [Sir James] Brisbane was serious to Bungaree, who had, with obtuse persistence, transformed the scene. The strange world of the white man had always been filled, for Aborigines like Bungaree, with difficult customs and power. He could negotiate these rituals with imitative ritual, and he seemed to have done it with great mastery.[46]

If Bungaree was aware of the role he played in Sydney's street theatre, no doubt his response to ridicule would have been sarcasm or satire. Although his source material may be challenged, there can be no argument against Dr Healy's statement that the references constantly made by nineteenth-century writers to the skill of Aborigines as mimics had the effect of denigrating them and implied that theirs was 'the speechless talent of gifted animals'.[47]

It seems likely, however, that the Warspite incident was 'worked up', perhaps by Charles Dickens, from the sentence in Bungaree's obituary in the *Sydney Gazette* (27 November 1830): 'The late Commodore, SIR JAMES BRISBANE, was particularly partial to him, and on one occasion presented him with a full suit of his own uniform'.[48]

Commodore Brisbane arrived in Port Jackson aboard *Warspite* on 17 October 1826. He was seriously ill by 22 October and died on 6 December 1826. Peter Cunningham was not in Sydney at the time. After his fourth voyage to New South Wales as surgeon of a convict ship, Cunningham was back in Britain in August 1826, preparing *Two Years in New South Wales* for the press.

In *White on Black: The Australian Aborigine Portrayed in Art* (1974), Geoffrey Dutton pulled together the strands of Bungaree as beggar, mimic and drunk. 'Among the scenes of drunkenness and squalor there rises one figure of tragic splendour, Bungaree, "King of the Blacks".' Bungaree, Dutton said, knew the reality of the situation of the Aborigines of New South Wales. 'When he wore the braided jacket and cocked hat given him by various Governors, he had only to look down at his bare feet to know where he really stood . . . Bungaree seems to have decided to treat the white men as a licensed jester, with scorn not far below the comedy and familiarity.'[49]

'Realising the hopelessness of his position and the loss of his heritage,' Dutton concludes, 'Bungaree determined to play it for laughs. He mocked the white men by mocking himself.'[50]

13 Images of Bungaree (2)

By definition, an artist has to see; he often sees what has become invisible to ordinary men. For reasons of his art he may be selective, or distort what he sees, but he cannot afford the dishonesty of turning his face away from his subject.
—Geoffrey Dutton *White on Black : The Australian Aborigine Portrayed in Art*, 1974,[1]

The way in which European artists portrayed black people throughout history tells us much about the attitudes of each period. From early times until about the Middle Ages, negroes were regarded as 'different but equal'. In the eighteenth century, the romantic idea of the 'Noble Savage' was put forward by French philosopher Jean-Jacques Rousseau (1712–78). Some of this philosophy of nature rubbed off on the artists of the First Fleet, including Thomas Watling and the Port Jackson Painter. However, by the 1830s there were few in New South Wales who could grasp the image of 'savage nobility' except as irony. The Aborigines had become the butt of colonial humour and were presented as grotesques or caricatures. In the words of art historian Bernard Smith: 'Clad in old European rags and divested of the last vestige of that nobility with which the eighteenth century had clothed him, the aborigine was depicted as a monstrous and comical absurdity'.[2] All too often, the overbearing attitude of religious, cultural and racial superiority displayed by 'educated' whites towards the native Australians spilled across the page in pencil, ink and watercolour as it did in life and literature.

As we have seen in the works of Pavel Mikhailov and Louis de Sainson, artists accompanying scientific expeditions to the South Seas were capable of adapting a painting to conform to classical tradition (or for other reasons) by adding or subtracting from what they actually saw with their own eyes. Yet the first portraits of Bungaree by Phillip Parker King (1819) and the Russian artist Pavel Nikolayevich Mikhailov (1820) appear as serious, honest reporting of their subject. Bungaree seems dignified and his facial expression is captured with some care and sympathy, although in the first instance his look is slightly sullen and in the second somewhat distracted.

The first known portrait (Fig. 24), *Boon-ga-ree Aboriginal of New St Wales 1819* . . . is a watercolour by Phillip Parker King, who described Bungaree as 'about forty-five years of age, of a sharp, intelligent and unassuming disposition'. King must have painted Bungaree sometime between February and May 1819, while in Port Jackson between voyages.

Bungaree's hair is curly but greying and he has not shaved recently. His face is lined and he seems older than in Mikhaylov's portrait of the following year, or in the later works of Augustus Earle. Bungaree wears a loose naval style topcoat with a wide collar. The chain of his brass gorget can be seen around his bare neck. His expression, in Dr Frederick McCarthy's view, is one of 'wary contempt'.[3]

The lithograph of Mikhailov's portrait (Fig. 26) of Bungaree is discussed in Chapter 8. His wife Matora, shown to the right of Bungaree, also has wavy hair, a headband across her head and body scars. She looks directly at the artist, with a suggestion of curiosity. She seems to have a more animated expression than Bungaree. In Mikhailov's original sketch of Matora she is shown at full length, seated. Neither lithograph differs much from the original sketches.

Jules Lejeune's quick head and chest ink sketches of 'Buggery' (Fig. 33) are hard to judge. The serious full face view at left has a 'modern' look, almost like a drawing by Jean Cocteau. The smiling lips and slight twinkle in Bungaree's eye in the profile accord with written descriptions of his manner. There is just a hint of the comic: Lejeune's finished works often tended towards satire. The drawings provide details of Bungaree's military jacket and his cocked hat (worn across the head) and its feather plume. The breastplate bears the inscription 'Roi des natifs' ('King of the Blacks'), otherwise mentioned only in suspected spurious accounts of Bungaree.

Penetrating Portraits

The portraits by Charles Rodius (1802–60) are astute studies which, although issued to the public after Bungaree's death, reveal a depth of insight into his character. Rodius, a specialist in the use of the 'French crayon', also worked in oils, watercolours and lithographs.

Born in Cologne, Rodius (also spelt Rhodius) spent several years in Paris, employed as a draughtsman and engraver. While in London he was convicted of theft at Westminster on 2 April 1829.[4] According to Sir Roger Therry, who happened to attend the trial, the charge against Rodius was for 'snatching a reticule from Lady Laura Meyrick's hand, on her coming out of the Opera-house'. The bag contained an opera glass, smelling bottle and handkerchief.

Rodius was sentenced to seven years transportation to New South Wales and arrived in Sydney on 7 December 1829 with 199 other male prisoners aboard the Sarah. The ship's papers described him as an artist and architect, aged 27 and a Roman Catholic. 'This person had taught drawing in several high families in England,' Therry wrote.[5] In Sydney Rodius was assigned to the Department of Public Works where he was employed without salary as an artist and architect. He also taught drawing to military officers and instructed the children of Sir Francis Forbes, first chief justice of New South Wales, in 'the elements of drawing and perspective'.[6]

Rodius was best known for his portraits of colonial notables of the day, many of which survive in the collections of the Mitchell and Dixson Libraries in Sydney. These include Judge Forbes, Edward Smith Hall, John Dunmore Lang, Francis Nicholas Rossi, Frederick Augustus Hely and Billy Blue.

Soon after his arrival in Sydney, Rodius published a portrait of Bungaree, probably using the same press as Augustus Earle. The Sydney Monitor commented: 'Mr C. Rhodius uses the lithographic press with great skill. He has executed front and profile likenesses of Bungaree in a most superior style.'[7] A hand-coloured version of this lithograph (Plate 18), titled BUNGAREE, Chief of the Broken Bay Tribe, is in the Rex Nan Kivell Collection at the National Library of Australia in Canberra. It is captioned 'Drawn upon stone by C. Rodius'. Bungaree is shown in right face head and shoulders profile, hatless, and in front face bust (head turned slightly to the right), with his cocked hat. Bungaree wears a blue naval jacket, but no gorget, though its chain can be seen. The colouring has given his face an unnatural-looking pinkish hue.

In 1831 Rodius began issuing lithographed portraits of the Aboriginal 'chiefs' and their 'queens', including Queen Gooseberry. His *Portraits of Aboriginal Kings*, six prints in a set priced at one guinea, was published in 1834 by J. G. Austin in Sydney. The *Sydney Herald* said the portraits reflected 'the highest credit on the talent and application of the Artist' and praised their 'extraordinary fidelity'.[8] The *Sydney Gazette* commented: 'Sets of these drawings would prove very acceptable present [*sic*] to friends in England'.[9] Included was Rodius' best known portrait, *KING BUNGAREE* (Plate 19). Several prints, on a range of paper types and colours, have survived and are now in the Mitchell and Dixson Libraries in Sydney and the National Library of Australia, Canberra.

This is a penetrating study of Bungaree in his later life. His expressive eyes stare keenly at the viewer with a rather arch and knowing look. His skin looks tough and leathery and the lines on his face are deeply etched, showing the effects of age and alcohol. Bungaree wears his familiar cocked hat and brass gorget over a blue naval jacket with a wide collar. The title wrongly states that Bungaree died in 1832 and adds 'Drawn from Life, 1831 and on Stone, 1834, by Chas. Rodius'. The hand-coloured version in the Nan Kivell Collection has a blue jacket and hat with gold highlights and gorget.

BUNGAREE (Fig. 44), 'Drawn on Stone by C. Pye' in London about 1831, is a mirror image of Rodius' *KING BUNGAREE*. There is no gorget, but its chain may be seen beneath Bungaree's jacket, which has a slightly different collar. The picture is captioned: 'This singular Countenance is an authentic Likeness from an original Drawing of the Chief of the Broka Bay Tribe, New South Wales, well known at Sidney'. The engraver may have been the artist Charles Pye of Birmingham or his son, also Charles (1777–1864), to whom he taught engraving. The Rex Nan Kivell Collection's hand-coloured print in the National Library of Australia, Canberra, makes Bungaree's cocked hat black and his jacket bright red, with gold buttons and neck chain.

It appears that these three lithographs derive from the one original, two pencil sketches, cut out and pasted on paper, titled in ink *King Bungaree 1829 Sydney* (Plate 16). This work, now in the Mitchell Library, Sydney, is attributed to Ambrose Wilson, who was tutor to the Forbes family and later caretaker at Judge Forbes' estate, Edenglassie, at Emu Plains.

This time we have the full-face portrait on the left and a left-face profile head at right. There is no evident chain or brass gorget, but Bungaree wears his cocked hat in both aspects. Here, surely, is the origin of Bungaree's steely gaze and hard, almost contemptuous expression in each of the Rodius lithographs, drawn 'from life'. We may make one of two possible conclusions: either the originals were drawn by Rodius in 1829 when Bungaree was still alive, or Rodius based his portraits on them. It is likely that the drawings were made by Rodius and came into Ambrose Wilson's possession while Rodius was teaching art to Judge Forbes' children.

Although Bungaree's mouth is open in the pencil sketch and the first Rodius lithograph, he does not appear to be missing the top tooth usually removed in initiation ceremonies of the Sydney-Broken Bay Aborigines. There is some similarity between the 1829 sketch of Bungaree and Lejeune's 1824 sketch (Fig. 33). Did Rodius see Lejeune's drawing after

Coquille returned to France in March 1825 and before his arrest in London? Unlikely—but possible.

Charles Rodius was granted a ticket of leave in February 1834 and a certificate of freedom in July 1841. In the following years he made his living in Sydney as an art teacher and portrait painter and from his lithographs of landscapes and Aborigines. He married twice. Rodius died at Liverpool Hospital on 9 April 1860.[10]

Oriental Dignity

A recently rediscovered watercolour and ink portrait, *Bungaree King of the Port Jackson Tribe Sydney* (Plate 17) has been attributed to artist and engraver John Carmichael. The painting came to light when it was sold to a private bidder at an auction at Sotheby's Fine Australian Paintings, Melbourne, on 17 April 1989.

Bungaree's cocked hat is pushed casually to the back of his head showing his wavy hair. The almost Oriental dignity of Bungaree's expression is enhanced by the colouring of his skin. His military jacket and gorget are not clearly shown as that part of the sketch has been blocked-in with squares to guide the artist. Although unfinished, this inspired portrait is just as technically sophisticated as those of Augustus Earle and Charles Rodius. Carmichael may have planned to issue a lithograph of Bungaree similar to his popular lithograph of *The Old Commodore, Billy Blue*, published by J. G. Austin.

William Dixson said he had never heard of 'any colour work' by John Carmichael. However, a watercolour portrait of Surveyor James Meehan has been attributed to the engraver.[11]

John Carmichael (1803–1857) arrived in Sydney on 28 October 1825 as a steerage passenger on the *Triton*, which sailed from Leith (Scotland) via Hobart Town. Carmichael, who

Fig. 45.

BARRACK
from George Street
John Carmichael, 1839.

Engraving.
Plate 23: Maclehose, J., *Picture of Sydney* . . . Sydney: J.
Maclehose, Hunter Street, 1839.

had served his apprenticeship in Edinburgh, earned his living in Sydney mainly as an engraver. He drew and engraved bookplates, bills, letterheads, advertisements, views and landscapes and painted miniature portraits to order.

In 1829, Sir Thomas Mitchell sought to employ John Carmichael in the Surveyor General's Department, but did not receive authorisation from the government. Years later, in 1851, Carmichael was paid the sum of £68 14 s. 0 d. by the department for engraving a map of New South Wales.[12]

At one time, Carmichael worked as a coach painter. He also engraved the copperplate for the New South Wales twopenny blue stamp (1850). Although the artist was thought to be deaf and dumb, as the handwritten note beside his portrait of Bungaree states, Carmichael advertised for pupils in drawing and engraving. John Carmichael died in Sydney on 27 July 1857.[13]

In his *Select Views of Sydney*, published in 1829, Carmichael included the figure of Bungaree and his people as part of his view *Sydney from the Parramatta Road* (Fig. 39). Bungaree, wearing a military jacket and plumed cocked hat, is seen, pointing a stick towards the campfire, while another Aborigine carries in a dead kangaroo. The scene is the present site of Railway Square. The printed caption reads: 'The last engraving is a view of Sydney from the south at the toll gate on the Parramatta road, where are represented a few of the homeless inhabitants of the forest accompanied by their Chief—Bungaree'.

Carmichael included a Bungaree-like figure in *Barrack from George Street* (Fig. 45), one of his engravings for *Picture of Sydney and Strangers Guide in New South Wales* (1838) by James Maclehose, but this is more likely to have been Bungaree's eldest son, known as 'Young Bungaree'.

Shadowy Profiles

Caricature enters the European images of Bungaree for the first time with the lithographic silhouettes of British artist and draughtsman William Henry Fernyhough (1809–49). Fernyhough succeeded William Romaine Govett as assistant surveyor and architect to New South Wales Surveyor General Major Sir Thomas Mitchell.

Bungaree had been dead and buried for more than five years when Fernyhough came to Sydney from Britain as a free man in 1836. As he was not able to make any 'life' sketches, Fernyhough's lithographs must have been based on the published portraits by Earle and Rodius. These black paper cut-out silhouettes appealed to the popular taste of the time for phrenology, whose practitioners claimed to be able to deduce the intelligence and character of a person by the shape of the subject's head.[14]

Fernyhough's *Twelve Profile Portraits of Aborigines of New South Wales* was published by J. G. Austin of Sydney in 1836 at a cost of 10 shillings and sixpence.

In *BUNGAREE, LATE CHIEF OF THE BROKEN BAY TRIBE SYDNEY* (Fig. 47), Bungaree assumes a cocky attitude, legs apart, left hand in his pocket and right hand holding a walking stick. Bungaree wears his familiar cocked hat, brass breastplate and a long-tailed uniform jacket, but any hint of former grandeur has faded; indeed he seems reduced even in stature. The face is merely a black outline. Fernyhough was a skilled draughtsman but his profile technique could not convey the character of his subject. The whole effect, heightened by the torn trousers and bare feet, is one of mockery. The original pen-and-ink-study for the lithograph (Fig. 46) is in the Dixson Library, Sydney. The hand-colouring

Fig. 46.

BUNGAREE.
LATE CHIEF OF THE BROKEN BAY TRIBE SYDNEY
William Henry Fernyhough, 1836.
Pen and ink sketch, 20.9 x 10cm.
Dixson Library, Sydney.

Fig. 47.

BUNGAREE.
LATE CHIEF OF THE BROKEN BAY TRIBE SYDNEY
William Henry Fernyhough, 1836.
Lithograph.
Fernyhough, W. H., A *series of twelve Profile portraits of Aborigines of New South Wales.* Sydney: J. G. Austin and Co., 1836.
Mitchell Library, Sydney.

in a copy of this lithograph in the Rex Nan Kivell Collection at the Australian National Library in Canberra is rather sloppy. Bungaree wears a blue cocked hat with gold braid decorations, a white shirt, red jacket and blue trousers.

Fernyhough's silhouette bust, *BUNGAREE, LATE CHIEF OF THE BROKEN BAY TRIBE* (Fig. 48), while showing Bungaree's facial features through bronze highlighting, is more like a sculpture or an eerie death mask than a portrait.

Many of Fernyhough's lithographs, including those of Bungaree and Gooseberry, were copied less expertly by William Nicholas (1809–54) and published in Sydney in his *Profiles, Aborigines* (1840). William Baker, a Sydney publisher, issued a pirated version of the Fernyhough portraits in the same year.

BUNGAREE.

LATE CHIEF OF THE BROKEN BAY TRIBE.

N. S. Wales.

Print.d & Publ.by J G Austin & Cº Nº 2 Bridge Street Sydney

Fig. 48.

BUNGAREE.   Sydney, J. G. Austin & Co.
LATE CHIEF OF THE BROKEN BAY TRIBE. N. S. WALES   Mitchell Library, Sydney.
William Henry Fernyhough, c. 1836.

Epilogue: Black Ulysses

Bungaree was flamboyant, intelligent and shrewd. He was an explorer, a go-between, a joker, a beggar, a mimic and a drunkard.

Judged by Homeric terms, he was a black hero of early Sydney. The young Aborigine who accompanied Matthew Flinders on his epic voyage around Australia fits the classic pattern of the hero in Greek mythology. Physically, he was strong, lean and active; mentally he was brave, alert and adventurous. His pronged spear seldom missed a fish. He sent his boomerang like a discus whirring and spinning to its target. His woomerah propelled his killing spear to a great distance. He was skilled at finding water and tracking humans or animals. He frequently shed his clothes to approach menacing groups of Aborigines, standing naked and unarmed between the opposing whites and blacks.

As the others on board HMS *Investigator* were British, Bungaree became the first Australian to circumnavigate the continent.

After his voyages Bungaree remained a warrior, often taking part with shield and spears in trials of strength and ritual punishment. He observed the religious beliefs of his people and kept the food taboo on stingrays. His eyes gleamed with excitement at the prospect of a corroboree or singing and dancing around the camp fire. He was powerful enough to order the punishment of an Aborigine who had murdered a woman.

In his later life, Bungaree had enough cunning to make humour and mimicry his weapons. Like Ulysses, he was a wily schemer, something of a con-man, or a 'master cheat' as Hyacinthe de Bougainville described him. He spoke English well and had a talent for mimicry. He wore his tattered uniform and old cocked hat with dignity and had the manners of a Regency fop. No visitor to Sydney could miss his cheerful grin. His bearing and uniform set him apart from the stereotyped image of the Aborigines.

Bungaree lived at Broken Bay and around the green shores of Port Jackson for about 50 years. In that time he saw his people dispossessed of their land and hunting grounds and their freedom to live their own way of life. He still preferred the bush to the white mens' houses and slept out at night under the open sky and the glittering stars of the Southern Hemisphere.

Bungaree could recall his friendship with Matthew Flinders and his playful cat Trim. He could look back through a line of transplanted British governors, navy and army men, from John Hunter to Sir Ralph Darling, who ruled the colony of New South Wales as it evolved from a convict settlement. He still wore the brass plate given to him by Lachlan Macquarie, who also gave Bungaree a fishing boat and made sure he was admitted to hospital when he was ill. Although he accepted Macquarie's gorget, Bungaree never laid aside his spear.

All heroes have their flaws. Bungaree's Achilles heel was alcohol. If the whites wished to call him 'King', he was ready to take advantage of it. So he met the foreign naval explorers and drank the health of many a ship's captain when he welcomed them to 'his' country. The hero, grown old, became a joker and mock 'King' of the Sydney Aborigines.

Sadly, by the 1820s the black peoples of the world were no longer judged by either Homeric terms or by Rousseau's philosophy as they had been until the eighteenth century. Bungaree's story is tragic, more so because it parallels the fate of so many of his people over the past 200 years.

On the eastern side of Port Jackson, below Bellevue Hill, there is a small bay with a narrow sandy beach fringed by a scrappy, untidy park running down a steep slope. In 1919, workmen there dug up a box which contained a cutting of Bungaree's obituary from the *Sydney Gazette* of 27 November 1830, stating that he would be 'interred at Rose Bay, beside the remains of his late Queen'.[1]

Nearby, carved into the rocks next to Captain John Piper's villa, there was once a gallery of the figures of Aboriginal men, whales, fish and kangaroos. Most of these images, like the villa, have been destroyed, but the outline of a whale remains under the garage floorboards of one of the fashionable homes at Point Piper. The foreshores of Rose Bay are crowded with yachts and boats at anchor. The high bluff of Georges Head can be seen in the distance past Shark Island. Somewhere in this greenery next to the shimmering harbour is the unmarked final resting place of King Bungaree.

Appendix I
The Name Bungaree

Most people today tend to pronounce Bungaree as BUNG-a-REE, with a hard accent on the 'g'. However, the majority of recorded variations in the spelling of his name point to a pronounciation sounding something like 'Boun-gurry', in which the first syllable is spoken softly and the remainder slurred but evenly stressed. Perhaps the word 'Boong', a perjorative name for an Aborigine, is derived from his name.

BANGARE	Robert Brown 1802
BANGAREE	Lieutenant James Grant 1801
BONG-REE	David Collins 1799
BONGAREE	Matthew Flinders 1802–3; Robert Brown 1802–3; Allan Cunningham 1818; Pavel Novosil'sky 1820; Robert Burford 1829
BONGARREE	Phillip Parker King 1827
BONGARRI	René-Primàvere Lesson 1838
BONGARIE	Robert Brown 1802
BONGARRY	Charles Rodius 1844
BONGARU	Philip Gidley King 1804
BONJARE	Robert Brown 1802
BONJAREE	Robert Campbell 1838
BONJARY	Dr John Harris 1801
BOON-GA-REE	P. P. King 1819
BOONGAREE	Matthew Flinders 1802; Lachlan Macquarie 1815/22; *Sydney Gazette* 1815/27/28/29; P. P. King 1817/21; Captain Faddei Fadeevich Bellingshausen 1820; Rev. Lancelot Threlkeld 1828; Robert Burford 1829
BOONGARIE	George Howe 1818; Captain Bellingshausen 1820; Rev. William Walker 1821; Rev. John McGarvie 1826; Hyacinthe de Bougainville 1827; Lachlan Macquarie 1828; *Sydney Gazette* 1830; *The Australian* 1830
BOONGARREE	P. P. King 1817; Peter Cunningham 1827; *Sydney Gazette* 1826/29
BOONGARRY	*Historical Records of Australia* 1917
BOONGARY	Lachlan Macquarie 1815
BOONGREE	David Collins 1799
BOUNGAREE	Lieutenant Charles Menzies 1804; P. P. King 1817; *Sydney Gazette* 1827
BOUNGARI	Hyacinthe de Bougainville 1827; Jules Dumont d'Urville 1834

BUGGARY	Jules Lejeune 1824
BUNGAREE	Dr Joseph Arnold 1815; Lachlan Macquarie 1816; Henry Ebsworth 1825; *Sydney Gazette* 1826/27/30; Peter Cunningham 1827; Dr Roger Oldfield 1828; John Carmichael 1829; Charles Rodius 1829/30/34; *Sydney Monitor* 1829; Augustus Earle 1826/30; Robert Dawson 1830; James F. O'Connell 1836; Charles Dickens (*All the Year Round*) 1859
BUNGARI	J. Dumont d'Urville 1830
BUNGARIE	Rev. John McGarvie 1829; *Sydney Gazette* 1829
BUNGARREE	*The Australian* 1828
BUNGARRIE	Alexander Berry 1838
BUNGARY	Samuel Smith 1802; *Sydney Gazette* 1804, Dr John Dunmore Lang 1834
BUNGERY	Colonel William Paterson 1801; Peter Good 1802
BUNJAREE	Captain James Wallis 1821

Appendix II
Picturesque Voyage

Jules Dumont d'Urville: *Voyage Pittoresque Autour Du Monde, Resumé général des voyages de découvertes*, Paris, 1834–35.

Jules Dumont d'Urville left an observant and lively description of Bungaree in *Voyage pittoresque autour du monde*, which became a French bestseller of the period. The two-volume book was published in Paris in 1834, six years after Dumont d'Urville had discovered the wreck and relics of La Pérouse's ship *Astrolabe* at Vanikoro in the Santa Cruz islands. It includes a general summary of voyages of discovery since Magellan. Although it draws on Dumont d'Urville's own adventures and observations during his years of exploration, it is, to a small degree, a work of fiction. By using this device the narrator is able to visit far-flung exotic places and describe them vividly in the style of a novelist.

While in Sydney, our storyteller, a passenger on board the brig *Kanguroo* (Kangaroo), meets a young English doctor called Harry, and asks him to be his guide and mentor. The story is set in 1832, two years after Bungaree's death. The following extract (Vol.2, pp. 292–4, translated by Leslie Lino) begins when the two men meet Bungaree:

On our return to Sydney, as we were approaching our hotel, we saw around the door about half a dozen people, one of whom was most noticeable by his hat ornamented with a twisted fringe and topped with a long black plume, with a large blue dress coat with frogs and loops, rather similar to those worn by senior English officers; and by his boots and trousers, the whole extremely dirty and almost in rags. On his chest shone a large copper plaque. This man's companions wore scarcely more than a torn shirt and holey drawers. 'What are these beggars doing here?' I asked Harry, 'and that great ruffian who seems to be their leader?' Harry burst out laughing. 'What!' he said 'Don't you know our King Boungari?' I shook my head.

'Boungari is the chief of the tribe to whom the territory of Sydney used to belong. It is you, doubtless, whom he is coming to see. No foreigner of some distinction arrives in Sydney unless he believes himself bound to greet him in order to receive a present. It is a burden on the foreigner, but it has its interesting side and besides it is not very costly. Boungari is easily pleased with a little gin and brandy. Look: there by his side, in that tattered robe, his noble and majestic spouse and behind them five or six gentlemen who constitute the principal officers and the most courageous leaders of the Gouia-Gal [Gweagal]. Doubtless, Boungari was away on the arrival of the *Kanguroo*; but today he has made up for his shortcomings; he is attending to his duties.'

Indeed, scarcely had we set foot on land than the illustrious Boungarie advanced towards me, raised his hat and made me a succession of deep bows which I gravely returned. Then, in very bad English, he welcomed me, insinuating rather shrewdly that as king of the country he had grounds for counting on my generosity.

Harry having prompted me, I lent a deaf ear. Then S. M. [Son Majesté] stated his request more earnestly and staked his claim for a bottle of brandy (*eau-de-vie*). 'Without a doubt.' I said to the great Boungari, 'one bottle for you; but not today, tomorrow'.

At this tardy answer, you should have seen the upheaval that took place on the face of my savage. There was no longer a smooth-talking suppliant, but rather a woeful and sullen sulkiness: 'No, massa,' he said in his jargon, '*no tamara; derekle, brandy, derekle*' (No, sir, not tomorrow, at once, some brandy at once).

I did not wish to vex this worthy brandy lover any longer, inasmuch as he could be useful to me for information on the customs of the natives before colonisation. I offered him a piastre [one Spanish dollar]. This unexpected generosity produced a dramatic turn of events. Beaming with joy, Boungari began to caper, alone at first, then making a signal to his wife and his troupe, he danced with everybody on a grand scale, making the most remarkable picture that one could see. This dance consisted of a sort of march which went along by leaps and bounds which were sudden and weighty, like the kangaroo running. Next, coming up to me and shaking my hand with the greatest cordiality, he declared that he and his wife were entirely at my service. I took advantage of this, with the help of Harry who understood him very well, by putting him through a kind of interrogation; to which he replied in his gibberish.

We went up to my rooms, to which I denied entry to all but Boungari and his wife, and so as to dispose my new friend to unlimited trust, I ordered him a glass of brandy which he swallowed without turning a hair, but not without giving each of us a deep bow, bending his head almost to the ground. In spite of his greed for brandy, he was careful to leave about a finger of it in the bottom of the glass, destined for his majestic better half who swallowed it as calmly as if it had been milk. Boungari then replied as agreeably as possible to my companion's questions.

We learned that, at this moment, the noble chief was absorbed by cares of the greatest importance. It concerned a kind of congress to settle for ever the differences existing between the diverse neighbouring tribes of Sydney. It was also the time when the Kerredais [Koradgees] had to perform the *gna-loung* [initiation] ceremony. This ceremony consists of taking out the front tooth of several young boys of the requisite age. Preparations for these two solemn ceremonies, the choice of sites for the scene of action and the numerous formalities which were linked to them, had already necessitated several meetings and conferences among the chiefs. King Boungari had been obliged to absent himself from his capital, Sydney, to go and settle various details with his neighbours. The brandy acting on the tongues of my savages, they spouted forth marvellous things about the *gna-loung*, so that I evinced the desire to be present at one or other ceremony. Boungari offered to take me there himself and I accepted eagerly. As it was now late, we sent off the two Majesties half drunk with the brandy they had consumed.

When our Australians had left, I turned to Harry. 'Doctor,' I said 'These are stupid brutes of the first degree. For forty years they have lived alongside European civilisation and they have remained as savage and stupid as ever. Brandy is the only thing they have understood.'

'You are right,' Harry replied. 'These beings derive from the animal as much as from man, however much one has tried to refine and humanise them. Nothing has done it, neither the philanthropic intentions of the colonists, nor the preaching of the missionaries. Everything has been tried to no purpose; the wild and roving instinct always has the upper hand.'

With the purpose of leading them into a more settled state, Governor Macquarie had a quite suitable small cottage built, at the gates of Sydney, surrounded by a garden. He put it at the disposition of the tribe which lives in the vicinity of Port Jackson. It was useless. The garden remained fallow, and they condescended to come from time to time to shelter beneath the roof of the house, without wishing to renounce their wandering life. One day an Englishman asked Boungari how they valued houses: '*Mari boudjiri, massa, poss i rain*', replied the savage 'Very good sir, supposing it rains'). The same Governor had founded, some distance from Parramatta, a free school for the education of young natives. The lure of easy, tasty food attracted some there at first, but soon, disliking the regular attendance demanded of them, they preferred the precarious and arduous existence of their compatriots to the sedentary life. Today the establishment is almost moribund.

These savages, so coarse and stupid in appearance have, however, an unquestionable intelligence. A very droll flash of memory is told about Boungari. Ten or twelve years ago, he accompanied Captain King on his reconnaissance of the northern part of Australia, and on this occasion, showed enthusiasm and dispatch. His presence was often useful because of the relations they wished to establish with the natives. As interpreter, he could do nothing: for the Australian idiom varies at very short distances. Thus, the dialect of the north of New Holland has no connection with that of New South Wales. On putting into Timor, Boungari having gone ashore, made a call on a merchant to drink a glass of gin; he drank and offered a piastre in payment, knowing well that he should be given small change in return for it. The shopkeeper, not having the exact change, took the piastre, saying that he would repay the balance another time. However, the ship having set sail, Boungari was forced to leave the credit. Nevertheless, he did not forget it, for the following year, the ship having put in again at the island, Boungari went off boldly towards the gin seller and asked him for spirits for the rest of his money.

As he had promised, Boungari came, on the day of the festival, to fetch me at my hotel. About nine o'clock in the morning, strange and piercing cries announced the arrival of his band. I went to the basement window and saw coming a dozen savages, painted white, black and red, at the head of whom Boungari walked solemnly. The latter came up alone to my room. He renewed his greetings, but with a more deliberate and much less free and easy air than the day before. He seemed imbued with the dignity of a tribal chief and with the important function he was going to fulfil. There was no longer anything about him of the humble beggar, who the day before was asking for money and gin. Cleaned up, his face and body daubed irregularly with red ochre, he had truly a better manner; he seemed twenty years younger. I offered him a glass of rum, but he drank only half of it, indicating to me that he should take care of his head because of the contests he was going to undertake. Then he urged me to hurry, for his warriors were waiting for him and seemed to be growing impatient with the idea of being the last to enter the lists.

So Harry and I followed, a few steps away from the wild troupe. It was made up of about twenty men, who marched quite peaceably while in the town, but once in the countryside, began their parades, sometimes rushing forward and winding through the bush, sometimes stopping suddenly to perform a national dance. Thus gambolling and leaping, they reached a small plateau which overlooks the road from Port Jackson to Botany Bay. This was a vast space, cleared of shrubs, which seemed marvelously set out for the jousts of the Australians. Already a number of tribes were camped in the surrounding bush. When we arrived at the field of combat, Boungari's troupe performed certain parades, the purpose of which seemed to be to challenge their enemies and to excite themselves to battle. These preliminaries accomplished, they withdrew, yielding their place to others who did the same thing.

Soon, at a signal, all the tribes came out of the bush and made their way towards the arena in groups of fifteen or twenty men, each one armed with spears, shields, war clubs and *womerangs* [woomerahs]. To serve as our guide, Boungari had placed beside us one of his subjects who had been prevented from taking his part in the affray because of a serious wound. He indicated to us the names of the tribes who were coming into the lists: Sydney, Parramatta, Emu, Botany Bay, Windsor, Illawarra, Marrigong, Murrumbidji [Murrumbidgee] and a crowd of others whose names escape me. All the warriors were adorned with red, white and black designs. Each tribe was distinguished by the shape and colour of its body paintings. Amongst all these warriors, I noticed mainly those of Marrigong, almost all of whom were small men, but vigorous and agile, whose plump and well-proportioned limbs contrasted remarkably with the emaciated and slender figures from the coast. Doubtless they owed this advantage to more abundant and substantial food. The decorations on their chests, representing coats-of-mail, added a great deal to their warlike attitude.

The action began towards midday. A young, fierce-looking man took up a position in the middle of the arena. Alone and naked, he was armed with only a narrow, oblong wooden shield. This champion was well known: in a single combat which had taken place some time before between himself and a member of a neighbouring tribe, he had felled his antagonist in a cowardly manner, just as he was picking up his war club. It was an act which cried out for vengeance. The victor did not wait, but fled into the bush. Tired of this wretched, wandering life he reappeared and offered himself for a public punishment. One after the other, five friends of the dead man let fly six spears at him from a distance of about 15 metres. This was the first test. He acquitted himself admirably, parrying each blow with his shield and a quick movement of his body. The second trial was to avoid the long spears thrown at one time and on different occasions. The condemned man avoided two flights of spears, but on the third a spear hit him in the thigh. A general shout followed this mishap; the friends of the wounded man intervened and, although the champions of death wished to push their vengeance further, it was decided that the reparation was sufficient. The wounded man withdrew among his people and had his wounds tended.

After this first act, five women appeared and were placed in a half circle, each furnished with a short stick. Then three men arrived unexpectedly and stood a little to one side, each one holding a shield. All these individuals were collectively accused by a neighbouring tribe. The punishment of the women consisted of receiving a certain number of blows on the head from a stick; which for four of them the executors were content to simulate, for they merely presented their sticks in front of their foreheads while the men hit the sticks with their clubs. The fifth did not get off so cheaply: she held her stick out well like the others, but avoiding the parry, the executor gave her such a violent blow on the chest that she was knocked down. Several times she fell like this and got up again. This woman, we were told, was much more seriously incriminated than her companions.

Next they passed on to the men. About twelve natives placed themselves fifteen or twenty paces from them and launched successive spears at them which were fended off with the greatest skill. These shafts were aimed, however, with remarkable skill. More than one buried itself an inch or two into the bark shields, while the others fell to the ground thirty paces further on. One person, posted near the accused, sent back the spears to their owners. At other times the men being punished sent them back themselves, adding a few mocking remarks about the clumsiness of the throwers. These men thus submitted, without accident, to a volley of about fifty spears, after which they were absolved of the accusation made against them . . .

[The description of the combats continues for some pages]

A fortnight had elapsed since my arrival in Sydney. I had profited by it: I had visited the whole colony and chance had given me the opportunity to be present at several native ceremonies. I was prepared to leave when Powell came to tell me that the *Kanguroo* was ready to set sail for Tasmania. I said goodbye to Harry and embarked on the 15th of January, 1832. A few hours later, the light brig was on course to the south and once more skirting the Australian coast.

Appendix III
'The Rum Cove'

James F. O'Connell, *A residence of eleven years in New Holland and the Caroline Islands: Being the adventures of James F. O'Connell, Edited from his verbal narration.* B. B. Mussey, Boston, 1836, pp. 29–31:

The pilot boarded us outside the heads; the next visiter was a much more interesting and august personage,—no less than KING BUNGAREE, of flash memory, by descent, ratified by H. B. M's government, chief of the Sydney Cove blacks, boarding officer and official welcomer and usher of new comers to Botany Bay. He paddled alongside of us in a whale-boat, for his safety in which, all riddled as it was, he had the sufficient guaranty that the boat 'carried Caesar'. His Bungaree Majesty's coat was of approved texture and quality, inasmuch as it had served a long apprenticeship to an English corporal, before falling into his hands. Upon his neck was suspended the order and insignia of his nobility,—a plate which might have been gold, but was brass, bearing the inscription,

'BUNGAREE,
KING OF SYDNEY COVE.'

Bungaree, like the ancient Pharaoh of the Egyptians, is the hereditary title of the royal family. His Majesty's pantaloons were of similar extraction with his coat; and as for shoes or sandals, it were sacrilege to suppose that the royal feet of the House of Bungaree need such plebeian defences. His head was surmounted with a cocked hat of magnificent dimensions, in which waved, and swam, and flaunted in air, a marital plume; the dependent feather's feathers of which kissed his sable cheeks, giving and receiving lustre. The brightness of darkness of his face, who shall describe? and who in fitting colours paint the glory of his suite, the tribe of Bungaree? The fair representatives of St Giles, Wapping, St Catherine's Lane, Ratcliffe High Way, Winnifield Bay, and St George's Fields [women convicts on board, characterised as prostitutes], entertaining high ideas of royalty, stood all abashed at the magnificence of the monarch, of whose fame the gossip of five month's passage had possessed them. In silver tones, their queries and comments rose in exquisite confusion, as they crowded round his Majesty of Port Jackson. 'The rum cove of this vile is up to lushing max, like a Billingsgate fish-monger.' [The king of this place drinks gin, &c.] 'The cove's kicksies [Trowsers] is rayther seedy.' ''His kelp [Hat] and his tug [Coat], stewed down, would fill the doctor's coppers [Cook's kettle] with soup'; with thousands of other observations, more various than edifying. King Bungaree, who is indeed better entitled to the rank than the English to his land, deigned no notice of the gadding women, but proceeded aft, to announce himself to the officers, and demand of them, in addition to the 'max', which he had received of course, the customary tribute. Even royalty must submit to disagreeables and King Bungaree was ordered away, upon the arrival on board of Dr Bowman, quarantine physician, and F. A. Healey, Esq., Superintendent.

The Tattooed Man

This tale of the 'rum cove' of Sydney is told by a seafaring character every bit as colourful as Bungaree himself. When James F. O' Connell (1808–54) appeared at the Lion Circus in New York in 1835, he was the first tattooed man to be exhibited in a public show in the United States of America.

A former sailor of Irish origin, O' Connell claimed that the blue, black and red patterns on his arms were acquired during four years spent as a captive after being shipwrecked at Ponape or Ascension, one of the Caroline Islands in the Pacific Ocean north of Papua New Guinea. Billed as the 'Celebrated Tattooed Man', O'Connell appeared on stage all over the United States with showman P. T. Barnum. He danced the Irish jig and the sailor's hornpipe and brought clog dancing to North America.

O'Connell had many imaginative stories to tell in his a book, *A residence of eleven years in New Holland and the Caroline Islands*, published in Boston in August 1836.

It seems, however, that the person known as James F. O'Connell sprang into being at the same time as the Tattooed Man. It was not his real name. There is no verifiable record of anyone by that name either being born in Dublin in 1808, as he claims, or being in the crews of the various ships he mentions. It is likely that O'Connell was a either a runaway convict from New South Wales or a sailor who deserted his ship and had changed his name to evade recapture and return to Australia.

By his own account, James O'Connell sailed from Ireland to Liverpool as a boy to join his parents in a travelling circus in which his mother was a horseback rider and his father a costumer for a male horse rider. After learning a few tumbling tricks, O'Connell says he shipped as a cabin boy at the age of 11 aboard the convict transport *Phoenix* to Port Jackson, where he arrived in 1820. This is just the first problem in what scholar Saul H. Riesenberg characterises as 'a maze of exaggerations, anachronisms, improbabilities, and outright fabrications, commingled with thoroughly accurate and original observations'. There is no record of the ship *Phoenix* in Port Jackson in 1820. However, the convict transport *Phoenix* left London in November 1821 and arrived in Sydney on 7 June 1822 after landing 182 prisoners at Hobart Town in Van Diemen's Land. Another convict transport, *Phoenix II*, landed 202 prisoners at Hobart after leaving Portsmouth on 6 August 1824. After running aground on the Sow and Pigs reef just inside Sydney Heads this ship was moored in Lavender Bay for many years as a prison hulk. The *Sydney Gazette* of Wednesday 31 December 1826 reported that a vessel called the *Phoenix* left Dublin on 29 August 1826 and arrived in Sydney on 27 December 1826 with 189 male prisoners.

To cloud matters further, O'Connell says 'his' *Phoenix* carried 200 female convicts, who were disembarked in Sydney.

The facts throw much doubt on O' Connell's story, the name of the ship on which he sailed and its date of arrival in Sydney—which must have been after 1824 and possibly as late as 1826. However, the bare facts in his description of Bungaree are accurate enough when compared with other contemporary accounts. On the other hand, the story may be a complete fabrication as all this material could have been cobbled together, using Peter Cunningham's *Two Years in New South Wales* (1827), from which the author has borrowed material on Aboriginal religious beliefs, and a work such as a *Classical Dictionary of the Vulgar Tongue*, which explained the 'cant' or 'flash' criminal language, first published in London in 1788 and again in 1811.

Dr James Bowman, who had been a Royal Navy surgeon, was principal surgeon at Sydney Hospital from 1819 to 1827 and afterwards inspector of colonial hospitals until 1836. Frederick Augustus Hely (Healey) was appointed superintendent of convicts in January 1823.

O'Connell's catalogue of adventures records that he spent six years in New South Wales and accompanied Surveyor General John Oxley (1781–1828) on an exploration of the Wellington Valley. In 1822 he was on a whaler, the *Cape Packet*, wrecked in northern Australia, and then took nine months to return to Sydney overland. In 1826, he claims, he was shipwrecked on the *John Bull* and held captive for four years in the Caroline Islands. Circus tricks and lively performances of 'Garry Owen' and other jigs saved his skin. He was tattooed in native fashion by a chief's daughter whom he married. He escaped and was thrown into gaol in the Philippines from which he escaped again, this time to China. He took ship to North America, arriving in New York in 1835.

O'Connell's book was 'edited from his verbal narration' by 'H.H.W.' identified by Riesenberg as Horatio Hastings Weld, a Boston writer, printer and newspaper editor who wrote on maritime subjects. The copy of *A residence of eleven years* . . . in the Mitchell Library, Sydney, once belonged to the library's founder James Mitchell. It is a tiny book of 256 pages, bound in the original green cloth covers embossed with leaves and flowers, with *O'Connell's Adventures* printed in gilt letters, surrounding a globe on the spine.

James O'Connell, the Tattooed Man, died in New Orleans on 29 January 1854 from the effects of chemicals used to produce electricity for stage lighting.

Notes

Chapter 1: Images of Bungaree

1. *Dictionary of National Biography* [DNB] (1885:3: 209).
2. Hyde, Ralph. *Panoramania!*, London, (1988: 57–64).
3. See *The entrance of Port Jackson, and part of the town of Sydney* (three engraved aquatints), c. 1821, Mitchell Library [ML] Sydney.
4. DNB (1886: 8: 301).
5. Burford (1829).
6. Hackforth-Jones (1980:149).
7. *Australian*, 10 February 1827.
8. Fox (1978: 27–8); Smith (1988:142–3).
9. Oldfield (1827: 14).
10. Richardson, ALS to Rev. Samuel Marsden, 4 April 1829.
11. *Australian Dictionary of Biography* [ADB] (1966:177); *Bibliography of Bungaree* Canberra, A.C.T. AIATSIS (1989); Cunningham (1966: 30–1).
12. *Sydney Gazette* [SG] 4 February 1815 (p. 1); Howe (1820: 74).
13. Burford (1829: 9) follows the description of Peter Cunningham in *Two Years in New South Wales* (1827).
14. See Neville (1991: 37–40).
15. Buscombe (1978:49–68; 191–201); Hackforth-Jones (1980: 7).
16. SG 21 October1826 (p. 2); Bonyhady (1987: 17–19).
17. Buscombe (1978: 192); PXN 685, ML. *Notes on the Lithographic Portrait of Bungaree* (1987); Wantrup (1987: 293).
18. *Monitor* 11 August 1826: 98 (not 16 June as in Wantrup [1987: 294]).
19. SG 21 October 1826 (p. 2).
20. SG 23 August1826 (p. 2). Richard Neville comments (1991:40: footnote 14) '50s is surely a typographical error for 5 shillings'.
21. SG 27 November 1830 (p. 2).
22. SG 6 December 1826 (p. 2).
23. Bonyhady (1987:17;19).
24. McGarvie, *Diary* Friday 27 October 1826.
25. SG 30 July 1829 (p.3).
26. T305, Curator's Report, National Library of Australia, Canberra, 3 April 1987.
27. Buscombe (1978: 194 a); Wantrup (1987: 294).
28. *Notes on the Lithographic Portrait of Bungaree*, 12 June 1987.

Chapter 2: A Boy at Broken Bay

For Aboriginal social life in the Sydney area (canoes, food gathering, shelter, initiation, languages, etc.) see Kohen and Lampert (1987), Turbet (1989) and First Fleet diarist cited.
1. Beaglehole (1955: 313).
2. Mulvaney, D. J. 'The End of the Beginning', in *Australians to 1788* (1987:75–6).
3. Tench (1961: 47); McCarthy (1938: 401–9); SMH 10 June 1958.
4. Mahroot (Boatswain), 'Report from the Select Committee on the Condition of Aborigines'. NSW Legislative Council Votes and Proceedings, Sydney (1845: 5)
5. Worgan, *Journal* 9 March 1788; Hunter (1793: 96).
6. Collins (1975:15).
7. Bradley, *Journal* 2 March 1788.
8. Phillip (1970: 41).
9. Worgan, *Journal* 9 March 1788.
10. Phillip (1970: 43–5).
11. Stanner (1977: 174).
12. Historical Records of New South Wales [HRNSW] (2: 124–36). Phillip to Sydney, 15 May 1788.
13. Worgan, *Journal* 9 March 1788.
14. HRNSW (2:131); Collins (1975: 370).
15. Collins (1975: 24–5).
16. HRNSW (2: 133). Phillip to Sydney.
17. Bradley, *Journal* October 1788.
18. Tench (1961:139–43).
19. Tench (1961: 146).
20. Collins (1975: 496).
21. Tench (1961:149–50).
22. Hunter, *Journal* 6 June 1789.
23. Hunter, *Journal* 15 June, 1789.
24. Tench (1961:153).
25. Collins (1975: 497).
26. Collins (1975: 2: 161–2).
27. SG 4 February 1815 (p.1).
28. Macquarie, *Journal* 11 February 1822.
29. Collins (1975: 453).
30. Quoted in Sadleir (1883: 39).
31. See Capell (1970: 20–2).
32. Bennett (1968:14).
33. Wallis (1821: 40).
34. Grant (1803:150–1).
35. Kohen and Lampert (1987: 345–48); Ross (1988).
36. Bellingshausen (1945: 337).
37. King (1827: xxxix).

Chapter 3: Sailing with Matthew Flinders

For Matthew Flinders life and voyages see Flinders' *Terra Australis* (1814), Scott (1914); ADB (1966: 389–91) and Austin (1964).
1. Trevelyan (1964: 2: 157–8); Scott (1914: 4–5;9).

2. Hughes, T. S. *Matthew Flinders.* Erskineville, N.S.W. (1984: 10).
3. ADB (1966: 389).
4. Scott (1914: 4–6); Flinders Petrie (1979: 25).
5. *Naval Chronicle* 32 (1814: 178).
6. Flinders Petrie (1979: 25); Scott (1914: 16).
7. Scott (1914: 18–19).
8. ADB (1966: 389); Austin (1964: 18–21).
9. Perry (1979: 55).
10. ADB (1966: 389); Austin (1964: 22–3); Scott (1914: 83).
11. Bradley, *Journal* November 1789; Tench (1961:159–61).
12. Brodsky, Isidore, *Bennelong Profile* Broadway, Sydney (1973: 65).
13. Austin (1964: 22).
14. Flinders (1814: xcvii); Scott (1914: 86).
15. Flinders (1814: xcvii–ciii); Scott (1914: 87–93).
16. Scott (1914: 94–5).
17. Flinders (1814: cvi–cxx); Collins

(1975: 2: 66–8); Scott (1914: 123–32).
18. Collins (1975: 2: 103–39); Flinders (1814: cxxxviii); Scott (1914: 123–32).
19. Scott (1914: 146–56).
20. Banks Papers (vii) 87. Hunter to Banks, 1 June 1799.
21. Collins (1975: 2: 85).
22. Banks (1963: 2: 63).
23. Beaglehole (1955: 319).
24. Banks Papers (vii:88–9) Hunter to Banks. 4 July 1799.
25. Flinders (1814: cxciv).
26. Narrative of 'The little sloop' draws on Flinders (1814: cxciii–ccii) and Collins (1975: 2: 161–80).
27. Flinders (1977: 20–1).
28. Tench (1961:160–1).
29. Welsby (1977: Preface).
30. Austin (1964: 26); Scott (1914: 163).
31. Banks Papers (vi: 119; 121; 129). Paterson to Banks, 18, 20, 22 February 1800.
32. Austin (1964: 30–2); ADB (1966: 52–5).

33. Austin (1964: 28–30).
34. ADB (1966: 389).
35. Flinders (1814: 4).
36. Scott (1914: 168; 184–6).
37. Scott (1914: 186).
38. Collins (1975:128–30).
39. Martin, James, 'Memorandums'. Bentham Papers, British Library, London (1791: 33–6).
40. Collins (1975: 2: 35.)
41. Grant (1803:149)
42. HRA (3: 60–2). Grant to King, 16 December, 1800.
43. Grant (1803:150–5).
44. Harris to P. G. King, 25 June 1801.
45. HRNSW (4: 416).
46. Collins (2: 239).
47. HRA (3: 172).
48. ML PXD388, fol. 2. Lewin, J. W. 'A sketch . . . on the banks of the Paterson's River, New South Wales...', 1801.
49. HRA (3: 168–9).

Chapter 4: Voyage of the Investigator

1. ML C218: 93–4. Bligh, W., Letters. Flinders (1814: 5–6); Scott (1914: 195).
2. Flinders (1814: 6; 12–14).
3. Flinders (1814: 8–12).
4. Flinders (1814: 15); Scott (1914: 178–80).
5. Flinders (1814: 19).
6. Brosse (1983: 99).
7. Flinders (1814: 60–1); White, Isobel M., 'The Birth and Death of a Ceremony.', *Aboriginal History* 4 (1) (1980): 33–36.
8. Flinders (1814: 185–7).
9. Brosse (1983: 100–3).
10. Flinders (1814: 188–90).
11. HRNSW (4: 269). Murray to King; Flinders (1814: 211–12).
12. Flinders (1814: 226–35).
13. Brosse (1983: 103).
14. ADB (1966: 177).
15. ML A3072: 60. Suttor, George, Memoirs (typescript). Mackaness, G., *Memoirs of George Suttor*, Sydney, (1948: 40).
16. Edwards (1981: 78–9).
17. Franklin, John., Letter to his sister, 19 October 1802.
18. Smith *Journal* 20 July 1802.
19. *Naval Chronicle* (July–December 1809: 385–90; 477–81); Scott (1914: 256–9).

20. ML CY Safe 1/24: 492 (Flinders Journal); HRNSW (4: 755). Flinders to King, 18 May 1802.
21. Flinders (1814: 235).
22. Collins (1975: 2: 48); SG 8 September 1821 (p.2).
23. Collins (1975: App. V1:483).
24. Flinders, Corres. (1925: 46–9).
25. Flinders, Corres. (1925: 50–2).
26. Flinders (1814: 2: 10).
27. Smith Journal 30 July 1802.
28. Edwards (1981: 82).
29. Brown, *Journal* 31 July 1802.
30. Flinders (1814: 2: 210).
31. Brown, *Journal* 31 July 1802.
32. Flinders (1814: 2: 11).
33. Edwards (1981: 82).
34. Brown, *Journal* 5 August 1802.
35. Flinders (1814: 2: 20).
36. Edwards (1981: 89).
37. Brown, Journal 30 August 1802.
38. Brown, Journal 9 September 1802.
39. Flinders (1814: 2: 87–8).
40. Flinders (1814: 2: 97). Nanbaree therefore did not circumnavigate the continent on this voyage as asserted in Bennett (1968: 13).
41. Flinders, Corres. (1925: 59).
42. Flinders (1814: 2: 104).
43. Flinders (1814: 2: 110).
44. Flinders (1814: 2: 135).
45. Flinders (1814: 2: 126).

46. Flinders (1814: 2: 135–6).
47. Flinders (1814: 2: 141–3).
48. Flinders (1814: 144).
49. Flinders (1814: 2: 188–9).
50. McCarthy, F. D., 'The Cave Paintings of Groote Eylandt and Chasm Island: American-Australian Scientific Expedition to Arnhem Land': Records (1960: 297–414).
51. Flinders (1814: 2: 196–8).
52. Edwards (1981: 112).
53. Brown, *Journal* 3 February 1803.
54. Flinders (1814: 2: 205–8).
55. Edwards (1981: 115).
56. Flinders (1814: 2: 208–10).
57. Edwards (1981: 116).
58. Flinders (1814: 2: 214).
59. Flinders (1814: 228–32).
60. Brown, *Journal* 17 February 1803.
61. HRNSW (2: 192). Phillip to Sydney, 28 September 1788.
62. Flinders (1814: 2: 238–9).
63. Brown, *Journal* 3 March 1803.
64. Flinders (1814: 2: 250).
65. Flinders (1814: 2: 272).
66. Flinders (1814: 276).
67. Flinders (1814: 2: 250).
68. Flinders (1814: 2: 279).
69. Flinders (1814: 2: 295–361); Brosse (1983: 112–14).

Chapter 5: 'The Most Intelligent of that Race'

1. SG 11 March 1804 (pp.1–3).
2. British Library [BL]. M.S. Royal 18E. i, ff. 172; 175. Quoted in Trevelyan (1964: 38; 279).
3. NK1127. Rex Nan Kivell Collection, National Library of Australia, Canberra.
4. SG 18 March 1804 (p. 2).
5. SG 25 March 1804 (pp.1; 4); 1 April 1804 (p. 2).
6. SG 29 April 1804 (p. 4).
7. HRA (5: 413–4).
8. HRA (5: 415–6).
9. SG 9 September 1804 (p. 2).
10. Smith *Journal* 30 July 1802.
11. Not Willeemarin, who speared Governor Phillip at Manly in September 1790.
12. SG 23 December 1804 (pp. 2–3).
13. Leubbers, R. A., 'Ancient Boomerangs Discovered in South Australia', *Nature* (1975) (253: 39).
14. Beaglehole, J. C., *The Endeavour Journal of Joseph Banks*. Sydney (1963: 2: 53).
15. White (1790: 292).
16. Phillip (1970: 77).
17. Tench (1961: 50).
18. HRNSW (5: App. A: 748–823; and footnote: 771). See Barrallier, F., *Journal of the Expedition into the Interior of New South Wales* [1802], Melbourne (1975).
19. Kohen, J. L., *A Dictionary of the Dharug Language*, Blacktown and District Historical Society (1987: 7).
20. SG 6 November 1808 (p. 2).
21. Welsby (1937: 116–26).
22. Flinders (1814: 2: 319).
23. Welsby (1937: 116–26).
24. Bennett (1968: 8).
25. Bennett (1968: 13).
26. Bennett (1968: 13).
27. HRA (5: 431–9). Flinders to King, 8 August 1804.
28. Clarke, C. M. H., *A History of Australia*, Melbourne (1962: 1: 174).
29. Flinders (1814: 2: 362–438).
30. Flinders, Diary, 25 October 1805. Quoted in Perry (1979: 58).
31. Flinders Papers. Quoted in Baker, Sidney J., *My Own Destroyer*, Sydney (1962: 133).
32. Flinders (1814: 2: 439).
33. Flinders (1814: 478–496); ADB (1966: 390–1).
34. Hill, Ernestine, *My Love Must Wait*, London (1966: 450).

Chapter 6: Macquarie's Favourite

M. H. Ellis, Lachlan Macquarie: His Life, Adventures and Times (1958), is the authority for this period.

1. ADB (1967: 187); Ellis (1958: xv-xviii); SG 31 December 1809 (p. 2).
2. Ellis (1958: 350–1); JRAHS (32 (5): 273–93).
3. ADB (1966: 470–2).
4. Ellis (1958: 343; 350; 504).
5. Huey, *Journal* 28–31 December 1809.
6. ML A1845: 491. Arnold to William Crowfoot, 1810.
7. ML A18492 : 2a–3a. Arnold to his brother, 25 February, 1810.
8. SG 14 May 1814 (p. 2).
9. HRNSW (5: 496; 503).
10. HRA (8: 250–1). Macquarie to Bathurst, 7 May 1814.
11. SG 4 June 1814 (p.2).
12. SG 7 May 1814.
13. SG 18 June 1814 (p. 1); SG 7 July 1814 (p. 2).
14. SG 9 July 1814 (p.2).
15. SG 23 July 1814 (p.2).
16. HRA (9: 365). Proclamation, 20 July 1816.
17. HRA (8: 367–70). Macquarie to Bathurst, 8 October 1814.
18. HRA (8: 371–3). Shelley to Macquarie, 20 August 1814.
19. SG 1 December 1814 (p.1).
20. Dixson Library [DL]. Add. 340. 'Points which the Committee are requested to Speak to the Natives Upon at the Meeting at Parramatta on Wednesday the 28th of Decr. 1814'.
21. SG 31 December 1814 (p.2).
22. HRA (8: 467). Macquarie to Bathurst, 24 March 1814.
23. HRA (11: 864). Brisbane to Bathurst, 3 October 1825.
24. Bonwick Transcripts [BT], Box 8. Bigge App. 3519. DL Add. 64. Rev. R. Hill, 22 January 1821.
25. SG 4 February 1815 (p.1).
26. HRA (8: 467). Macquarie to Bathurst, 24 March 1815.
27. SG 22 April 1815 (p.2).
28. Howe (1820: 74).
29. Arnold, *Journal* 13 July 1815.
30. Macquarie *Memoranda*, 17 July 1815.
31. Macquarie, *Journal* 5 November 1815.
32. ML D. 1. Wentworth Papers (153), 31 December 1816.
33. Cowper (1838).
34. Debenham (1945: 188).
35. Debenham (1945: 162).
36. Debenham (1945: 162).
37. Ellis (1958: 572: note 18).
38. ML ZR251(b) Relics.
39. Reg. No. B8454, Australian Museum, Sydney; McCarthy (1952: 328–9).
40. ADB (1967: 187); Ellis (1958: 4; App. 11: 528).
41. Jacobs (1950: 51–2); See Peets, Orville H., *American Antiquity* 31 (1) (1965): 113–16.
42. Webster's Collegiate Dictionary Springfield, Mass. (1939: 430).
43. Macquarie, *Diary* 1 January 1818.
44. Howe (1820: 74).
45. McCarthy (1952: 327). See Bridges (1971: 107–17).
46. SG 9, 16, 21 March 1816.
47. HRA (9: 54). Macquarie to Bathurst, 8 March 1816.
48. HRA (9: 139–40), Macquarie to Bathurst, 8 June 1816.
49. Macquarie, *Diary* 10 April 1816 (3; 12).
50. HRA (9: 139: note 39). Macquarie to Bathurst, 8 June 1816; Reece, R. H. W., *Aborigines and Colonists*, Sydney (1974: 109).
51. HRA (9: 139–145). Macquarie to Bathurst, 8 June 1816.
52. Macquarie, *Diary*, 7 May 1816.
53. Macquarie, *Diary*, 25 May 1816.
54. HRA (9: 362–4). Macquarie to Bathurst, 1 April 1817.
55. SG 31 August 1816 (p. 2).
56. SG 4 January 1817 (pp. 2–3); Macquarie, *Diary*, 28 December 1816.
57. HRA (10: 95). Macquarie to Bathurst, 24 March 1819.
58. Oldfield (January 1828) (2: 105). Barry Bridges in *Descent* 5 (3) (1971): 110 mistakenly identifies Bungaree as the 'chief' mentioned in this anecdote.
59. HRA (9: 342). Macquarie to Bathurst, 4 April 1817.
60. Macquarie, *Diary*, 1 January 1818.

Chapter 7: Voyage of the Mermaid

1. HRA (8: 544). Macquarie to Bathurst, 10 December 1817.
2. ADB (1966: 61–2).
3. ADB (1966: 61).
4. ADB (1966: 265–6).
5. King (1827: xxxix).
6. Lee (1925: 310).
7. HRA (8: 605). Macquarie to Bathurst, 18 April 1816.
8. King (1827: 4).
9. King (1827: 5–6).
10. King (1827:15–16).
11. Lee (1925: 319–20).
12. Lee (1925: 329).
13. King (1827: 38–9).
14. Lee (1925: 337).
15. King (1827: 40–1).
16. Lee (1925: 338).
17. King (1827: 41–2).
18. Lee (1925: 339).
19. King (1827: 45; 47).
20. Lee (1925: 340).
21. Lee (1925: 350).
22. Lee (1925: 351); King (1827: 65).
23. King (1827: 66–8).
24. King (1827: 68–9).
25. King (1827: 72–3).
26. Lee (1925: 360).
27. King (1827: 87–80).
28. King (1827: 100–15).
29. Lee (1925: 391).
30. King (1827: 129).
31. D'Urville (1824: 294).
32. As claimed in Bennett (1968: 9).
33. ADB (1966: 62).
34. Cassell's *Picturesque Australasia* [1889], Hornsby, N.S.W. (1980: 257).
35. Bassett (1961:181).
36. HRA (10: 283–4). Macquarie to Bathurst, 28 February 1810; Bassett (1961: 181; 184); Macquarie, *Journal* 18 November 1819.
37. Bassett (1961:184).
38. JRAHS (24: 24–31; 250–1).
39. Brosse (1988: 45).
40. Archives N.S.W. Berry (1838: 557–8).

Chapter 8: The Russians at Kirribilli

The main authorities are translations of Bellingshausen and other Russian voyagers in Debenham (1945) and Barratt (1981).
1. SG 22 April 1820 (p. 2).
2. Debenham (1945: 162–3).
3. Debenham (1945: 163–4).
4. Stringer, M., *Sydney Harbour*. Narrabeen, N.S.W. (1984: 202).
5. Debenham (1945: 190).
6. Barratt (1981: 47–8).
7. Barratt (1981: 49).
8. Barratt (1981: 29).
9. Macquarie, *Journal*, 11 April 1829.
10. Ellis (1958: 140).
11. Macquarie, *Journal*, 19 April 1820.
12. Macquarie, *Journal*, 28 April 1820.
13. Debenham (1945: 186).
14. Debenham (1945: 188).
15. Debenham (1945: 188).
16. Debenham (1945: 189).
17. Barratt (1981: 50).
18. Debenham (1945: 189).
19. Barratt (1981: 52).
20. Debenham (1945: 189–90).
21. McCarthy, F. D. (1989) MS Research Notes.
22. Russian State Museum [RSM], St Petersburg, 'Boongaree—'Nov. Zeland', RSM - R29212/210. 'Gouroungan and Matora'. RSM - R29214/211.
23. SG 4 February 1915 (p. 1).
24. McCormick (1987: Plate 174b).
25. 'Gagolbi', RSM- R29289/278.
26. 'Native of New Holland—Couz-chou-bari-cal', RSM - R29302/301.
27. 'Nouvelle-Hollande—Cou-rou-bari-gal', Plate 21, Historique Atlas de MM. Lesueur et Petit, in Péron, F., *Voyage de découvertes aux terres australes . . .*, Paris,1824 (2nd ed.).
28. 'Bara Bara vilam miny', RSM-R25210 [not seen].
29. 'Bourinoan', RSM- R29210/208; 'Gulanba Duby', RSM - R29205/203; 'Toúbi', RSM - R292Q6/204; 'Gouroungan and Matora',.RSM - R29214/211; 'Ga-ouen-ren', RSM - R29215/212; 'Female Aborigine', RSM - R29216/213.Note: Colour transparencies of Mikhailov's original sketches in the Russian State Museum, St Petersburg, were kindly made available for study by Tim McCormick in Sydney. Copies of many of these are also held by AIATSIS in Canberra.
30. Debenham (1945:190).
31. Barratt (1981: 81).
32. SG 20 May 1820 (p.3).
33. Debenham (1945: 332).
34. Debenham (1945: 335–8).
35. Barratt (1981: 50).
36. Barratt (1981: 32).
37. Howe, George, *New South Wales Pocket Almanac*, Sydney 1821.

Chapter 9: The Native Settlers

1. Debenham (1945: 162).
2. King (1827: 2: 4–5).
3. Tench (1979: 218).
4. Collins (1971: 147).
5. Mann, D. D., *The Present Picture of New South Wales*, London, Booth (1811: 47).
6. King (1827: 2: 131).
7. See McCormick (1987: Plates 180, 182, 184).
8. Field (1825: 224–5). Genesis 3: 7 and 3: 10–11. Field compares the innocent nakedness of the Aborigines to that of Adam and Eve.
9. Field (1825: 435–6).
10. Macquarie, *Journal*, 28 March 1820.
11. Macquarie, *Journal*, 1 January 1822.
12. Macquarie, *Journal*, 31 January 1822.
13. HRA (14: 596–8). E. S. Hall to Sir George Murray, 26 November 1828.
14. Oldfield (January 1828) (2: 104).
15. Campbell (1838: 491).
16. Macquarie, *Journal*, 11 February 1822.
17. Bennett (1834: 338).
18. Comment by Margaret McWilliams, Resource Officer, Mosman Historical Society (31 March 1989).
19. Heaton (1887: XIV: Pt 1).
20. Cunningham (1827: 2: 18–19).
21. 1900.55.57. Original catalogue entry (1900). Pitt Rivers Museum, University of Oxford. A drawing of the club appears as Plate 41 in McBryde, Isabel, *Guests of the Governor*, Sydney, 1989.
22. SG 29 December 1823 (p.2).
23. Tyerman and Bennet (1841: 2: 178).
24. SG 30 December 1826 (p. 2).
25. See note 21.
26. Aust Museum Acquisition Papers, 5 August 1897 *et al.*

Chapter 10: French Connections

1. Lesson (1838: 288–9); Rosenman (1987: lx).
2. SG 22 January 1824 (p. 2).
3. Rosenman (1987: xlv); Brosse (1983: 210).
4. Rosenman (1987: xli-liii); JRAHS (24: 4: 278).
5. Brosse (1983: 149).
6. JRAHS (1918) (4: 349–50); (1924) (10: 215–226).
7. Lesson (1838: 276).
8. Lesson (1838: 277).
9. Lesson (1828: 291).
10. Rosenman (1987: 85–90).
11. Lesson (1838: 291–2).
12. Lesson (1838: 278–80).
13. Ellis (1958: 520).
14. Ellis (1958: 522).
15. Lang (1838: 263).
16. Brosse (1983: 98; 104; 209).
17. JRAHS (1918) (4: 350–3).
18. Bougainville (1837: 485–7).
19. Berry (1838: 83: 557–8).
20. Bougainville (1837: 2: 225).

Chapter 11: 'A King of Shreds and Patches'

1. Macquarie, *Journal*, 11 February 1822.
2. Debenham (1945: 188).
3. Dutton (1974: 29).
4. ML B852-1. 'H.T.E.', *Observations*, 13 November 1825.
5. ML B852-2 (1826).
6. SG 25 March 1826 (p. 2).
7. Sadlier (1883: 56).
8. McGarvie, *Diary*, 21 May 1826.
9. Cunningham (1827:74).
10. ADB (1966: 282–236).
11. HRA (12: 125).
12. Rowley, C. D., *The Destruction of Aboriginal Society*. Ringwood, Victoria, (1970: 19).
13. Scott, T. H., *Letterbooks* (291).
14. HRA (12: 795–6). Darling to Bathurst, 22 December 1826.
15. SG 19 January 1826 (p.2).
16. *Australian* 19 January 1826 (p.3).
17. SG 30 December 1826 (p.2).
18. SG 21 October 1826 (p.2).
19. SG 21 October 1826 (p.2 [sep. item]).
20. Lind, Lew, *Fair Winds to Australia* Frenchs Forest, N.S.W. (1988: 41).
21. SG 1 November 1826 (p.2).
22. SG 6 December 1826 (p.2).
23. SG 20 December 1826 (p.2).
24. SG 6 December 1826 (p.2).
25. Rosenman (1987: 70).
26. Oldfield (January 1828) (2: 104).
27. SG 24 March 1827 (p.3).
28. See Mackanness, G., *Fourteen Journeys over the Blue Mountains*, Sydney (1950–1: 166).
29. SG 28 November 1827 (p.2).
30. Oldfield (1828) (3: 279).
31. Oldfield (1828) (2: 103–4).
32. Oldfield (1828) (2: 128).
33. Oldfield (1828) (2: 104).
34. Cunningham (1827: 67–8).
35. Oldfield (1828) (2: 102–4).
36. Oldfield (1828) (3: 278).
37. *Australian*, 4 January 1828 (p. 3).
38. Dawson (1830: 269–70).
39. ML. Bonwick Transcripts. Box 53: (5: 1789–90).
40. SG 7 July 1829 (p.2).
41. SG 27 November 1830 (p.3).
42. Hood (1843: 447–8).
43. SG 27 November 1830 (p.2).
44. *Australian*, 3 December 1830 (p. 3).
45. Bellingshausen (1945: 163).
46. 'Old Chum' (J. M. Forde) in 'Old Sydney' *Truth* 28 August 1910.
47. Mann, J. F., 'Notes on the Aborigines of Australia', *Volume of Proceedings, Royal Geographic Society of N.S.W.* (1885: 28).
48. Angas (1847: 2: 202; App: 272–3).
49. SG 27 November 1830 (p. 3).
50. A. G. Foster, Mr and Mrs, *Epitaph Book*, 1901. Quoted in Johnson and Sainty (1973: 120).
51. SG 22 January 1829 (p. 2).
52. Debenham (1945: 163).
53. Cunningham (1827: 28–9).
54. Lesson (1838: 278).
55. *Sydney Herald* 14 November 1831.
56. Hood (1843: 478).
57. Waterman, J. C., JRAHS (1923) (8:359).
58. Mann, J. F., 'A few Notes on Australian Aborigines', SMH 1886 [ML Newspaper cuttings: (116: 169); See ML Am 1.]
59. 1828 Census of N.S.W. (Sainty and Johnson,1980); Hunter Valley Directory (1841).
60. *Australian* 15 December1840 (p.2.); 18 December 1841 (p.2).
61. D14 Dixson Library [DL]. Wilkie (1852: 1–7).
62. Ridley, Rev. William, App. C.,'Report of the Select Committee on the Native Mounted Police', Queensland Legislative Assembly. Brisbane (1861: 116).

Chapter 12: An Actor in the Streets

1. Cunningham (1827: 2: 19).
2. Cunningham (1827: 2: 23).
3. Cunningham (1827: 2: 20).
4. See App. ll.
5. Oldfield (1828) (4: 319).
6. Dawson (1830: 263).
7. ML A1849 ll (25 Feb 1810).
8. Field (1825: 435).
9. Halloran, Rev. L. H., *The Gleaner* 26 April 1827 (p. 3).
10. Debenham (1945: 335).
11. *Australian*, 3 December,1830 (p.3).
12. Debenham (1945: 163).
13. Debenham (1945: 189; 335).
14. Bougainville (1827: 485).
15. See App. ll.
16. McGarvie, *Diary*, 22 May 1826 (221).
17. Barratt (1981: 29).
18. Dawson (1830: 269).
19. Jacobs (1950: 53; 55).
20. Moorehead, Alan, *The Fatal Impact*, London, Hamish Hamilton (1966: 82; 84–5).
21. Neville (1991: 38).
22. Hackforth-Jones (1980: 13).
23. Worgan, *Journal*, 9 March 1788.
24. SG 23 December 1804 (pp. 2–3).
25. Debenham (1945: 337).
26. Macquarie, *Journal*, 11 February 1822.
27. SG 27 November 1830 (p.3).
28. ADB (1966: 177).
29. Earle, Augustus, *Views in New South Wales . . .*, London, J. Cross,1830.
30. Lang (1834: 263).
31. Dickens (1859: 77–83). Too lengthy to reproduce here.
32. Dickens (1859: 77).
33. Dickens (1859: 78).
34. 'Tales and Sketches', *Australian Home Companion* (1859: 4: 359–60).
35. Sadleir (1883: V11: 56–61).
36. Macmillan, David S. (ed.), *Two years in New South Wales* [Peter Cunningham] Sydney (1966: xxi-xxv).
37. ADB (1966: 267–8).
38. Pope-Hennessy, Una, *Charles*

Dickens: 1812–1870, London (1968: 305).
39. *The Dickensian*, June 1915. Quoted in Lansbury (1966: 125).
40. Dickens to Mrs Watson, 3 July 1850. Quoted in Lansbury (1966: 115).
41. Lansbury (1966: 115).

42. Hardwick, Michael and Mollie, *As they saw Him . . . Charles Dickens*, London (1970: 40–1).
43. Hardwick (1970: 28).
44. Dickens (1859: 78).
45. Dickens (1859: 79); Healy (1977: 28–31).
46. Healy (1988: 10).
47. Healy (1977: 20).
48. SG 27 November 1830 (p.3).
49. Dutton (1974: 28–9).
50. Dutton (1974: 31).

Chapter 13: Images of Bungaree (2)

1. Dutton (1974: 13).
2. Smith, Bernard, *European Vision and the South Pacific*, Melbourne (1989: 269).
3. McCarthy (1989) MS Research Notes.
4. ADB (1966: 389). See Hackforth-Jones (1977: 84–5); JRAHS (1919) (5: 287).
5. Therry (1863: 110–11).
6. ADB (1966: 389).
7. Sydney *Monitor*, 6 March 1830.
8. *Sydney Herald*, 2 October 1834 (p. 3).
9. SG 7 October 1834 (p. 3).
10. ADB (1966: 389); Hackforth-Jones (1977: 86).
11. JRAHS (1919) (5: 287); Neville (1991: note 15).
12. ML QA923.5/C. N.S.W. Surveyor General's Department, typescript of letters regarding employment of J. Carmichael.
13. JRAHS (1919) (5: 287); DAA (1984: 134–5).
14. DAA (1984: 250–1). See also Moore, W., *The Story of Australian Art*, Sydney (1934: 23).

Epilogue: Black Ulysses

1. Pollon, Frances, *The Book of Sydney Suburbs*, Sydney (1988: 225).

Bibliography

Primary Sources

Manuscripts in the Mitchell Library [ML], State Library of New South Wales, Sydney

Arnold, Dr Joseph, Journals 27 August 1810–17 Decenber 1815. C720.

—, Letter to his brother, 25 February 1810. A18492.

—, Letter to William Crowfoot, 25 February 1810. A1846.

Cowper, Rev. Wm, Letter to W. W. Burton in Supreme Court Papers Relating to Aborigines 1796–1819. A1161.

Flinders, Matthew. Journal on HMS *Investigator*, 1801-02. Safe 1/24.

—, Correspondence, June 1791-July 1803. Extracts from Flinders papers, State Library of Victoria [Typescript copy 1925]. A1592–1.

Harris, Dr John, Letter to Gov. P. G. King. King Family Papers. V. 8, Further Papers, 1775–1806. A1980–2.

H. T. E. [Henry Thomas Ebsworth], Observations during a voyage on the Ship *York*, from England to N.S.W., 18 June–25 November 1825. B852 –1.

Huey, Alexander, Journal. Typescript. B1514.

McGarvie, Rev. John, Diary 1825–1828. A 1332.

Macquarie, Lachlan, Memoranda and Related Papers. 22 December 1808–14 July 1823. A772.

—, Diary, 10 April 1816–1 July 1818. A773.

—, Journals, 9 July 1818–28 February 1820. A774.

Mann, John F., Aboriginal Names and words of the Cammeray Tribe, obtained from Long Dick, son of King Bungaree and Queen Gooseberry. Ms and typescript. Am 1.

Richardson, John, Letter to Rev. Samuel Marsden, 4 April 1829. A1992.

Smith, Samuel, Journal of Samuel Smith, 26 May 1801–7 October 1803. ZC222.

Threlkeld, Rev. L. E., London Missionary Society. Mission to the Aborigines of New South Wales [circular letter]. Bonwick Transcripts [BT] Box 53, Missionary Vol. 5.

Wentworth, D'arcy, Police Reports and Accounts, 1810–1827, Wentworth Papers, D. I.

Walker, Rev. William, Letter to Rev. R. Watson (c. 1821). BT Box 52, Missionary (4: 984).

Other MS Sources

Berry, Alexander, Recollections of the Aborigines, 1838. In Supreme Court Misc. Correspondence Relating to Aborigines, No. 83. Archives Office of N.S.W., Sydney.

Brown, Robert, Diary, 7 December–9 May 1801. British Museum (Natural History), Kensington (London).

Campbell, Robert, Letter to Mr Justice Burton, June 22 1838. In Supreme Court Papers. No. 71. Archives Office of N.S.W., Sydney.

Flinders, Matthew, A Biographical Tribute to the Memory of Trim. Isle de France, 1809. Flinders Papers 60/017/FLI/11A. National Maritime Museum, Greenwich.

McCarthy, Dr Frederick David, 'The Art and Life of the Aborigines of the Sydney-Hawkesbury area'. MS Research Notes loaned to author, Sydney, November 1989.

Wilkie, John Perrett, ALS to Henry Hughes, 25 October 1852. D14, Dixson Library, Sydney.

Bibliographies, Published Records, Reference Works

[ADB] *Australian Dictionary of Biography*, Melbourne, Melbourne University Press, 1966–1981.

Bibliography of Bungaree (computer printout), Canberra, A.C.T., Australian Institute of Aboriginal Studies, 1989.

Cumpston, John Stanley (comp.), *Shipping Arrivals and Departures: Sydney, 1788–1825*, Canberra, Roebuck Society, 1964.

[DNB] *Dictionary of National Biography*, London, Smith Elder, & Co., 1885–1888.

[HRA] *Historical Records of Australia*, Series 1, Canberra, A.C.T., Library of the Commonwealth Parliament, 1914–22.

[HRNSW] *Historical Records of New South Wales*, 7 Vols, Sydney, Government Printer, 1892–1901.

Johnson, K. A., and Sainty, M. R. (eds.), *Gravestone Inscriptions N.S.W.*, Vol. 1, Sydney Burial Ground. North Sydney, Genealogical Publications of Australia, 1973.

—, *Census of New South Wales*, November 1828, Sydney 1980.

[JRAHS] Royal Australian Historical Society, *Journal and Proceedings*, Sydney, Vol. 1, 1906 to date.

Printed Primary Sources

(Includes reprints and facsimile editions)

Angas, George French, *Savage Life and Scenes in Australia and New Zealand*, 2 Vols, London, Smith, Elder & Co.,1847. Facs: Adelaide, Libraries Board of South Australia,1969.

Bennett, George, *Wanderings in New South Wales . . .* 2 Vols, London, Richard Bentley, 1834.

Burford, Robert, *Description of a View of the Town of Sydney, New South Wales; the Harbour of Port Jackson, and Surrounding Country*, London, J. and C. Adlard, 1829.

Cunningham, Peter Miller, *Two Years in New South Wales . . .* 2 Vols, London, Henry Colburn, 1827. Reprint (2nd ed.): Macmillan, David S. (ed.), Sydney, Angus & Robertson, 1966.

Dawson, Robert, *The Present State of Australia . . . and a Particular Account of the Manners, Customs, and Conditions of its Aboriginal Inhabitants*, London, Smith, Elder & Co., 1830.

Edwards, Phyllis I. (ed.), *The Journal of Peter Good*, London, Bulletin of the British Museum (Natural History),1981.

Field, Barron, *Geographical Memoirs of New South Wales . . .*, London, John Murray, 1825.

Flinders, Matthew, *A Voyage to Terra Australis . . .* 2 Vols, London, W. Nichol, 1814. Reprint: Adelaide, Libraries Board of South Australia, 1966.

Grant, James, *The Narrative of a Voyage of Discovery, Performed in His Majesty's Vessel The Lady Nelson . . .*, London, T. Egerton, Military Library, Whitehall,1803.

Hood, John, *Australia and the East . . .*, 2nd ed., London, John Murray,1843.

Howe, George, *New South Wales Pocket Almanack*, Sydney, 1820; 1821.

King, Phillip Parker, *Narrative of a Survey of the Intertropical and Western Coasts of Australia. Performed between the years 1818 and 1822*, 2 Vols, London, John Murray 1827.

Lang, John Dunmore, *An Historical and Statistical Account of New South Wales . . .*, 2 Vols, London, Cochran and McCrone, 1834.

Lee, Ida (Mrs C.B. Marriott), *Early Explorers in Australia*, London, Methuen & Co., 1925 [Journal of Allan Cunningham].

Mann, David Dickinson, *The Present Picture of New South Wales*, London, Booth, 1811. Facs: Sydney, John Ferguson, 1979.

Montgomery, James, *Journal of Voyages and Travels*, by the Rev. Daniel Tyreman and George Bennet, Esq. London 1831.

O'Connell, James F., *A residence of eleven years in New Holland and the Caroline Islands: Being the adventures of James F. O' Connell. Edited from his verbal narration*. Boston, B. B. Mussey, 1836. Reprint: Riesenberg, Saul H.(ed.), ANU Press, Canberra, 1972.

Sadleir, Richard, *The Aborigines of Australia*. Sydney, Thomas Richards, Government Printer, 1883.

Therry, Judge Roger, *Reminiscences of Thirty Years Residence in New South Wales and Victoria*. London, 1863.

Wallis, James, *An Historical Account of the Colony of New South Wales . . . in Illustrations of twelve views . . .*, London, Rudolph Ackermann,1821.

Wentworth, W. C., *A Statistical, Historical & Political Description of the Colony of New South Wales . . .*, London, G. & W. Whittaker,1819.

First Fleet Diaries

Bradley, William, *A Voyage to New South Wales: The Journal of Lieutenant William Bradley RN of HMS Sirius, 1786–1792*. Facs. reprint: Sydney, Trustees of the Public Library of NSW, 1969.

Collins, David, *An Account of the English Colony in New South Wales . . .*, 2 Vols, London, T. Cadell Jnr and W. Davies, 1798–1802. Facs. reprint: Adelaide, State Library, 1971.

Hunter, John, *An Historical Journal of the Transactions at Port Jackson and Norfolk Island . . .*, London, John Stockdale, 1793.

Phillip, Arthur (attrib.), *The Voyage of Governor Phillip to Botany Bay, with an Account of the Establishment of the Colonies of Port Jackson and Norfolk Island*. London, John Stockdale, 1789. Reprint: Auchmuty, J. J. (ed.), Sydney, Angus & Robertson/ Royal Australian Historical Society, 1970.

Tench, Watkin, *A Narrative of the Expedition to Botany Bay; with an Account of New South Wales, Its Productions, Inhabitants & c . . .*, London, Debrett, 1789.

—, *A Complete Account of the Settlement at Port Jackson, in*

New South Wales . . ., London, 1793. Both reprinted in one title as Sydney's First Four Years, Sydney, Angus & Robertson, 1979.

White, John, Journal of a Voyage to New South Wales . . ., London, 1789. Reprint (1790 edition): Sydney, 1962.

Worgan, George Bouchier, Journal of a First Fleet Surgeon, Sydney, Library Council of N.S.W., 1978.

The Russians

Barratt, Glynn, The Russians at Port Jackson, 1814–1822, Canberra, A.C.T., Australian Institute of Aboriginal Studies, 1981.

Bellingshausen, (Fabian Gottlieb von), Dvukratnyye izyskaniya v Yuzhnom Ledovitom Okeane i plavaniye vokrug sveta, v prodolzhenii 1819, 20, i 21 goduv . . . na shiupakh Vostok i Mirnyy (Repeated Investigations in the Southern Icy Ocean and a voyage around the world during 1819, 20 and 21 . . .), St Petersburg, 1831.

Debenham, Frank (ed.), The Voyage of Captain Bellingshausen to the Antarctic Seas 1819–1821, 2 Vols, Cambridge, Hakluyt Society, 1945.

The French

Arago, Jacques Etienne Victoire, Promenade autour du Monde, pendant les années 1817, 1818, 1819 et 1820 sur les corvettes du Roi l'Uranie et La Physicienne, Commandés par. M. Freycinet, par J. S. Arago . . ., 2 Vols, Atlas Historique et Pittoresque, Paris, Leblanc, 1822.

—, Narrative of a Voyage around the World in the Uranie and Physicienne Corvettes . . ., London, Treuttel and Wurz, 1823. Facs. reprint: Amsterdam, N. Israel/New York, Da Capo Press, 1971.

Bassett, Marnie, Realms and Islands: The world voyage of Rose de Freycinet in the Corvette Uranie 1817–1820, London, Oxford University Press, 1962.

Bougainville, M. Le Baron de [H. Y. P. P.], Journal de la navigation autour du Globe de la Frégate La Thétis et de la corvette L'Espérance pendant les annees 1824, 1825 et 1826 . . ., 2 Vols, Atlas, Paris, Arthus Bertrand, 1837.

Brosse, Jacques, Great Voyages of Exploration: The Golden Age of Discovery in the Pacific. Stanley Hochman (trans.), Lane Cove, N.S.W., Doubleday Australia, 1983.

Dumont d'Urville, Jules, Voyage de la corvette l'Astrolabe Exécuté par Ordre du Roi, pendant des années 1826–1827–1828–1829, sous le commandement De M. J. Dumont D'Urville, Capitaine de Vaisseau, 14 Vols, 5 atlases, Paris, J. Tartu, 1830–35.

—, Voyage Pittoresque Autour Du Monde, Resumé général des voyages de découvertes, 2 Vols, Paris, 1834–35.

—, Voyage au Pole Sud et dans l'Océanie sur les corvettes l'Astrolabe et la Zélée . . ., 2 Vols, 7 atlases, Paris, 1842.

—, Two Voyages to the South Seas, by Captain (later Rear-Admiral) Jules S.-C. Dumont D'Urville . . ., Vol 1, Astrolabe, 1826, 1829. Translated from the French and edited by Helen Rosenman. Melbourne, Melbourne University Press, 1987.

Freycinet, Louis de, Voyage Autour du Monde, Enterpris par Ordre de Roi . . ., Exécuté sur les corvettes de S.M. l'Uranie et la Physicienne, pendant les anées 1817, 1818, 1819 et 1820 . . ., Paris, Chez Pillet Aîné . . ., 1824–29.

Lesson, René-Primevère, Voyage médical autour du monde, 1822–1825 . . . Paris, 1829.

—, Voyage autour du Monde, sur la Corvette La Coquille, par P. Lesson, 2 Vols, Paris, 1838.

Péron, Francois, and Freycinet, Louis de, Voyage de Découvertes aux terres Australes . . . pendant les anées 1800, 1801, 1802, 1803 et 1804. 2 Vols, & atlas, Paris, 1807–1816.

Péron, M. F., A Voyage of Discovery to the Southern Hemisphere performed by order of the Emperor Napoleon during the years 1801, 1802, 1803 and 1804, London, 1809.

Newspapers and Periodicals

Australian, The. Sydney, relevant dates.

Daily Mirror, Sydney 26 February. 1988 (Anon., 'Bungaree King of the Blacks').

Monitor, Sydney, relevant dates.

Old Times, Sydney, June 1903.

Oldfield, Roger (ed.), South-Asian Register, Sydney, 1827–1828.

[SG] Sydney Gazette, Sydney, 1804–1834.

Sydney Herald, 15 September 1836.

[SMH] Sydney Morning Herald, relevant dates.

Secondary Sources

Printed

Austin, K. A., *The Voyage of the Investigator, 1801–1803*. Adelaide, Rigby, 1964.

Bassett, Marnie, *The Governor's Lady: Mrs Philip Gidley King*, Melbourne, Melbourne University Press, 1961 (1940).

Beaglehole, K. C., *The Voyage of the Endeavour, 1768–1771* Vol. l, Cambridge, Hakluyt Society, 1955.

Bennett, F. C. (ed.), *The Story of the Aboriginal People of the Central Coast of New South Wales*, Historical Monograph No.1, Wyong, N.S.W., Brisbane Water Historical Society,1968.

Colwell, Max, *The Voyages of Matthew Flinders*, Dee Why West, N.S.W., Paul Hamlyn, 1970.

Dickens, Charles (ed.), 'Bungaree, King of the Blacks', *All the Year Round*, London, Vol. 1, No. 4, May 1859.

Ellis, M. H., *Lachlan Macquarie: His Life, Adventures and Times*, Sydney, Angus & Robertson, 1958 (1947).

Flinders, Matthew, *A Biographical Tribute to the Memory of TRIM*, Ile de France, 1809. Reprint: *Advertiser*, Adelaide, 22 & 29 December 1973.

—, *Trim*, Illustrated by Annette Macarthur-Onslow, Sydney, Collins, 1977.

Flinders Petrie, Ann Lisette, 'Flinders—The Family', in Russell, R. W. (ed.), *The Ifs of History*, Flinders University, South Australia, 1979.

Fox, Len, *Old Sydney Windmills*, Potts Point, N.S.W., Len Fox, 1978.

Gunson, Niel (ed.), *Australian Reminiscences & Papers of L. E. Threlkeld Missionary to the Aborigines, 1824–1859*, 2 Vols, Canberra, A. C.T., Australian Institute of Aboriginal Studies, 1974.

Healy, John Joseph, *Literature and the Aborigine in Australia*, St Lucia, University of Queensland Press, 1988 (1978).

Ingleton, Geoffrey C., *Matthew Flinders: Navigator and Chartmaker*, Guildford, Surrey, Genisis, 1986.

Jacobs, Wilbur R., *Diplomacy and Indian Gifts, 1748–1793*, Stamford, Conn., 1950.

Kohen, J. l., and Lampert, Ronald, 'Hunters and Fishers in the Sydney Region', in Mulvaney, D. J., and White, J.P. (eds.), *Australians to 1788*. Sydney, Fairfax, Syme and Weldon, 1987.

Ly-Tio-Fane Pineo, Huguette, *In the Grips of the Eagle: Matthew Flinders at Ile de France, 1803–10*. Moka, Mauritius, Mahatma Gandhi Institute, 1988.

Perry, Dr T. M., 'Flinders—The Man', in Russell, R. W. (ed.), *The Ifs of History*, Flinders University, South Australia, 1979.

Ross, A., 'Tribal and Linguistic Boundaries: A Reassessment of the Evidence', in Aplin, G. (ed.), *A Difficult Infant: Sydney before Macquarie*, Kensington, New South Wales University Press, 1988.

Scott, Ernest, *The Life of Captain Matthew Flinders*, R. N., Sydney, Angus & Robertson, 1914.

Smith, Keith and Irene, *Sydney City*. Epping, N.S.W., Smith's Guides, 1988.

Tregenza, John, *George French Angas, Artist, Traveller and Naturalist, 1822–1886*, Adelaide, Art Gallery Board of South Australia, 1980.

Trevelyan, G. M., *Illustrated English Social History*, 4 Vols, Ringwood, Victoria, Penguin Books, 1964 (1942).

Welsby, Thomas, *The Discoverers of the Brisbane River*, Brisbane, 1913 (reprinted 1977).

—, *Bribie —The Basket Maker*, Brisbane, Barker's Bookstores, 1937.

Willey, Keith, *When the Sky Fell Down: The Destruction of the Tribes of the Sydney Region 1788–1850s*, Sydney, Collins,1985 (1979).

Journal Articles and Papers

Bridges, Barry John, 'The Aborigines' Breast-Plate Insignia: Lachlan Macquarie's Scheme for an Aboriginal Meritocracy', *Descent* 5 (3) (1971).

Capell, A., 'Aboriginal Languages in the South Central Coast, New South Wales: Fresh Discoveries', *Oceania* 41 (1)(1970).

Healy, John Joseph, 'A Most Tragic Theme', *Hemisphere* 21 (5) (1977).

—, 'Dimensions and Grandeur', *Hemisphere* 21 (6)(1977).

Heaton, J. Henniker, 'On the Origin, the Manners, Customs, of the Aborigines of Australia', *Transactions of the Royal Society of Literature*, Vol. 1X, Part 1, London, 1887.

Kohen, J. L., 'Aborigines in the West: Prehistory to Present', Western Sydney Project, Seven Hills, N.S.W., 1985.

Lansbury, Coral, 'Charles Dickens and his Australia', *JRAHS*, 52 (5)(1966).

McCarthy, F.D., 'Breast-Plates: The Blackfellow's Reward', Sydney. *Australian Museum Magazine* 10 (10) (1952).

Reece, R.H.W., 'Feasts and Blankets: The History of Some Early Attempts to Establish Relations with the Aborigines of N.S.W. 1814–1846', *Archaeology and Physical Anthropology in Oceania*, 11 (3) (1967).

Stanner, W.H.E., 'The History of Indifference thus Begins', *Aboriginal History* 1(1) (1977).

Art

Bonyhady, Tim, *The Colonial Image: Australian Painting 1800–1880*, Sydney, Australian National Gallery/Ellsyd Press, 1987.

Buscombe, Eve, *Artists in Early Australia and their Portraits*, Sydney, Eureka Research, 1979.

—, *Portraits of the Aborigines*, Sydney, Eureka Research, 1980.

[DAA] *Dictionary of Australian Artists*, Kerr, Joan (ed.), Power Institute of Fine Arts, University of Sydney, 1984.

Dixson, William, *Notes on Australian Artists*, Sydney, *JRAHS*, Vol. 1X, Parts 4 & 5, Sydney, 1919–20.

Dutton, Geoffrey, *White on Black: The Australian Aborigine Portrayed in Art*, South Melbourne, Macmillan, 1974.

Evans, Susanna, *Historic Sydney as seen by its Early Artists*, Sydney, Doubleday,1983.

Hackforth-Jones, Jocelyn, *Augustus Earle: Travel Artist*, Canberra, National Library of Australia, 1980.

McCormick, Tim et al ., *First Views of Australia 1788–1825: A history of Early Sydney*. Sydney, David Ell Press, 1987.

Neville, Richard, 'The Many Faces of Bungaree', *Australian Antique Collector* 42, July-December 1991.

Norst, M. J., *Ferdinand Bauer: Australian Natural History Drawings*, London, British Museum (Natural History), 1989.

Notes on the Lithographic Portrait of Bungaree, PXN685, Mitchell Library, Sydney, 12 June 1987.

Perry, T. M., and Simpson, D. H. (eds.), *Drawings by William Westall*, London, Royal Commonwealth Society, 1962.

Wantrup, Jonathan, *Australian Rare Books, 1788–1900*, Sydney, Hordern House, 1987.

Index

Australian Aborigines

alcohol (brandy, bull, gin, grog, rum, etc.), 9, 10, 73, 76, 80, 84, 85, 86, 99, 100, 103, 105, 107, 113, 121, 122, 126, 128, 129, 131, 133, 134, 135, 136, 141, 142, 143, 145, 148, 149, 150, 151, 152, 153, 167, 170, 171, 172, 174
art 17, 57, 67, 109, 146, 147
badges (see gorgets)
bags, 16, 31, 110
barter and gifts, 10, 31, 33, 34, 36, 45, 57, 73, 93, 94, 95, 96, 97, 98, 108, 113, 114, 141, 149, 151
basket 30, 54, 97
begging, 10, 113, 114, 117, 128, 131, 140, 142, 149, 150, 151, 158, 166, 170, 172
belt (fillet), 31, 112
breastplates (see gorgets)
body painting, 10, 109, 128, 129
canoe, 16, 18, 19, 20, 33, 49, 55, 56, 91, 96, 97,108, 113, 129, 134, 172
ceremonies, 17, 18, 25, 36, 49, 52, 55, 72
chief, 23, 80, 82, 85, 86, 90, 108, 121, 125, 127, 129, 131, 132, 136, 140, 142, 143, 144, 145, 154, 171, 172
clothing (European), 10, 12, 57, 77, 78, 79, 83, 84, 85, 91, 100, 103, 106, 107, 109, 114, 121, 133, 134, 140, 141, 142, 143, 144, 147, 150, 159
    blanket, 83, 84, 85, 103, 112, 114, 115, 128, 129, 140, 153
    bonnet, 76, 145
    cap, 31, 33, 34, 53, 54, 57, 66, 76, 85, 93, 140
    coat, 10, 13, 131, 134, 139, 147, 154, 155, 160, 170, 174
    cocked hat, 9, 10, 12, 13, 129, 131, 134, 136, 139, 142, 143, 144, 147, 148, 150, 154, 155, 158, 160, 161, 163, 164, 166, 170, 174
    dress, 146
    gown, 140
    greatcoat, 115, 128, 129, 154
    helmet, 128, 154
    jacket, 9, 66, 76, 85, 106, 107, 109, 134, 136, 140, 148, 153, 154, 158, 160, 161, 162, 163, 164
    petticoat, 85
    shift, 76
    shirt, 10, 85
    skirt, 140
    shoes, 139
    suit, 12, 142, 154
    top hat, 136
    trousers ('trowsers'), 76, 85, 106, 107, 109, 139, 140, 153, 154, 163, 164, 170, 174
    uniform, 121, 122, 129, 133, 136, 144, 148, 153, 154, 166
conflict, 19, 20, 21, 31, 32, 34, 95, 96, 97, 98, 137
    armed, 32, 34, 36, 54, 55, 56, 59, 65, 67, 96, 97

brawls, 100, 101, 108, 109, 140, 147, 149, 151, 153
    corn raids, 73, 74, 83, 149
    ritual, 66, 72, 100, 123, 126, 127, 147
corroboree, 10, 47, 80, 109, 128, 136, 147, 153, 166
dancing, 35, 36, 80, 108, 126, 127, 143, 166, 171, 172
drunkenness, 104, 105, 108, 128, 134, 142, 147, 149, 150, 151, 158, 166
fishing, 16, 77, 106, 108, 113, 119, 141, 153
    boat (European), 10, 109, 114, 119, 121, 126, 127, 129, 131, 133, 141, 142, 143, 154, 174
    nets, 31, 32, 33, 35, 37, 54, 59, 121
    spear (fiz-gig), 16, 37, 92, 96, 108, 113, 166
gorget, 9, 11, 12, 13, 78, 80-3, 85, 103, 105, 107, 110, 115, 133, 134, 147, 148, 150, 160, 161, 162, 163, 166, 170
hair coiffure, 109, 110, 111
headbands, 109, 110, 111, 128, 129, 160
huts, 30, 32, 77, 79, 96, 118, 119, 121, 122
hunting, 16, 75, 113, 141, 153, 166
infanticide, 150
initiation, 17, 18, 171
kidnapping of, 93, 94
king, 108, 133, 136, 142, 144, 150, 155, 157, 158, 160, 161, 167, 170
'King Billys', 83
kingplates (see gorgets)
koori (kuri), 24
kooringals, 18
koradgees, 18, 25, 146, 171
Ku-ring-gai, 24, 25
languages, 16, 24, 25, 36, 37, 43, 49, 53, 56, 60, 68, 73, 91, 114, 118, 143
medals (see gorgets)
messengers, 143
mimcry, 9, 10, 20, 128, 150, 153, 154, 155, 157, 158, 166
name exchange, 36, 55, 149
Native Conference, 75, 80, 82, 84, 85, 86, 123, 135, 136, 139, 140, 142, 146
Native Police, 148
Native School (Institution), 75, 76, 77, 80, 84, 85, 99, 107
Native Village (Elizabeth Bay), 118, 119
nosepeg, 18, 106, 109, 111
rations, 75, 78, 83, 84, 143
raft, 57, 94
rock painting, 17, 52
rock engraving, 17, 146
scarification, 18, 20, 93, 109, 110
sexual favours, 149
shelter, 16, 17, 30, 32, 77, 108, 110, 115, 122, 142, 171
singing, 35, 36, 72, 80, 166
smallpox, 21, 22, 25, 52
tobacco, 66, 80, 84, 103, 105, 108, 113, 114, 118, 128, 139, 142, 146, 149, 151, 152
taboos, 62, 166
tooth extraction, 18, 20, 52, 171
tracks, 18, 20, 21

tribes (social and language groups),
    Awaba, 25, 143
    Awabagal, 143
    Bidjigal, 22
    Botany (Bay), 25, 82
    Broken Bay, 19, 23, 25, 77, 78, 79, 80, 90, 103, 107, 109, 131, 133, 142, 145, 149, 160, 163, 164
    Cadigal, 22
    Cammeraigal (Cammeray), 24, 25, 27, 148
    Cannalgal, 25
    Carigal, 25
    Cow-Pastures, 73, 74, 82, 123, 127, 136
    Darling Harbour, 144
    Dharawal, 24
    Dharug, 24, 73
    Eora, 24
    Five Dock, 123
    Gandangara, 73, 74, 83
    George's River, 82
    Goruagal, 25
    Hawkesbury, 82
    Gweagal, 24, 170
    Illawarra, 123, 136
    Kayimai, 25
    Kissing Point, 25
    Ku-ring-gai, 24, 25
    Liverpool, 123, 136
    Pitt Water, 23, 121
    Port Jackson, 119, 132, 162
    Sydney Cove, 127, 174
    Sydney, 118, 127, 133, 142, 143, 144, 145, 146, 150
    Terramerragal, 25
    Turubul, 37
    Undanbi, 37
    Womerah, 25
waddie, 84, 139, 147
weapons, 16, 19, 35, 37, 38, 55, 56, 57, 59, 66, 67, 68, 73, 83, 84, 85, 91, 110, 113, 122, 126, 127, 140, 149, 173
    axes, 16, 19, 97, 143
    boomerang, 66, 67, 68, 113, 122, 123, 126, 147
    club, 16, 19, 68, 84, 91, 98, 113, 122, 123, 127, 128, 129, 172
    shield, 16, 31, 38, 113, 167, 173
    spears, 19, 32, 35, 37, 38, 54, 55, 57, 58, 60, 66, 73, 83, 84, 85, 96, 97, 98, 107, 110, 113, 128, 129, 139, 145, 166, 173, (see fishing spear)
    woomerah, 16, 35, 37, 54, 55, 57, 58, 68, 113, 166, 172

Names

Abaroo (Boorong), 21
Aken, John, 57
Alexander 1, 103
Allen, John, 45, 46
Angas, George French, 146
Arabanoo (Manly), 21, 27
Arago, Jacques, 100, 140
Arnold, Joseph, 72, 78, 79, 151
Austin, J. G., 162
Baker, William, 73, 164
Banks, Joseph, 15, 27, 29, 30, 38, 39, 42, 43, 45, 49, 52, 67, 87, 104
Barker, Henry, 8
Barker, Robert, 8
Barnum, P. T., 175
Barrallier, Francis, 42, 43, 67, 68
Barratt, Glynn, 104, 105, 113
Bass, George, 27, 28, 29, 39, 46
Bathurst, Earl, 73, 77, 83, 135
Baudin, Nicolas, 39, 46, 47, 60, 64, 111
Bauer, Ferdinand, 45, 46, 59, 63, 65
Bedwell, Frederick, 87, 92, 93, 96, 97
Bell, Hugh, 46, 54, 58
Bellau, 'Captain', 114
Bellingshausen, Fabian von, 25, 79, 103, 104, 105, 106, 107, 108, 109, 110, 112, 113, 114, 116, 122, 131, 133, 147, 151, 153, 154
Bennelong (Bennilong), 27, 36, 140
Bennett, Frederick, 24, 69
Bennett, George, 122
Bent, Jeffrey, 116
Berry, Alexander, 101, 127
Bidgee Bidgee (Bidji-Bidji), 84, 127
Bitugally, 74
Blackmore, Edward, 157
Blang, 136
Bligh, William, 2, 41, 56, 69, 72
Blue, Billy, 139, 160, 162
Blücher, G. von, 107
Bo-ma-ri-go, 36
Bonyhady, Tim, 12
Boodeny, 148
Borton (Berton), Edward, 145, 146
Bosch, John, 68
Bougainville, Antoine de, 130
Bougainville, Hyacinthe de, 130, 131, 132, 134, 151
Bourinoan, 112, 113
Bourke, Richard, 77, 155
Bouzet du, 131
Bowman, James, 174, 176
Boyle, Mary, 156
Bradley, William, 19, 20, 21
Brisbane, James, 12, 137, 139, 144, 157, 158
Brisbane, Lady, 137
Brisbane, Thomas, 11, 12, 80, 118, 119, 121, 125, 130, 135, 137, 154, 157
Broughton, William, 84
Brown, Robert, 45, 46, 47, 52, 53, 54, 55, 58, 59, 62, 63, 64
Bryant, Mary and William, 41
Budgery Dick, 42, 43
Bundell, 84, 116
Bunduck, 84
Bungaree, Diana (see Ga-ouen-ren)
Bungaree, John, 145, 148
Bungaree, Rose, 145
Bungaree, Young, 145, 147, 148, 163
Burford, Robert, 8, 10, 13
Burra Burra, 106, 111, 113
Burton, Mr., 119
Caley, George, 42, 65, 66
Campbell, John, 76
Campbell, Robert, 50, 117, 118
Carmichael, John, 162, 163
Carnanbigal, 84
Chappell, Ann (see Flinders, Ann)
Charles X, 126, 137
Clark, Manning, 70
Cocteau, Jean, 160
Cogy (Cogai, Cogie, Cogle, Gogy, Kogee), 68, 74, 82, 86, 127, 136

Coleby, 22, 27, 52, 84
Collins, David, 20, 21, 22, 23, 24, 25, 30, 31, 34, 35, 36, 37, 41, 43, 51, 52, 126
Cook, James, 15, 25, 27, 29, 31, 32, 36, 39, 56, 59, 104, 153
Cooribah, 142
Cornell, Geoffrey, 140
Cour-rou-bari-gal, 110, 112
Cowper, Mrs., 79
Cowper, William, 79, 135
Cox, Edward, 74
Cox, George, 74
Cox, William, 74
Coxen, Charles, 148
Coxen, Stephen, 148
Crossley, John, 45, 46
Crowfoot, Edward, 73
Cunningham, Allan (botanist), 87, 90, 91, 92, 93, 95, 96, 98, 125, 149
Cunningham, Allan (poet), 156
Cunningham, Peter, 122, 125, 134, 141, 147, 156, 158, 175
Cunningham, Phillip, 65
Daly, James, 74
Daniel, 131
D'Arifat, Delphine, 70
Darling, Ralph, 9, 11, 119, 135, 136, 137, 138, 140, 143, 155, 166
Darwin, Charles, 153
Dawes, Charles, 83
Dawes, William, 20
Dawson, Robert, 142, 143, 150, 151
Debenham, Frank, 104
Dickens, Alfred, 156
Dickens, Charles, 155, 156, 157
Dickens, Edward, 156
Dickens, Mamie, 157
Dixson, William, 162
Douglas, James, 29
Drury, Dru, 43
Dual, 136
Dumaresq, Eliza, 135
Dumaresq, Henry, 9, 135, 136, 140
Dumaresq, William John, 140
Dumont d'Urville, Jules, 98, 122, 124, 125, 126, 127, 137, 138, 139, 147, 150, 151, 170–173
Dunlop, James, 11
Duperry, Louis-Isidore, 124
Dutton, Geoffrey, 133, 158, 159
Earl, James, 11
Earle, Augustus, 9, 10, 11, 12, 13, 80, 136, 139, 153, 154, 159, 160, 162, 163
Ebsworth, Henry, 133, 134
Elder, John, 70
Ellis, M. H., 80, 140
Fernyhough, William, 148, 163, 164
Field; Barron, 97, 99, 100, 116, 151
Flinders family, 27
Flinders, Ann (Mrs.), 39, 52, 55, 56, 71
Flinders, Matthew, 25, 26–63, 68, 69, 70, 71, 87, 90, 99, 103, 129, 131, 154, 166
Flinders, Samuel, Ward, 27, 30, 36, 45, 46, 61, 64, 70
Forbes, Francis, 160, 161
Foster, A. G., 147
Fowell, Newton, 21
Fowler, Robert, 46, 58, 59, 64
Franklin, John, 46, 49, 64
Fraser, Charles, 138
Freycinet, Louis de, 47, 99, 100, 124
Freycinet, Rose de, 99
Fridrits, Ivan, 110, 111
Fulford, George, 148
Ga-ouen-ren ('Miss Diana' Bungaree), 112, 145,146, 147
Gaimard, Joseph-Paul, 137
Gaunt, M., 99
Geary, Patrick, 78
George III, 27, 38, 82, 129
Gill, John, 79
Gipps, George, 155
Good, Peter, 45, 46, 49, 53, 54, 55, 58, 59, 60, 63
Goondel, 74

Gooseberry (Cora; Queen Gooseberry), 80, 81, 82, 145, 146, 147, 148, 153, 155, 161, 164
Gouroungan, 112
Govett, William, 163
Grant, James, 42, 43, 50
Greenway, Francis, 72, 138
Gulanba Duby, 102
Hacking, Henry, 52
Hall, Edward Smith, 11, 160
Halloran, Laurence, 151
Hamelin, Emmanuel, 46
Hardy, Norman, 123
Harris, John, 42, 43
Harry, 84
Healy, John Joseph, 157
Heaton, J. Henniker, 122
Hely (Healey), Frederick 160, 174, 176
Hill, Ernestine, 71
Hill, William, 116
Hood, John, 147
Howe, George, 78, 83, 144
Howe, Robert, 144
Huey, Alexander, 72
Hunter, John, 20, 21, 27, 28, 30, 38, 39, 41, 154, 166
Jacky Jacky, 147
Jamison, John, 137
Jansz, Willem, 57
Jobinge, 136
Johnson, John, 52
Johnston, George, 21, 65
Johnston, William, 65
Jorgensen, Jorgen, 52
Kable, George, 140
Keltie, James, 19
Kenyon, Mr., 123
King, Anna Josepha, 52
King, Philip Gidley, 9, 20, 42, 43, 47, 51, 52, 64, 65, 68, 69, 87
King, Phillip Parker, 25, 87, 91, 92, 93, 94, 95, 96, 97, 98, 99, 103, 116, 131, 159, 172
Kiselyov, Yegor, 105, 114
Knight, Mr., 65
Kongate, 84
Kurringy ('Carbone Jack'), 84
La Pérouse, Jean-François, 126, 130, 137, 170
Lang, George, 129, 154
Lang, John Dunmore, 129, 154, 160
Lansbury, Coral, 157
Laycock, Thomas, 65
Lazarev, Mikhail, 107
Lear, George, 157
Lejeune, Jules, 80, 129, 130, 139, 160, 161
Lesson, Pierre, 137
Lesson, René-Primevère, 124, 125, 127, 128, 147
Lesueur, Charles Alexandre, 17, 49, 50, 110
Lethbridge, Harriet, 87
Lewin, John William, 42, 43
Lino, Leslie, 170
Lockyer, Edmund, 138
Long Dick, 145, 148
Macarthur, Elizabeth, 73, 83
Macarthur, John, 69, 72, 135
McCarthy, Frederick, 57, 109, 154, 160
McCormick, Tim, 110
McGarvie, John, 12, 13, 134, 151
McLeay, Alexander,119, 136, 143, 144, 147
Maclehose, James, 163
Macquarie, Elizabeth Henrietta, 72, 77, 79, 85, 99, 118, 119, 121, 149
Macquarie, Lachlan, 10, 23, 69, 72–86, 87, 91, 99, 101, 105, 107, 108, 118, 119, 121, 122, 124, 129, 130, 133, 134, 143, 149, 150, 154, 155, 166, 171
Macquarie, Lachlan (Jnr.), 118, 121, 129
M'Quarie, 142
Mahroot (Boatswain), 18
Mailiez, Bernard de, 19
Mann, David, 116
Mann, John Frederick, 145, 148
Mansfield, Ralph, 144
Marley (Marlay), Edward, 126, 147
Marsden, Samuel, 9, 130, 135, 138
Mart, Russell, 57

Martens, Conrad, 153
Martin, James, 41
Martin, William, 28
Mason, Edward, 118
Mason, Martin, 43
Matora, 103, 104, 107, 109, 110, 112, 145, 151, 160
Matterer, Armand, 124
Meehan, James, 162
Melville, Herman, 153
Menzies, Charles, 65, 66, 69
Meyrick, Laura, 160
Mikhailov, Pavel, 80, 109, 110, 111, 112, 114, 147, 159, 160
Miles, W.A., 146
Millam (Mileham), John, 65,
Mitchell, James, 176
Mitchell, Thomas, 163
Morgan, Thomas, 58
Munnan, William, 143
Murrah, 74, 84
Murray, John, 43, 47, 52, 53
Murray, William, 57
Myles, 84
Nanbaree, 21, 22, 51, 53, 54, 55, 69
Napoleon, 64, 70
Narragingy (Creek Jemmy), 84
Narrange Jack, 84
Neville, Richard, 13, 153
Nicholas, William, 148, 164
Nöel, Alexis, 139
Norwong, 82
Novosil'sky, Pavel, 105, 107, 151
O'Connell, James, 174, 175, 176
O'Donnell, 118, 119
Oldfield, Roger, 9, 85, 119, 139, 140, 141, 142, 150
Oxley, John, 99, 176
Palmer, G. T., 83
Palmer, John, 9
Park, Mungo, 45
Parker, John, 87
Parkes, Henry, 118
Pasley, Thomas, 27
Paterson, Elizabeth, 52
Paterson, William, 38, 42, 43
Petit, Nicolas Martin, 110, 112
Péron, François, 50, 64, 112
Phillip, Arthur, 9, 18, 19, 20, 21, 22, 25, 27, 36, 41, 62, 67, 87, 154
Piper, John, 100, 130, 167
Pitot, Thomas, 70
Platt, John, 42
Pobasso (Probasso), 61, 62
Pomare, 153
Port Jackson Painter, 159
Powell, 173
Port Stephens Robert, 68
Pulpin, 82
Pye, Charles, 161
Queen Gooseberry (see Gooseberry)
Quoy, Jean-René, 137
Rachel, 84
Raffles, Thomas Stamford, 92
Receveur, Father, 125
Reiby, Thomas, 65
Richard II, 65
Ricketty Dick, 147
Ridley, William, 148
Riesenberg, Saul, 175
Robinson Crusoe, 27, 36, 70, 71
Rodius (Rhodius), Charles, 13, 81, 146, 160, 161, 162, 163
Roe, John Septimus, 87, 91
Rosenman, Helen, 126
Ross, Robert, 20
Rossi, Francis, 130, 133, 160
Rousseau, Jean-Jacques, 159, 167
Rowley, C. D., 135
Sadleir, Richard , 134, 135, 155
Sainson, Louis de, 137, 138, 139, 159
Saint Pierre, Bernadin de, 70
Schanck, John, 42
Schaw, W. G. B., 83

Scott, Thomas, 135
Selkirk, Alexander, 71
Shakespeare, William, 9, 149, 150, 157
Shelley, William, 75, 77
Shortland, John, 27, 41, 114
Simonov, Ivan, 105, 107, 109, 131
Smith, Bernard, 159
Smith, Christopher, 46
Smith, Mr., 123
Smith, Samuel, 49, 53, 66
Smith, Sydney, 156
Solander, Daniel, 15
Spencer, Earl, 38
Spillers, John, 68
Stanner, W.E.H., 19
Stockdale, Harry, 123
Strangeways, Thomas, 140
Sullivan, Mary, 73
Sultan of Mysore, 72
Suttor, George, 49
Sydney, Lord, 19
Tattooed Man (see O'Connell, James)
Taylor, James, 8
Taylor, William, 47
Tench, Watkin, 20, 21, 36, 67, 73
Therry, John Joseph, 143, 144
Therry, Roger, 160
Thistle John, 46, 47
Threlkeld, Lancelot, 24, 135, 140, 143
Tindall, 82, 83, 84
Tippo Sahib, 72
Tommy ('Jackey Jackey'), 140
Touanne, Edmund de la, 130
Toúbi, 102
Townson, John, 29
Trim, 34, 52, 64, 70, 166
Tucker, John, 65
Tyler, Wat, 65
Tyler, William, 39
Underwood, James, 139
Uniacke, John, 126
Venus de Milo, 124
Verge, John, 119
Vermuyden, Cornelius, 26
Victoria, Queen, 66
Wallah ('Warren'), 74, 84
Wallis, James, 24, 83, 84
Waterhouse, Henry, 27, 28, 38
Waterman, J. C., 147
Watling, Thomas, 159
Weld, Horatio, 176
Welsby, Thomas, 37, 68, 69
Wentworth, d'Arcy, 78, 79
Wentworth, William Charles, 144
Westall, Richard, 46
Westall, William, 45, 46, 57, 58, 59, 62
White, Andrew (see Nanbaree)
White, John, 20, 21, 52, 67
Whitewood, Mr., 57
Wiles, James, 27
Wilkins, R. F., 123
Willamannan, 66
Williams, Barney, 121
Wilson, Ambrose, 161
Woga (Woogah), 59, 60
Wolaworee, 36
Woolstonecraft, Edward, 100, 101
Woottan, 84
Worgan, George, 19, 29, 21, 154
Yallaman, 74, 84
Ye-woo, 84
Yehangeree, 59
Yel-yee-bah, 36
Yemmerrawannie, 27
Zavadovsky, I., 10

Places

Adventure Bay, 27
Airds, 74, 83
Albany, 46
Appin, 68, 73, 74, 83, 84
Argyle, 137
Arnhem Bay, 62
Arnhem Land, 61, 92
Barranjoey, 19
Barrow Island, 99
Bass Strait, 29, 39, 42, 43, 45, 47, 50, 92
Batavia, 78
Bathurst, 135, 140
Bathurst Island, 96, 98
Bengal, 43, 71
Bennelong Point, 47, 50, 105, 142, 144
Bentinck Island, 57, 61
Black Town (Blacktown), 77, 119
Blue Mountains, 24, 63, 67, 74, 99, 138, 140
Blue Mud Bay, 57
Boongaree (Qld.), 32
Botany Bay, 15, 18, 20, 22, 24, 28, 67, 125, 126, 130, 172, 174
Bountiful Island, 57
Bowen, 43
Break Sea Spit, 3, 52
Bribie Island, 32, 37
Brickfields, 126
Bringelly, 74
Brisbane River, 37
Brisbane Water, 23, 148
Brisbane, 37, 57
Britain, 50, 66, 71, 129, 156, 158, 163
Broad Sound, 55
Broken Bay, 12, 13, 14, 15–25, 30, 32, 42, 43, 47, 50, 52, 62, 66, 67, 69, 134, 139, 143, 148, 154, 166
Bungary Norah, 24, 25
Bunker Hill (Boston), 20
Burragorang Valley, 73
Bustard Bay, 54
Caledon Bay, 58, 59, 60, 61
Camden, 73, 83
Cammeray, 25
Cape Arnhem, 61
Cape Banks, 47
Cape Byron, 31
Cape Horn, 28, 38, 103, 125
Cape Howe, 92
Cape Keer-Weer, 57
Cape Leeuwin, 46, 92
Cape Moreton, 31
Cape Naturaliste, 92
Cape of Good Hope, 28, 29, 45, 46, 50, 56, 64, 71
Cape Town, 34, 38
Cape Wilberforce, 61,
Cape York, 52, 56
Caroline Islands, 174, 175, 176
Castle Hill, 65
Central Coast, 69, 143
Ceylon (Sri Lanka), 72, 137
Chasm Island, 57
Church Hill, 63
Clarence River, 31
Coal River, 39, 42, 43
Coochie Mudlow, 37
Coupang (Coepang, Kupang), 30, 41, 62, 98
Cow-Pastures (Cowpastures) 68, 73, 83, 86
Crow's Nest, 101, 127
Cumberland Islands, 55
D'Entrecasteaux Channel, 47
Dampier Archipelago, 93
Darling Downs, 87, 148
Dawes Point, 5
Deerubin (Hawkesbury River), 15, 21
Depuch Island, 92
Elizabeth Bay, 118, 119, 144
Elizabeth Town, 118, 119, 121, 122
Encounter Bay, 47
Endeavour River, 36
England, 43, 45, 63, 64, 68, 87, 107, 160

English Company Islands, 62
Exmouth Gulf, 92
Falkland Islands, 101, 124
Farm Cove, 25, 49, 52, 66, 69
Fig Tree Point, 25
Flinders Passage, 56
Fort Macquarie (Bennelong Point), 11, 12, 110, 144
France, 39, 45, 50, 64, 156
Fraser Island, 52, 144
Furneaux Islands, 29
Garden Island, 63, 118, 144
George's River, 28, 68
Georges Head, 10, 69, 77, 78, 79, 118, 119, 121, 122, 167
Gladstone, 54
Glass House Bay, 31, 37
Glass Houses, 29, 30, 32, 33, 35, 37
Goulburn Island, 92, 96
Government Domain, 9, 143, 147
Government House (Parramatta), 107, 136
Government House (Sydney), 11, 21, 69, 78, 107, 118, 135, 137
Great Australian Bight, 47, 86, 92
Great Barrier Reef, 52, 55, 56
Green Island, 37
Grose River, 83
Groote Eylandt, 57
Gulf of Carpentaria, 45, 52, 56, 61, 62, 68
Harvey Bay, 30, 37, 38, 52, 54
Hastings River, 99
Hawkesbury District, 67, 72
Hawkesbury River, 15, 63, 69, 83
Hobart Town, 99, 162, 175
Horseshoe Island, 57
Hunter (Hunter's) River, 24, 39, 41, 42, 43, 47, 65, 66, 68, 134, 137, 148, 155
Hyde Park (Sydney), 147, 148
Ile de France (Mauritius), 34, 47, 64, 70, 71, 135
India, 50, 56, 72, 80, 87, 103, 107
Indian Ocean, 64, 69, 92
Intercourse Islands, 95
Jervis Bay, 73, 138
Kangaroo Island, 47
Keppel Bay, 54
Keppel Island, 54
Kew Gardens, 38, 46, 87
King George Sound, 45, 46, 64, 92, 138
King's Town (Newcastle), 43, 68, 69
Kirribilli, 105, 106, 108, 111
Knocker's Bay, 97
Lake Macquarie, 24, 25, 135
Lane Cove River, 25
Launceston, 29
Lewis Island, 93
Lincolnshire, 26, 27, 39, 46, 47, 49
Lion Island, 19
London, 38, 42, 70, 86, 91, 104, 117, 129,135, 153, 157, 175
Luxmore Head, 97
Macleay Island, 37
Macquarie Harbour, 99
Macquarie Light, 107, 138
Macquarie Place, 137
Macquarie Street, 72
Manly, 25
Mauritius (see Ile de France)
Melville Island, 96, 97
Middle Harbour, 25
Middle Island, 63
Millicent, 67
Monte Bello Islands, 99
Moreton Bay, 29, 34, 37, 39, 52, 56
Moreton Island, 29
Morgan's Island, 57
Moscow, 107, 110, 111
Mosman, 122
Mount Warning, 31
Mud Island, 37
Mulgoa, 74, 84
Mullet Bay, 96
Murray Islands, 56
Nepean River, 83, 85, 137

Neutral Bay, 47, 130, 137
New Guinea, 45
New Holland, 28, 38, 39, 42, 45, 46, 51, 63, 103, 107, 109, 116, 129, 172
New South Wales, 27, 34, 38, 39, 42, 43, 56, 62, 63, 65, 69, 73, 87, 101, 121, 125, 126, 129, 133, 134, 135, 143, 153, 156, 158, 159, 160, 163, 172, 175
New Zealand, 50, 113, 136, 138, 139
Newcastle, 24, 25, 39, 43, 68, 69, 78
Noosa Heads, 37
Norfolk Island, 28, 29, 87, 116
North Head, 131, 146
North West Cape, 92
Otway, 47
Oyster Harbour, 92, 138
Pacific Ocean, 28, 30, 41, 56, 99, 113, 137
Palmer's Hill, 9
Pamplemousses, 70
Papua, 125, 175
Paris, 107, 139, 160, 170
Parramatta River, 129, 154
Parramatta Road, 163
Parramatta, 49, 76, 84, 86, 99, 107, 123, 129, 130, 135, 136, 138, 139, 142, 147, 154, 171, 172
Paterson's River, 43
Patonga, 23, 24
Peel Island, 37
Penrith, 137
Pitt Water (Pittwater), 20, 21, 23, 143
Point Alexander, 59
Point Piper, 167
Port Curtis, 54
Port Essington, 92, 97
Port Hacking, 28
Port Jackson, 8, 15, 22, 24, 25, 27, 28, 29, 30, 31, 33, 34, 35, 36, 37, 38, 39, 41, 42, 45, 47, 51, 52, 54, 55, 57, 58, 59, 60, 62, 63, 64, 65, 66, 67, 69, 70, 72, 75, 78, 87, 90, 91, 101, 103, 105, 107, 108, 110, 113, 114, 115, 116, 125, 126, 130, 131, 133, 134, 137, 141, 142, 146, 149, 150, 151, 158, 159, 166, 167, 172, 175
Port Lincoln, 58
Port Macquarie, 99, 105
Port Phillip, 47
Port Stephens, 30, 133, 142, 151
Portland, 49
Portsmouth, 87, 175
Prince of Wales Island, 56
Providental Bank, 64
Pumicestone Passage, 32, 33
Raffles Bay, 92
Recherce Archipelago, 63
Red Point, 91
Redcliff Point, 33, 37
Reed's Mistake, 24, 25, 42
Revesby, 26, 39
Richmond Hill, 22
Rocks, The, 8, 49, 99
Rose Bay, 144, 145, 167
Rouse Hill, 65
Rowley Shoals, 92
Rushcutters Bay 25
St. Asaph's Bay, 97
St. Petersburg, 103, 104, 107, 110, 111, 113
Sandy Cape, 37, 52
Seal Island, 92
Shoal Bay, 30, 31
Shoalwater, 55
Skirmish Point, 32
Smithfield, 65
Snug Cove, 91
South Australia, 47
South Georgia Islands, 103
South Head, 22, 24, 107
South West Bay, 96
Spencer Gulf, 51, 70
Spithead, 38, 45, 46, 71
Stradbroke, 37
Sulawesi, 61
Surry Hills, 126
Sweers Island 57, 61

Sydney Cove, 12, 18, 20, 28, 29, 41, 49, 50, 63, 66, 99, 105, 117, 128, 137, 139, 154
Sydney Heads, 28, 52, 72, 121, 175
Sydney Town 69, 110, 130, 151
Sydney, 8, 9, 10, 11, 15, 17, 29, 39, 43, 47, 49, 50, 55, 63, 64, 67, 68, 69, 72, 75, 78, 86, 105, 110, 113, 114, 117, 123, 124, 125, 126, 133, 135, 136, 139, 140, 142, 143, 145, 147, 149, 150, 151, 155, 160, 162, 163, 166, 170, 171, 175, 176
Tahiti, 113, 125, 130, 131, 153
Tamar River, 29
Tank Stream, 49
Thirroul, 24
Timor, 30, 41, 46, 47, 61, 62, 87, 98, 99, 172
Tonga, 75, 125
Torres Strait, 2, 45, 52, 56, 64
Townsville, 55
Turramurra, 25,
Twofold Bay, 91
Van Diemen Gulf, 92, 96, 97
Van Diemen's Land (Tasmania), 11, 27, 29, 30, 46, 47, 113, 116, 175
Vinegar Hill, 65, 66
Wattamolla, 28
Wednesday Island, 56
West Head, 25
Westernport, 29, 47, 138
Whilhelm's Plains, 70
Wide Bay, 37
Wilson's Promontory, 29
Windsor, 65, 123
Woody Point, 33
Wooloomooloo, 49, 118, 144
Wreck Reef, 64, 68
Wyrie Swamp, 67
Yoo-lahng-erah-ba-diahng, 52

Ships

Admiral Cockburn, 11
Alert, 27
Amity, 138
Aquilon, 124
Asia, 155
Assistant, 56
Astrolabe, 126, 137, 139
Bathurst, 116
Beagle, 153
Bellerophon, 27
Boongaree, 77
Bounty, 27, 41
Bridgewater, 64
Britannia, 50
Cape Packet, 176
Cato, 64, 68
Chevrette, 124
Coquille, 124, 125, 127, 128, 137, 138, 162
Coromandel, 103
Cumberland, 41, 64, 69, 70
Cyprus, 11
Diana, 87
Dick, 87
Dromedary, 72
Dundee, 68
Duyfken, 57
Endeavour, 15, 29, 38, 56
Espérance, 130
Fly, 12, 137
Fram, 39
Francis, 29, 42, 43, 66
Géographe, 39, 46, 47, 50, 64, 130
Gorgon, 87
Greenock, 134
Halcyon, 68
Harriet, 71

Hindustan, 72
Hope, 64, 68
Indefatigable, 78
Investigator, 39, 45–63, 66, 68, 70, 71, 87, 90, 99, 166
James, 65, 66
John Bull, 176
Kanguroo, 170, 173
Lady Nelson, 42, 43, 45, 47, 50, 51, 52, 54, 55, 65, 66, 68, 69, 87
Marquess Cornwallis, 43
Martha, 24
Mary Hope, 9
Mermaid, 87–99, 103, 116
Mirnyy, 103, 107, 113, 115
Naturaliste, 39, 46, 47, 50

Nautilus, 29
Norfolk, 25, 29, 30, 31, 32, 33, 34, 35, 38, 42, 46, 47, 51, 52, 69, 90
Northampton, 78
Otter, 71
Phoenix, 175
Porpoise, 43, 47, 49, 64, 68, 69, 70
Providence, 27, 56
Reliance, 27, 28, 30, 34, 38, 52
Resolution, 27
Resource, 65, 66
Rolla, 64
Salamander, 116
Sarah, 160
Sirius, 18, 28
Success, 137

Supply, 18, 22, 63, 116
Surry, 122
Suvorov, 107
Sydney Cove, 29
Tees, 124
Thétis, 130, 151
Tom Thumb, 28
Triton, 162
Uranie, 99, 101, 124
Venus, 29, 50
Volage, 12, 137
Vostok, 103, 107, 108, 110, 113, 115, 151
Warspite, 12, 137, 157, 158
William and Ann, 66
Xenephon, 39, 46
York, 133

A NEW CHART OF NEW HOLI

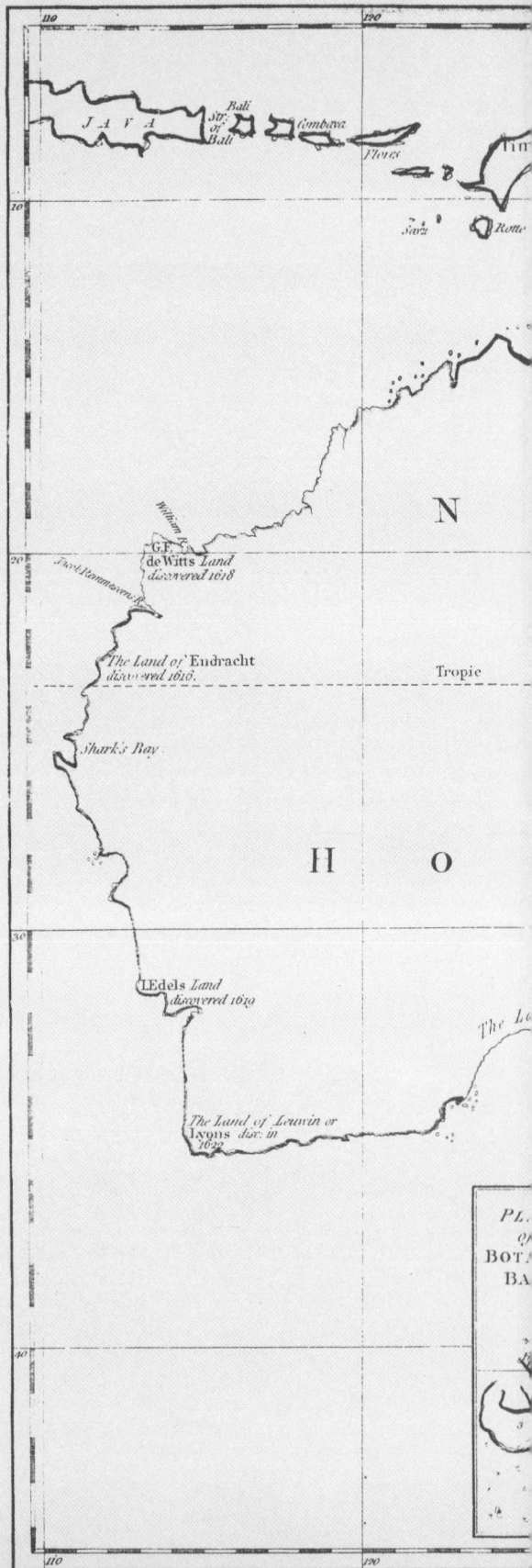

JAVA
Bali
Str: of Bali
Combava
Flores
Tin

Sava
Rotte

William I.
G.F. de Witts Land
discovered 1618

Wert Pennasvisy

N

The Land of Endracht
discovered 1616.

Tropic

Shark's Bay

H   O

LEdels Land
discovered 1619

The La

The Land of Leuwin or
Lyons dis: in
1622

PL.
of
BOT.
BA

Map 3. *A NEW CHART OF NEW HOLLAND*
[The map of Australia before the voyages of Matthew Flinders and George Bass]
London, Publish'd as the Act directs, 1 Jan.ᶜ, 1787 by Jnᵒ. Stockdale, Piccadilly.
Anon. *The Voyage of Governor Phillip to Botany Bay.* London, John Stockdale, 1789.